Philosophers of the Enlightenment

edited by
Peter Gilmour

Edinburgh University Press

© Edinburgh University Press 1989
22 George Square, Edinburgh

Set in Linotron Plantin by
Photoprint, Torquay, and
printed in Great Britain by
Redwood Press Limited,
Trowbridge, Wilts

British Library Cataloguing
   in Publication Data
Philosophers of the Enlightenment
1. European philosophy, history
1. Gilmour, Peter
190′.9

ISBN 0 7486 0110 4
       0 7486 0147 3 pbk

CONTENTS

CHRISTOPHER J. BERRY BA, PH.D.,
Lecturer then Senior Lecturer, Department of Politics, University of Glasgow since 1970. His doctoral thesis was on an aspect of the Scottish Enlightenment and he is the author of *Hume, Hegel and Human Nature* (1982), *Human Nature* (1986), *The Idea of a Democratic Community* (1989) and many articles on problems in political philosophy and the history of political thought.

STUART BROWN
is Professor of Philosophy at the Open University. His publications include a book on *Leibniz* and an edition of articles on *Philosophers of the Enlightenment*.

STEPHEN R.L. CLARK
is Professor of Philosophy at Liverpool University; author of Aristotle's Man, The Moral Status of Animals, The Nature of the Beast, From Athens to Jerusalem (all OUP), The Mysteries of Religion (Blackwells), and Civil Peace and Sacred Order (OUP); editor of Berkeley: Money, Obedience and Affection (Garland Press). He is married, with three children.

PETER GILMOUR
has taught Philosophy at the University of Glasgow, Literature at the University of Strathclyde, and both at the Open University, where he is mainly employed.

PETER JIMACK
has been Professor of French at the University of Stirling since 1972. He previously taught French at the University of Birmingham. His doctoral thesis was on the genesis of *Emile*, Rousseau's pioneering work on education. He has also written other books and articles on Rousseau and Diderot, and French educational thought in the eighteenth century.

I.D. LLOYD-JONES
is Senior Lecturer in Politics at the University of Glasgow. He studied at St John's College, Cambridge where he was awarded his MA and Ph.D.

MURRAY MACBEATH
studied at the universities of Glasgow, Oxford and Rochester, and is now a lecturer in Philosophy and in Religious Studies at the University of Stirling. He wrote his contribution to this book while on secondment to the University of Zimbabwe, teaching philosophy there.

ANGUS MCKAY
studied at the Universities of Aberdeen, Glasgow, and Cambridge. He has taught Philosophy at Glasgow University since 1972, and has written on medical ethics and philosophy of religion.

R.F. STALLEY
studied Classics and Philosophy at Worcester College, Oxford. After postgraduate work at Harvard and Oxford Universities he began teaching at the University of Glasgow where he is now Senior Lecturer in Philosophy. He has a special interest in Scottish Philosophy of the eighteenth century and has published articles on Hume and on Reid.

JOHN WILLIAMSON

PETER GILMOUR

Introduction

Although the nine philosophers in this volume can be described as Enlightenment philosophers (or, at least, as philosophers who touch on the Enlightenment in some way), it would be a mistake to think that therefore they have a project, or set of ideas, in common. There are similarities, of course, resemblances – their inclusion together in the volume would otherwise be arbitrary – but there are also differences, divergences. The first to be considered is Leibniz who, with his belief that the truth is revealed to pure reason rather than to the senses, cannot be placed at the centre of the Enlightenment. Nor can the last, Fourier, with his concern to develop a science of man that explains the spirit and the imagination. Within the thought of both, however, there are elements which link them importantly to the Enlightenment. Even within that group usually held to be essentially of the Enlightenment, the British Empiricists, there are important differences. Students new to the philosophers of this age, therefore, would do well to be alert to this diversity. Here as elsewhere the search for common ideas, common beliefs, is limiting and misleading.

The dominant element in Enlightenment philosophy is the belief that the methods of the natural sciences should also be those of philosophy. To understand why this should have been believed, it is necessary to appreciate the enormous impact of Newton. With his theory of gravity, he had made it possible to explain the material world. The movements of all the bodies in it, regardless of size, could be explained by a few fundamental laws. This spectacle of the material world triumphantly fathomed was intoxicating, particularly perhaps for philosophers, whose own subject was beset by obscurities and confusions. It was believed that the mechanical model of investigation and explanation, if brought into philosophy, would be as liberating and clarifying there as it had been in physics. A science of the material world had emerged, so why not of man also?

For the mind to be susceptible to this kind of empirical

investigation, it had to be conceived of as a kind of material universe in microcosm, with ideas and sensations as the equivalents of particles. And indeed this was how Locke, Berkeley and Hume regarded it. But the empiricism of these three was employed to different ends and with different results, as we shall see.

The first important statement of the empirical theory of knowledge was Locke's *Essay Concerning Human Understanding* (*1690*). As a member of the Royal Society, Locke met Newton and Robert Boyle, and discussions with them and other scientific friends appear to have been the main inspiration behind *An Essay Concerning Human Understanding*. He begins by criticising the theory of innate ideas, the view that is, that 'stamped upon the mind of man' at birth are certain innate principles upon which our knowledge is founded. But if our ideas are not innate, Locke asks, how are we to account for them? What is their origin? He answers by saying that the mind at birth is a *tabula rasa* and that it is from experience therefore that our ideas come – experience providing us with two sources for these, sensation and reflection. All of our ideas, whether simple or complex, come from one or the other of these two sources, some (such as the ideas of rest, motion and extension) coming from the senses (here, the senses of touch and sight), others (such as willing and doubting) from reflection alone, others still (such as our ideas of pleasure and pain) from a combination of sensation and reflection. Locke now asks which of these ideas resemble how objects actually are, the qualities they have, and which do not; this leads him to the distinction between primary and secondary qualities, a distinction which he believed necessitated the idea of substance (extremely difficult in all of its appearances in philosophy, from the Greeks onwards). Experience shows us that simple ideas often occur together, in combination, and we suppose that, since they cannot subsist on their own, there must be a thing to which they belong. This thing we think of as a substratum, more commonly called a substance, and it is in this that the primary qualities are held to inhere. The essay by John Williamson in this volume is an investigation of substance as understood by Locke and Boyle. If it is difficult, it is not only because the idea of substance is difficult, but because Locke, caught between the old and the new thinking about material objects, between that of the Scholastics on the one hand, Galileo and Newton on the other, is himself confused about it.

In Stuart Brown's essay on Leibniz, the emphasis is on Leibniz the inspired eclectic, the borrower of the best from rival schools or systems of philosophy, the philosopher who appreciated that between, say, a version of Plato's theory of reminiscences and some of the ideas of Locke there could be an enlightening relationship. Like Locke, he held that reality is material, but rejected Locke's view that the mind at birth is a *tabula rasa*. For him, the appropriate simile is a block of marble with veins: ideas rise into consciousness when the mind, under pressure of experience, is stimulated to consider the necessary principles which underpin the empirical world. It is possible to discover empirically a truth about, for example, the sides of a triangle (this Leibniz called 'a truth of fact'), even although the truth of reason which lies behind it has not been grasped. He thus, in his defence of innate ideas, makes a distinction between truths which depend on the senses and truths which depend on reason, and in his concern with the former foreshadows the Enlightenment. He also held that perception is a much more complex matter than it was thought to be by Locke, and went on not only to criticise Locke's conception of simple ideas, but to claim that the distinction between primary and secondary qualities does not hold up and is unnecessary anyway. Here he anticipates Berkeley's rejection of this distinction, though it does not lead, as it did with Berkeley, to a denial of the materiality of the external world. And he disagreed with Locke with regard to substance, holding that it does not make sense to describe substance as a mere collection of properties. Because, for human reason, a property must be a property of something, it is not intelligible, Leibniz held, to say that there can be properties which do not belong to anything, or which belong to something not definable apart from the properties.

Another of Locke's profound critics was Berkeley. He too, as we have seen, rejected Locke's distinction between primary and secondary qualities, where the former are held to exist in some material substratum, the latter in the mind. Such a distinction cannot be upheld, Berkeley argued, because where it is held that secondary qualities exist in the mind, it must be accepted that primary qualities exist there too. There are three reasons for this. First, it is impossible to imagine an extended, moving body (the primary qualities) which does not have colour or temperature (the secondary qualities). Secondly, when relativity is invoked – as it was to prove the subjectivity of secondary qualities – it is found that it applies equally to primary qualities. (The size of something, no less than its colour, is determined by the position of the observer.) Thirdly, an idea can only resemble another idea, not be a copy of material reality, so by setting up a distinction between appearance and reality Locke assumed the existence of an external

world, with its material substratum or substance, which cannot
be known.

So if for Locke empiricism led to the claim that there is an
external world and that it is material, for Berkeley it led to a
denial of this materiality. For him, reality was not material, it was
spiritual. He does not deny reality, as was thought by Dr Johnson
(and many since), he seeks to refute the materialist explanation of
it. In place of material substance, there is Spirit, there is spiritual
activity, and it is to the challenge of this account of reality that
Stephen Clark responds in his essay.

The age of the Enlightenment was an optimistic one. Man and
society were held to be perfectible. The science of man, it was
thought (by believers and atheists alike), could be used to create a
world that was just, harmonious and happy. Even if tempted by
vice, man was spontaneously capable of virtue. Such a view was
held by David Hume, a point developed by Angus Mackay in his
discussion of Hume's attack on Hobbes's view that men are
incapable of altruism. But, as this essay also shows, Hume's
empiricism led to conclusions disturbing to common sense, such
as the conclusion that because induction, unlike deduction, does
not involve necessity, there can never be certainty about matters
of fact. In his attempt to show how the mind operates, how we
come by the knowledge we have, Hume used the experimental
method with great rigour and consistency, though it is arguable
that, in the case of a science of man, he did not wholly understand
what it involved. Perhaps more clearly than in the case of the
other empiricists, we see in Hume the attempt to make the
methods of the natural sciences – observation and generalisation –
those of philosophy. The scepticism this led to brought reactions
from other empiricists, the most famous of whom is Thomas
Reid. In his essay on Reid, Richard Stalley considers the attempt
to return philosophy to common sense, to rescue it from the
paradoxical extremes to which Berkeley and Hume had taken it.

Empiricism also had its confusions, however, its misapprehen-
sions, these having their source in the failure adequately to
distinguish questions of fact (answerable by empirical methods)
from questions about the categories of propositions (not answerable by such methods). And it was these confusions which awoke
Kant from his 'dogmatic slumbers'. For him, the main questions
of philosophy were to do with the concepts and categories – such
as those of space, time and causality – which shape and inform
our thinking inescapably, and are not empirically determinable.
He saw that the exhaustive science of man desired by the
empiricists would not answer all the questions they thought it

would answer, that there were questions whose logical status placed them beyond the reach of empirical enquiry. And he saw that the empiricists suffered from this misapprehension because they had failed to distinguish questions about how we come by our knowledge (which do fall within the province of this science) from questions about what sorts or categories of knowledge we have (which do not fall within it). In the *Critique of Pure Reason*, in fact, he tried to effect a reconciliation between two rival theories of knowledge, that of the European rationalists (Descartes, Leibniz and Wolff) on the one hand, who held that knowledge is arrived at by pure reason, independently of the senses, and that of the British Empiricists (Locke, Berkeley and Hume) on the other, who held that knowledge is dependent on the senses. He argued that there were faults in both epistemologies, but finally accepted much in both of them. There is therefore an important sense in which Kant belongs to the counter Enlightenment. He is also, however, self-consciously and importantly an 'enlightenment' thinker, and the sense in which he held himself to be is the starting point for Murray MacBeath's essay.

Adam Smith, the third member of the Scottish Enlightenment considered here, was no less concerned than his friend Hume with the experimental method. But where Hume applied it to the mind, Smith applied it to the economy. Once again, Newton was the model, the inspiration. As in Newtonian mechanics, there were to be first principles, and these were to be drawn from experience. For Smith, the most important of these first principles was the division of labour, itself the consequence of what he saw as the natural human inclination to barter and exchange. While he stressed that men were self-interested, and would always be so, he argued in the *Wealth of Nations* that, where there is natural liberty, this self-interest will work to the benefit of others. The 'invisible hand', which regulates and prevents excess, ensures that private and public interest are in harmony, that from the selfishness of successful individuals in the market place civic virtue arises. There is therefore no cause for pessimism about the human condition, for the economy, on Smith's conception of it, works so that from private vice a tide of public virtue is released, the ripples of this benison reaching even to the very poor. It is with the character of this system of natural liberty that Chris Berry is concerned in his essay.

As Peter Jimack says, Voltaire is not a great or original philosopher, yet his is the name most commonly associated with the Enlightenment. He was many things: philosopher, tragedian, essayist, poet, scientist, novelist, historian. Locke was the contemporary he most admired, and he did much to make people aware of the nature of empiricism in philosophy, passionately insisting on how liberating it was, how, were it to be widely applied, it would reveal man to himself as never before, his nature and his needs and the means of satisfying these needs. And yet, as Peter Jimack shows, this faith in the power of the new philosophy to reveal and liberate did not prevent Voltaire from being periodically haunted by the problem of evil, as well as challenged by religious belief. Deep metaphysical unease seems to have co-existed with the wit and polemical power – used both to communicate the best of the thought of his age and to expose what was dangerously false – for which he is famous.

Fourier, the last philosopher in the volume, shared with the British Empiricists a concern to develop a science of man. But what he understood by a science and what he understood by man were very different from what the empiricists understood by them (the nature of this original and difficult understanding uncovered by David Lloyd-Jones in his essay). Fourier held not only that the imagination was superior to the reason, but that it and the spirit could be explained scientifically. Largely for this reason, he is not in the habit of giving his science of man coherence in the normal way, by employing connections which are either causal or those of logical entailment. Rather he defines and orders his thought through a pattern of analogies and metaphors. In this sense, his cast of mind is romantic or poetic rather than empirical. It is a different way of doing philosophy, and it requires different expectations and habits on the part of the student. What the other Enlightenment thinkers would have held to be beyond the province of science, Fourier claimed for science, seeking a physiology of the imagination, as it were, of spirituality (though, in common with many of his contemporaries, he was not a believer). The form and manner of his enquiry mark him as of the Enlightenment, but the features of man that he singles out for this enquiry – the spirit and the imagination – anticipate the romantics. It is possible to see him as a figure midway between two ages, that of the Enlightenment, with its passionate belief in science, and that of Romanticism, with its rage against the presumptions of science, its belief that (in the words of William Blake) Newton, Locke and Bacon made up a kind of 'Trinity of Evil', sinning in their insistence that the higher faculties could be fathomed by science, the Spirit and the Imagination accommodated to the laws of mechanics. The belief that there could be a science of man equal to the science of the material world, and serving the quest for happiness and equity, did not last. Nor, as a result, did the great confidence and optimism which went with the Enlightenment, and which have not been seen since.

None the less, while the marriage of philosophy and science may have been misguided, based as it was on misconceptions about the nature of philosophical enquiry and explanation, it was passionate while it lasted and immensely fruitful: a fruitfulness to which the present volume bears testimony.

STUART BROWN

Leibniz and the Fashion for Systems and Hypotheses

> . . . the taste for systems . . . is today almost entirely banished from works of merit . . . a writer among us who praised systems would have come too late . . . (d'Alembert, *Preliminary Discourse*, 1751, 94)

> Men are now cured of their passion for hypotheses and systems in natural philosophy, and will harken to no arguments but those which are derived from experience. (Hume, *Enquiry Concerning the Principles of Morals*, 1751, Sect. I)

My initial excuse for talking about a *fashion* for systems and hypotheses in the pre-Enlightenment period is that this is invited by the language in which d'Alembert and Hume contrast the philosophical trends of the mid-eighteenth century with the trends that had previously prevailed. D'Alembert explicitly associates the taste for systems with Descartes, Malebranche and Leibniz, whose disciples had become few and far between by the middle of the eighteenth century, at any rate in France. In saying that anyone who wished to perpetuate the taste for systems 'would have come too late', d'Alembert comes close to saying that this style of philosophy had gone out of fashion. Hume, in talking of a curable 'passion', implies that the enthusiasm for systems and hypotheses was more of a temporary mental derangement. But the difference between what we would call a 'craze' and a fashion is a difference largely of degree.

It is tempting to treat these remarks of d'Alembert and Hume as dismissive rhetoric. This temptation will be strong in those who think that philosophy is not the kind of subject in which 'fashions' or 'crazes' or anything much like them can occur. But I want to suggest, on the contrary, that in certain circumstances serious intellectual pursuits can be strongly affected by something like fashions. And this is what I shall be exploring in what follows. I shall suggest that in late seventeenth and early eighteenth-century French philosophy[1] the conditions were right for the emergence of fashions in metaphysics and that this was the high-

point of the fashion for systems and hypotheses. The case of
Leibniz is particularly interesting since, in his native Germany,
the conditions for the emergence of such fashions did not exist.
The Francophile Leibniz, I shall try to bring out, dressed up his
philosophy to suit the French fashion when he wrote for the
French-reading public. But he presented it rather differently
when he wrote for that part of the intellectual world in which
Latin remained the *lingua franca*. Leibniz became a fashionable
author in France, particularly on account of his *Theodicy*, and his
reputation suffered in the French and Francophile Enlightenment
in virtue of his association with the fashion for systems and
hypotheses. In Germany, by contrast, where philosophy was not
subject to the same fluctuations, many of Leibniz's ideas were
accommodated to the thought of the still dominant Scholasticism.
In consequence, whereas in France Leibniz came to epitomize
what the *philosophes* were opposed to in past philosophy, he was
for the philosophers of the German Enlightenment a respected
figure.

I

The emergence of a new fashion is always an expression of a sense
of discontinuity with the immediate past. In general – though
there are interesting exceptions – educational institutions have
inhibited the emergence of fashions. For, at least in large
measure, they have been concerned to transmit to the next
generation a received or accumulated wisdom in which continuity
with the past is stressed. This was just as true when the teachers
believed that theirs was a subject in which steady progress was to
be made as it was when they were concerned to transmit age-old
or even timeless truths. At all events, universities in the seventeenth century mostly remained strongholds of Scholasticism.[2]
The development of Modern philosophy was largely fostered by
intellectuals who did not make a living teaching in academic
institutions. This was particularly true of France, where the
opposition between the ultra-Modernist Cartesianism and the
then established 'school' philosophy became highly polarised and
politicised, with each party aiming to exclude the teaching of the
opposing philosophy.[3] It was less true of Germany, perhaps
because it could be nowhere boast of the sizable group of *savants*
to be found in Paris, who were at the centre of intellectual life and
yet had no formal association with the University. In Germany
the debates between Modern and Scholastic philosophy were
conducted within the universities – affecting Leipzig when Leibniz

was an undergraduate there in the 1650s – and the tendency was
towards finding ways of harmonising them rather than for one to
triumph at the expense of others.[4] This may partly explain why the
influence of Scholasticism on German philosophy remained strong
throughout the eighteenth century, whereas in other countries of
Europe it was either superceded or had become largely peripheral.
The accent in Germany was on continuity. And even that giant
amongst the philosophers of the German Enlightenment, Imman-
uel Kant, made no attempt to dissociate himself completely from
the Scholastic tradition.

The ultra-Modernism of the Cartesians was, however, to create
a quite different environment in France, in which it became the
custom not to acknowledge past philosophy. Paris philosophy
became sectarian and, with many unable to accept the doctrinaire
approach of either the Cartesians or the Scholastics, the conditions
seem to have been ripe for yet more new philosophies to emerge.
They seem to have favoured a wholesale scepticism about metaphysics or at any rate a more or less frankly speculative and
undogmatic metaphysics. The trend-setter for this more speculative metaphysics was a Cartesian of sorts: Nicolas Malebranche.
His *Search after Truth* (1674–5) aroused much interest and
controversy, and it was his metaphysics to which the words
'system' and 'hypotheses' seem to have first been applied in the
relevant senses.

The word 'system' had previously been used in at least two
senses. Firstly, it was used of large-scale scientific theories and
particularly of the Copernican system. But it was also used of
works of theology in which the connections between various
doctrines were elaborated. Malebranche's metaphysics was a
highly God-centred one and yet he did not pretend to be able to
demonstrate his key doctrine that we see all things in God. It was
rather a hypothesis that explained the phenomena and did so,
according to Malebranche, much better than other available
hypotheses.[5] In presenting his metaphysics in this way, Malebranche seemed to give to metaphysical theories something of the
character of systems of astronomy. Instead of claiming that
metaphysics was a demonstrable science like geometry, as others
had wanted to do, Malebranche was willing to argue that it was a
matter of which account was the most satisfactory. In view of
both the theological associations and the comparison with astro-
nomical theories, it was a natural step for Malebranche's contemporaries to use the word 'system' of his metaphysics.

By the 1690s the words 'system' and 'hypothesis' had become
vogue words in French and Francophile philosophical circles.

The use of these words, moreover, was accompanied by new expectations of what a piece of metaphysics should be like and perhaps even by a sense of liberation from the problems that beset the attempt to defend metaphysics as a demonstrative science. Metaphysics itself became for a while a more entertaining, accessible and even fashionable subject.[6] Yet alongside this fashion for metaphysical systems there went a scepticism about whether, in the end, it was possible to choose between them. This ambiguity is well-captured in Pierre Bayle's *Historical and Critical Dictionary*. This work both catered to the fashion and yet seemed to encourage the thought that there is such a plethora of metaphysical systems and hypotheses (with deep difficulties for the ones usually favoured and much more to be said in defence of others) that we should be sceptical of all of them. Bayle's *Dictionary* was an outstanding success, perhaps partly because of this ambiguity. But it was his scepticism that was to prove an enduring influence on the Enlightenment, notably on David Hume.

The fashion for systems and hypotheses had some following in Holland, where Bayle had taken refuge. But it did not extend to Germany, where Christian Wolff complained in 1713 about the fact that, to conform to it, Nicolas Hartsoeker had changed the title of his *Principles of Natural Philosophy* to *Physical Conjectures*. The tendency in Germany seems to have been to despair of philosophy when it was merely conjectural and to reject presentations unless they promised something more solid. In the 1690s, as I shall now try to bring out, Leibniz found himself caught between these different expectations of a work of philosophy.

II

The terms 'system' and 'hypothesis' seem to have become attached to Leibniz's metaphysical theory initially insofar as it was thought of as an alternative to that of Malebranche. And it may briefly be explained as arising from the problems of the Cartesians. It was natural enough in the seventeenth century, as perhaps it still is, to think of the world as consisting of a very large number of interacting substances. According to Descartes, however, there were basically only two kinds of substances: minds, or simple non-extended things whose essence is consciousness, and matter, whose essence consists in being extended. Descartes held that mind and matter were interacting substances. But few even of his disciples could see how this position could be maintained. For, in brief, Descartes conceived of mind and matter as completely different from one another. And, having nothing in common, there were no features of a mind in virtue of which any effect on a body could be made intelligible, or vice versa.

What became known as the 'hypothesis' or 'system' of *occasional causes* emerged as a solution to this difficulty. It was accepted that no substance, strictly speaking, acted on any other. The action of one substance on another was to be explained, rather, by saying that God intervened to produce the effect. In short, the only true cause is God. What we think of as causes in the natural order are no more than *occasions* on which, in accordance with His own laws, God regularly intervenes.

There are many other reasons why this striking theory should have recommended itself to seventeenth-century philosophers. Malebranche was not the originator of the system of occasional causes but his writing talents did much to spread interest in it and indeed to make it an attractive one to accept. Malebranche himself came to occupy the centre of the French philosophical stage in the 1680s and 1690s and it is natural that Leibniz should have sought to advertise his own metaphysics among the *savants* by presenting it as an alternative to that of Malebranche. He did this in his 'New System of the nature and communication of substances' in successive issues of the *Journal des Savants* in 1695.

This is the first work in which Leibniz publicly claimed to be the author of a 'system', though he used the phrase 'my system' in notes he made on one of Malebranche's controversies, probably in 1685.[7] More striking was his willingness to stress the novelty of his system. To be sure, he went out of his way in the 'New System' to stress that he had arrived at this system some years before and had delayed its publication while he sought the opinion of others about it. But in the earlier (unpublished) version of his system known as the *Discourse on Metaphysics*, written in early 1686, his mode of presentation is hostile to novelty. The term 'innovator' in metaphysics – though not indeed in mathematics, in which Leibniz also excelled – was for him a pejorative term at that time. And indeed, when Antoine Arnauld complained that the summary he had been sent smacked of fatalism and could not be approved by a Catholic, Leibniz was quick to protest:

> '. . . I want Mr Arnauld to realise that I make no claim to the glory of being an innovator, as he seems to understand my views. On the contrary I usually find that the oldest and more generally accepted opinions are the best ones . . .
> (*Philosophische Schriften*, ii, 20f.)

Although Leibniz went on to admit that he was producing

'certain new truths', he stressed this was not tantamount to innovation. An innovator was someone who showed a disregard for established opinions. The German compromise, to judge from Leibniz's own rhetoric, was to presume that established opinions were the correct ones unless the contrary could be established.

New truths need not contradict established opinions, of course. But anyone who claimed something new that *did* contradict established opinions, or even appeared to do so, was guilty of what Leibniz called a 'paradox'. Leibniz himself put forward what he admitted to be 'paradoxes' in the *Discourse* (e.g. in Section 9). But he goes on to defend these by saying that they were much the same as had been put forward by a reputable authority before, or by showing how they followed from established opinions. The onus of proof, in short, lay with the propounder of paradoxes and not with the defender of established opinions. In this way the Scholastics, with their high profile in defending established opinions, were given their due and yet it was allowable for a German also to be a Modern philosopher, engaging in new problems and putting forward new truths.

In accordance with this style of presentation it was the usual practice to acknowledge both established opinion and earlier authorities. The Cartesians, by writing as if no one had written before them, were quickly accused of innovation. Leibniz, to avoid this charge, often exaggerated the extent to which what he was saying had been said before, ascribing to Aristotle, Aquinas or the Scholastics views that it is difficult to trace in their works, or are not quite what they said. In this way he seemed inclined to disguise the novelty of his metaphysics. And Leibniz, it should be said, was not a modest and unassuming man. When it came to the question of who was first to produce the infinitesimal calculus, he was quick to insist on his originality. But the ethos in which mathematical prodigies vied with one another (and allowed one another only unintelligible accounts of work in progress) was quite different from that in which metaphysicians worked. Metaphysics was viewed as a close cousin of theology and so greater restraint and greater respect for the past was to be expected.

This restraint lay firmly on German metaphysics and there were many in France who sought to keep it imposed there. The fashion for systems and hypotheses and the interest in novelty in metaphysics amongst the *savants* should not be seen as marking a more liberal French culture. It testifies rather to the emergence of an intellectual élite who enjoyed at least some degree of freedom from the authoritarian institutions of State, Church and University, interrupted however by sporadic assertions of orthodoxy. The fashionable philosophers were by no means free of harassment. Malebranche's works were, after a while, put on the Index (as the works of Descartes had been) and he was frequently denounced in print. But his works were still available, and there were doubtless those who were more inclined to read them as a result of their receiving these marks of disfavour.

Leibniz himself had spent a few years in Paris in the 1670s and often longed to return there. He continued to keep in touch by correspondence and to take a keen interest in the activities of the *savants*. Amongst his pleasanter and less formal duties in Hanover by the 1690s was to advise the Electress Sophie on philosophical matters. Sophie asked for Leibniz's opinion about books that seemed to set new trends in metaphysics, and she seems to have been the motivating force behind Leibniz's writing books on Locke and Bayle. Leibniz was, however, largely a solitary philosopher. Most of his communications about philosophy – including not a few to or for Sophie – were written down. And, since a large number of these have been preserved, they provide a valuable outside perspective on the *savants* and on the fashion for systems and hypotheses. For rather different reasons in each case, parts of his correspondence with Foucher and Bayle are of particular relevance, as are his books against Locke and Bayle. As I shall bring out in the next three sections, they reveal Leibniz's willingness to accommodate himself to the fashion up to a point, but also how this led to his being misunderstood.

III

Leibniz's 'New System' was advertised as an alternative to what was thought of as Malebranche's 'new system', indeed as arising out of its difficulties. But Leibniz had shown little inclination to use the word 'system' previously of his own metaphysical theory, not even in correspondence. In 1686, when he had put together a version of this theory, he introduced it to his old Paris friend, Simon Foucher:

> 'I also feel you are right . . . to doubt that bodies can act on minds and vice versa. On this matter I have a pleasing opinion, which seems necessary to me and is very different from that of the author of the *Recherche* [Malebranche] . . . (*Philosophische Schriften*, i, 382.)

Leibniz went on to explain why he rejected the Scholastic 'hypothesis' of a real 'influence' of one created substance on another and the 'hypothesis of occasional causes'. But he did not describe his own view – that everything that happens to a substance arises from within itself and yet in perfect harmony with what happens to every other substance in a way pre-established by God – as a 'hypothesis'. His view was not a mere hypothesis but was something 'necessary', in a way he does not make explicit to Foucher. But his use of the phrase 'plaisante opinion' would hardly invite the sceptical Foucher to expect that Leibniz thought he could demonstrate the correctness of his account of the relation between mind and body. On the contrary it seems likely that Leibniz was caught between two strategies – between claiming that all he had produced was an interesting new hypothesis that was worth considering along with these others, and claiming that he had a definitive and demonstrable solution to the problem.

Foucher had proved himself an exacting critic of Descartes and Malebranche.[8] His strategy was usually to identify the 'suppositions' of an argument and then complain that there was no obligation to accept them. The sceptical moral he drew from this was that, since such systems are based on arbitrary suppositions, we should not take them as adding to our knowledge of the world. Leibniz knew that Foucher would have been much provoked if he had claimed that he could demonstrate his system. It may be, therefore, that he was hoping Foucher would lower his guard at the offer of a 'pleasing opinion'. At all events the response it brought from Foucher was a friendly one. Foucher would not attempt to pass a final judgement on what he was quick to call Leibniz's 'system' but would assist in getting a good reception for it that would allow Leibniz to explain himself further.

Leibniz was encouraged by this response to think that he had an understanding with Foucher and that, if he published some of his original thoughts in the *Journal des Savants*, Foucher would make the kind of reply that would encourage favourable attention. In the event, however, Foucher let Leibniz down. He was the first to reply to Leibniz's 'New System' but his reply was far from what Leibniz had hoped. He accused Leibniz and Malebranche of producing the kind of 'system' that was 'manufactured after the event' and designed to 'save' their favoured principles (*Philosophische Schriften*, iv, 489). He did not rule out the possibility of such matters being decided. But the problems with which Leibniz and Malebranche were concerned could only be solved if philosophers would go back to first principles and agree on the infallible criteria of truth (*Philosophische Schriften*, iv, 490). Descartes had been right, in other words, to look for a demonstrative metaphysics, even if he had failed to provide one.

Foucher thus diverted attention from Leibniz's system and

from serious consideration of it by calling in question the methodology involved. By doing so, he was also attacking the fashion for systems in metaphysics. Leibniz was forced in his reply, to defend his methodology. He claimed not to understand what Foucher meant by objecting that such systems were manufactured after the event to save certain principles:

> All hypotheses are formed *with a set purpose*, and all systems come *after the event* to save phenomena or appearances. But I do not see which are the principles in favour of which I am supposed to be prejudiced, and which I want to save.
>
> If this means that I am led to my hypothesis by *a priori* reasons also or by settled principles, as is in fact the case, this is more a commendation of the hypothesis than an objection to it. It is usually enough for a hypothesis to be proved *a posteriori*, because it satisfies the phenomena; but when we have other reasons as well, and those *a priori*, it is so much the better. (*Philosophische Schriften*, iv, 496.)

Leibniz went on to deny that he was interested in producing 'novelties' rather than solid truths, and to repeat the hope that the value of his hypothesis would be recognised 'in view of the difficulty which the ablest philosophers of our time have found in the communication of minds and bodies'. But he failed to reply directly to Foucher's suggestion that since he, Leibniz, was no Cartesian, he need not enbroil himself in their difficulties. In fact Leibniz was involved in very similar difficulties because of his view that all true substances must be simple and indivisible.[9] And it seems that this is one of what he would have counted as the 'settled principles' on which his system was based and from which it drew *a priori* support. This is implicit in his earlier response to Foucher's charge that his hypothesis of harmony was arbitrary, when he suggests (probably rightly) that Foucher 'did not realise that it follows from my view of unities, and that my whole contention stands or falls together.' (*Philosophische Schriften*, iv, 494). The 'view of unities' is Leibniz's principle that true substances must be simple and indivisible. But this reply to Foucher does not go to the heart of his objection. For is not that 'view of unities' itself arbitrary, in the sense of being an assumption that need not be made, and which Leibniz is saving by producing his system? The problem about what looks like a *priori* support is that it may only shift the problem one stage further back.[10]

Perhaps Foucher would have made just this point had he replied to Leibniz's reply. Unfortunately, he died before he was able to do so, leaving Leibniz with the last word but without the

excuse to expand on his system in the way in which he had
envisaged.

IV

Leibniz's 'New System' was to receive attention from others. But
the attention he received from Bayle was particularly gratifying.
Bayle, like Foucher, was a sceptic but of a rather different kind.[11]
Whereas Foucher distanced himself from the fashion for systems
and hypotheses and called for a return to demonstrations from
first principles, systems like that of which Leibniz appeared to
Bayle to be the author were grist to his mill. Bayle delighted in
setting one system or hypothesis against another and was undis-
turbed at the prospect of not being able to choose between them.
The attitude he was happy to recommend was a suspense of
judgement. But it was possible to read Bayle's *Dictionary* and
enjoy his writing and penetrating expositions without feeling that
this moral was being drawn too forcibly. Bayle went out of his
way to present the most outlandish hypotheses in as favourable a
light as possible. And he probably did think Leibniz's system of
pre-established harmony was outlandish. None the less he offered
everything that an author could hope for from a critic, as far as
Leibniz was concerned.[12]

Perhaps for this reason Leibniz was willing to debate the
virtues of his 'New System' with Bayle on Bayle's terms. Bayle, in
his *Dictionary* article 'Rorarius', had rightly pointed out that
Leibniz's criticism of the system of occasional cases was mistaken
insofar as he claimed that it required God to intervene continually,
and so called for a perpetual miracle. He also raised a number of
difficulties for Leibniz's own system. In a 'clarification' inserted
in the Dutch journal *Histoire des ouvrages des savants* in 1698,
Leibniz hinted that he might be able to demonstrate his system
but was willing to allow that 'for the present the question is
merely to maintain it as a possible hypothesis which is suitable for
explaining phenomena' (*Philosophische Schriften*, iv, 518). In
doing so, however, he was encouraging the view that his system
was no more than a possible way of explaining what called for
explanation. He thus played into Bayle's hands. For Bayle could
then argue that there are several possible systems, for each of
which certain advantages could be claimed but none of which was
free of difficulties. The moral that the reasonable person would
suspend judgement between them was one he hardly needed to
insist on.

The example of Bayle made a considerable impact on Leibniz's style of writing in the early eighteenth century. Here was a philosopher who could combine depth of insight with clarity, and whose wit and conversational style of writing made his works readable and accessible. This 'popular' style of writing seemed to Leibniz the one he should also adopt if he wished to succeed in making his philosophy influential. It is the one he sought to adopt in his two most substantial writings of this period, most particularly in his *New Essays on Human Understanding*, a kind of critical commentary on the *Essay* of John Locke.

Locke was seen by the *philosophes* in the mid-eighteenth century as a severe critic of metaphysical systems and indeed, in d'Alembert's words, as having 'reduced metaphysics to what it really ought to be: the experimental physics of the soul' (*Preliminary Discourse*, 84). Locke's *Essay* of 1690 is sufficiently different from the metaphysics of his time for him to be regarded as a forerunner of the *philosophes* (who held him in the highest esteem), and even as anticipating in some respects the 'critical philosophy' of Kant. But in its own time the *Essay Concerning Human Understanding* could be seen as belonging in a particular tradition of metaphysics that was previously associated with Aristotle and Pierre Gassendi. In short, he could be seen, not as a critic of metaphysical systems, but rather as the exponent of a rival system. And this was how he was read by Leibniz.

Leibniz's plan, in writing his *New Essays*, was to contrast Locke's system with his own, by means of a dialogue between two imaginary philosophers, one of whom spouts from Locke's *Essay* and the other of whom comments upon it. The commentator is a recent convert to Leibniz's philosophy, who had previously attached himself to the opinions of Descartes and Malebranche. The Locke spokesman is a French disciple of Gassendi, who has found his position much strengthened by Locke's *Essay*, of which he says:

> This author is pretty much in agreement with M. Gassendi's system, which is fundamentally that of Democritus: he supports vacuum and atoms, he believes that matter could think, that there are no innate ideas, that our mind is a *tabula rasa*, and that we do not think all the time; and he seems inclined to agree with most of M. Gassendi's objections against M. Descartes. He has enriched and strengthened this system with hundreds of fine thoughts . . . (*New Essays*, 70)

Leibniz had himself been attracted by Gassendi's system as a youth but had come to regard such a philosophy as one that should be resisted. In a letter to Malebranche (undated but

probably written before he embarked on writing the *New Essays*),
Leibniz wrote:

> I have also tried to combat, in passing, certain lax philosophers,
> like Mr Locke, Mr le Clerc and their like, who have wrong
> and base ideas about man, about the soul, about the under-
> standing and also about the divinity, and who treat as
> illusory whatever goes beyond their popular and superficial
> notions. They have failed to do justice to them because they
> are poorly informed about the mathematical sciences and are
> not sufficiently familiar with the nature of eternal truths.
> (*Philosophische Schriften* i, 361)

But, if the *New Essays* were written to 'combat' Locke's
system, this is not at all obvious from the way in which Locke is
treated. On the contrary, Leibniz is highly deferential and indeed
seems to be leaning over backwards to present Locke fairly. In
the early 1690s he had still been writing in the heavy style of
critique and refutation. Perhaps he had learnt a lesson from the
unfavourable response to his critiques of Descartes, which brought
against him the charge that he was trying to build his reputation
on the ruins of Descartes'. Perhaps he came to realise that the
style of critique and refutation only served to increase sectarianism
and was hardly suited to someone like himself who claimed not to
be a sectarian philosopher. Perhaps something of Bayle's tolerance
of different systems had rubbed off on Leibniz. At all events the
New Essays was an experiment in what was, for Leibniz, a new
style of writing.

Leibniz's *New Essays* seem to have been designed to cater to a
fashion for systems. But his purpose was quite different from that
of Bayle. Whereas Bayle wanted to persuade his readers to
distance themselves from any particular system, and to tolerate
diversity of opinion, Leibniz did, after all, have a system of his
own to offer and was not at all happy, to judge from his remarks
to Malebranche (quoted above), simply to tolerate Locke. Leibniz
found, however, that there was a way in which he could present
his system consistently with retaining many Bayle-like features
and treating Locke with respect. This was to present himself as an
eclectic. Thus he has his disciple tell of the 'new system' of which
he has read in the learned journals of Paris, Leipzig and Holland
and in Bayle's 'marvellous *Dictionary*':

> This system appears to unite Plato with Democritus, Aristotle
> with Descartes, the Scholastics with the moderns, theology
> and morality with reason. Apparently it takes the best from
> all systems and then advances further than anyone has yet
> done . . .' (*New Essays*, 71).

Such an eclecticism can be seen as a counterpart to Bayle's scepticism. Leibniz did indeed agree with Bayle that there were difficulties for all of the systems that vied with one another for public credence. And Bayle agreed with Leibniz that there was often much to be said for systems that were not widely favoured. But, whereas Bayle stressed the negative side, and so anticipated the scepticism about systems characteristic of the *philosophes* half a century later, Leibniz stressed the positive side. In one of his responses to Bayle he claimed that it was a virtue of his system that it brought out the truth in so many different schools of thought:

> . . . the lack of substantial reality in the sensible things of the skeptics; the reduction of everything to harmonies or numbers, ideas, and perceptions by the Pythagoreans and Platonists; the one and the whole of Parmenides and Plotinus, yet without any Spinozism; the Stoic connectedness, which is yet compatible with the spontaneity held to by others; the vitalism of the Cabalists and hermetic philosophers who put a kind of feeling into everything; the forms and entelechies of Aristotle and the Scholastics; and even the mechanical explanation of all particular phenomena by Democritus and the moderns; etc – all of these are found united as if in a single perspective centre from which the object, which is obscured when considered from any other approach, reveals its regularity and the correspondence of its parts. Our greatest failure has been the sectarian spirit which imposes limits upon itself by spurning others. (*Philosophical Papers*, 496)

Leibniz has been taken to be an eclectic by some of his commentators and undoubtedly there was an eirenic side to his character that led him to present himself as a reconciler and his philosophy as a harmonisation of the views of others. But his commitments were too strong for him to settle happily in such a role. In particular, as has recently been argued,[13] he was anxious to curtail the spread of materialism and for this reason to 'combat' the philosophy of Locke. While he was no one's disciple, he was more than anything else a kind of Christian Platonist.[14] It was Plato whom he, in common with a number of other leading seventeenth-century philosophers, regarded as a bastion against materialism. Plato was not a systematic philosopher, compared with Aristotle.[15] But Leibniz was probably stating the simple truth when he wrote to a correspondent: 'If someone were to reduce Plato to a system he would render a great service to mankind, and it would then be clear that my own views approach his somewhat' (*Philosophische Schriften*, iii, 638).

Leibniz, I am suggesting, never entirely adapted himself to the fashion for systems and hypotheses. He shared the widespread worry about the possibility of resolving disagreements in metaphysics and the proliferation of systems that results. But too much seemed to be at stake for him to be content with the scepticism of either Foucher or Bayle or with a tolerant eclecticism.

V

Leibniz was always hesitant about becoming embroiled publicly in metaphysical controversy and he made Locke's death in 1704 an excuse for not publishing his *New Essays*. He was, however, finally induced to publish a book in metaphysics, his *Theodicy*, subtitled *Essays on the Goodness of God, the Freedom of Man and the Origin of Evil*. Like the *New Essays*, the *Theodicy* is written in a popular style and it is also written as a corrective, this time against Bayle. Here he claimed to be presenting 'a certain system concerning the freedom of man and the co-operation of God', one that 'appeared to me to be such as would in no wise offend reasonable faith' (*Theodicy*, 68). In calling it a 'system', however, Leibniz was using the word in its old sense of an organised and supposedly defensible body of doctrine, and not in the new (fashionable) sense in which a 'system' is an explanation of phenomena. A confusion of the theological with the quasi-scientific use of the word 'system' may have been partly responsible for Leibniz's 'system of optimism' being misunderstood by the *philosophes*. Leibniz may partly be blamed for the confusion.[16] But the upshot was that in attacking the 'system of optimism' they attributed to Leibniz, the philosophes were attacking a strawman, as I shall bring out in Section VI below.

The *Theodicy* is primarily a set of essays 'written to oppose M. Bayle'. That Leibniz should have been 'exhorted and urged' (63) to write them is in itself a tribute to the impact of Bayle's *Dictionary*. Most notorious, perhaps, was Bayle's article on 'Manicheans', which in effect presented this heresy as rationally the equal of orthodox Christianity in its explanation of good and evil. 'It was fortunate that St Augustine, who was so well versed in all the arts of controversy, abandoned Manicheanism; for he had the capability of removing all the grossest errors from it and making of the rest of it a system, which in his hands would have perplexed

the orthodox' (*Dictionary: Selections*, 144). Perhaps Bayle wrote
this with his tongue in his cheek. At all events the effect of his
own contribution seems to have been to perplex the orthodox. It
seemed as if he were seeking to compensate the cause of Manicheanism for the loss occasioned by Augustine's conversion to
Christianity.

Bayle in fact thought it was quite proper that the orthodox
should be perplexed, if they sought to put their faith on a rational
basis. Bayle was an ardent fideist who sought to destroy natural
theology in order to give proper emphasis to revelation.[17] Doubts
have been expressed about his sincerity in this respect. But that is
perhaps because Bayle is often ironical and others, like Hume,
were later to use a similar irony in order to appear to espouse
fideism.

Whatever Bayle's intentions, however, his *Dictionary* was widely
regarded as subversive of established religion. And it seems
Leibniz was put under pressure from his patroness to produce the
Theodicy as a defence of orthodoxy. In his Preface, Leibniz
alludes to Manicheanism as one of those 'extravagant dogmas'
that happily no longer held sway among theologians. But he goes
on, in what seems an oblique reference to Bayle, to add:
'Nevertheless some astute persons, who are pleased to make
difficulties, revive them: they seek to increase our perplexity by
uniting the controversies aroused by Christian theology to the
disputes of philosophy' (*Theodicy*, 59). Bayle indeed treated
theological systems as if, like philosophical ones, they were
explanations of phenomena. And he thought that those who
opposed the Manicheans would be hard put to explain how moral
evil could exist in a world that is governed by an infinitely good
and holy principle. It would be easier to explain the existence of
evil, he suggested, as the Manicheans do, by appealing to a
separate evil principle and therefore to present the world as
governed ultimately by two conflicting principles.

Bayle was accused of defending Manicheanism because of his
claim that the hypothesis of two principles (one good, one evil)
governing the world could not be rationally refuted. But Bayle
himself seems to have been concerned to make a point about
reason itself:

> It is a principle of destruction and not of edification. It is
> only proper for raising doubts, and for turning things on all
> sides in order to make disputes endless . . . It is only fit to
> make man aware of his own blindness and weakness, and the
> necessity for another revelation. That is the one of Scripture.
> It is there that we find the means to refute invincibly the

hypothesis of the two principles and all the objections of Zoroaster. (*Dictionary: Selections*, 151)

Leibniz was wholly opposed to Bayle's way of putting faith and reason in opposition to one another. Faith goes *beyond* reason, he claimed in the Preliminary Dissertation to his *Theodicy*, but it is not *contrary* to reason. A philosophical theology does not seek to prove the mysteries of religion or to make them comprehensible. Rather it seeks to show how, for instance, belief in a good and wise omnipotent Creator of all things can be upheld in the face of evident objections such as the existence of evil. That is what Leibniz's 'system of optimism', as it came to be known, purports to do.

By replying to Bayle along these lines, Leibniz was in this case refusing to meet him on his own ground. He was retreating from offering an explanatory system in the fashionable sense. He was not putting forward the 'optimistic' view as the hypothesis that best explains the existence of evil. On the contrary he was assuming it and trying to show why it was not unreasonable in spite of the existence of evil. By the same token, he was not undertaking to show that Manicheanism was an unsatisfactory hypothesis. He was not, therefore, replying directly to Bayle's challenge. It was one thing to allow his system of pre-established harmony to be treated as a hypothesis and accepted or rejected on its merits as an explanation of the phenomena. It was quite another to allow the existence of a perfect Creator to be treated as a hypothesis. This Leibniz was never tempted to do.

Leibniz's accommodation to the fashion for systems and hypotheses was thus at most a partial one, relating to aspects of his metaphysics where his views had been novel and did not touch on central points of theology. The *Theodicy* makes some mention of these. But it caters to the fashion by its willingness to give an airing to extravagant opinions. Leibniz mainly assigns to himself the role of narrator and commentator, in a conversational style not unlike that of Bayle. The *Theodicy* was a success, being taken by many as a definitive solution to the problems relating to the existence of evil that had perplexed the orthodox since the publication of Bayle's *Dictionary*.

VI

I suggested earlier that the fashion for systems was one symptom of the crisis of metaphysics amongst those interested in Modern philosophy. Metaphysical disputes had come to seem endless and the very status of metaphysics as a pre-eminent science was in doubt. Leibniz, Locke and Bayle all showed an awareness of this crisis but of these three, only Leibniz sought to retain for metaphysics anything of its former role. By the mid-eighteenth century Bayle's scepticism about metaphysics had become pervasive in French philosophical circles. d'Alembert was able to report that the fashion for systems had been dealt a death-blow by the publication of Condillac's highly critical *Traité des Systèmes* (1746). And Condillac had done much to promote interest in Locke, not as himself the author of a system, but as the inventor of a quite different way of doing metaphysics. Metaphysics had become divorced from natural philosophy and become instead the study of the human mind and its ideas. With this change, Leibniz had come to appear as a philosopher of a past age.

In Germany, however, the course of philosophy in the same period was quite different. Leibniz, in his Latin writings, expressed his sense of the critical state of metaphysics as 'first philosophy' but not without holding out the hope that it could yet be done in a more exact and rigorous way.[18] The principles he stressed, like the principle of contradiction and the principle of sufficient reason, were ones familiar to Scholastic philosophers. The sense of crisis was largely defused in Germany, insofar as it existed, by an accommodation between Modern and Scholastic philosophy. It was only the influence of Locke and Hume on Kant in the late eighteenth century that re-awakened concern with how far metaphysics was possible.[19]

The *philosophes* shared with Bayle a scepticism about metaphysical systems but whereas Bayle (and evidently some of his readers) found them interesting and amusing, some of the leading *philosophes* were positively hostile to them. This is particularly true of Voltaire and d'Alembert. It is not true of Diderot, whose interest in speculation made him an admirer of Leibniz. But Voltaire and d'Alembert had been involved in the protracted controversy between the Newtonians and the Cartesians, as Diderot had not been. And it is this controversy, in which the Newtonians ultimately triumphed, that led to a hostility towards systems like that of Leibniz.

Newton's theory involved the thought that every object in the universe exerts a gravitational pull on every other, in accordance with his Inverse Square Law. This thought could not be reconciled with the mechanical philosophy of which the Cartesians (the followers of Descartes) were the outstanding defenders. According to the mechanical philosophy, one body could only act on another in virtue of acting on bodies in between. For there to be gravitational attraction, on this theory, the universe would need to be a *plenum*, i.e. it would need to be filled with matter and in this way there might be some hope of explaining how, for instance, the earth is kept in orbit round the sun. The Cartesians postulated such a *plenum* and sought a theory that would fit in with the requirements of the mechanical philosophy. Newton's theory did not postulate a *plenum* but, on the contrary, suggested that the sun exerted its influence on the earth directly, without the need of intervening matter. Newton declined to advance any 'hypothesis' as to how such a gravitational attraction was possible, declaring himself content with the experimental support he could claim for his mathematical principles.

The Cartesians were outraged at this, claiming that Newton's failure to give an intelligible account of how gravitation was possible made him no better than the Scholastics. Was not Newton's gravitation an 'occult quality'?[20] The Newtonians, for their part, rejected the metaphysics-led insistence that only 'intelligible' properties could be ascribed to matter. Their hostility to systems was grounded on their rejection of those dogmas that came to be seen as integral to Descartes' system – the insistence on a *plenum*, the denial of action at a distance, and the claim to know the essential properties of matter – that stood in the way of Newton's theory being readily accepted in France.

Newton's theory required a new modesty about how far the operations of nature could be understood, a new modesty that Hume well captured in his *History of Great Britain* (1754–63):

> While Newton seemed to draw off the veil from some of the mysteries of nature, he shewed at the same time the imperfections of the mechanical philosophy; and thereby restored her ultimate secrets to that obscurity in which they ever did and ever will remain.

The Newtonian dislike of systems was based above all on their pretence of explaining more than it seemed possible to explain. But d'Alembert, writing after the triumph of the Newtonians in France, seems to have been anxious to make peace with any whose sympathies remained residually with Descartes. Descartes was excused for the over-boldness of his theorising and was even presented as having, in a sense, prepared the way for Newton by overthrowing the authority of the Scholastics. No such palm was offered in Leibniz's direction. Leibniz bore the full brunt of the hostility to systems expressed in d'Alembert's *Preliminary Discourse* to the *Encyclopédie*.

D'Alembert, although outstanding in the mathematical sciences, was no historian or scholar. He respected Leibniz as a mathematician, but did not consider his metaphysics worth reading. Indeed he omits Leibniz from his proper chronological place in his section on the history of the sciences, coming to him as an afterthought when he had not been central to his story. 'Among these great men there is one whose philosophy, which is today both very well received and strongly opposed in the north of Europe, obliges us not to pass over him in silence. This is the illustrious Leibniz' (op. cit., 86).

D'Alembert credits Leibniz with seeing difficulties in Descartes' metaphysics but not with having made any advance in this subject. Since metaphysics is a subject which, as traditionally conceived, is not one in which d'Alembert thought anyone made advances, this part of his verdict is unsurprising. What is surprising is that d'Alembert should have claimed that Leibniz's 'system of *Optimism* is perhaps dangerous because of the alleged advantage it has of explaining everything' (op. cit., 87). For Leibniz, as we saw in the previous section, alleged no such advantage. Indeed his system of optimism was not the kind of system that purported to explain the phenomena (of suffering, or whatever) but a system of philosophical theology of an old-fashioned sort.

There are several possible explanations for this serious distortion of Leibniz's 'optimism' at the hands of the *philosophes*. It may be that Leibniz was confused with other fashionable optimists like Pope. It may be that the *philosophes* simply imposed on Leibniz their expectations of what a 'system' should be like – expectations that would certainly have been encouraged by their reading of Bayle. It may be that this was how Leibniz was defended by his enthusiasts in the controversies 'in the north of Europe' to which d'Alembert alludes. One way or another, it became possible to present Leibniz's thought in a debased form, a process that is taken to an extreme in Voltaire's *Candide*. The Leibnizian disciple, Dr Pangloss, is a stupid, woffling, pedantic figure who has mastered a little jargon and a few formulas and serves them up without any sense of their inappropriacy to the circumstances in which he finds himself. If the fashion for such systems of optimism survived d'Alembert's *Preliminary Discourse*, it could hardly survive Voltaire's satire.

VII

I have tried, in this paper, to link the presentation of Leibniz's philosophy with a particular phase in French philosophy. I have suggested that Leibniz went too far in presenting his philosophy so as to make it appear more in tune with the then current trends than it really was. In particular I have tried to bring out how Leibniz accommodated himself to the fashion for systems and hypotheses. If, in so doing, he became a more fashionable figure than he would otherwise have been,[21] he was later to pay the price for misrepresenting himself by being himself misrepresented by leading figures of the French Enlightenment. For the very existence of such a fashion cloaked a benign scepticism as to what could be established in metaphysics. It was not a large step from the benign scepticism of Bayle to the hostile and positivistic scepticism of d'Alembert.

If my account of Leibniz's major French writings in the period 1695–1710 is correct, it suggests that we should be wary about basing our interpretations of Leibniz's philosophy too much on them. If we do so, then we are liable to think that his system was merely hypothetical or that Leibniz was a kind of eclectic. The Leibniz of his Latin writings of this period presents a different face and shows a concern to achieve a more rigorous and demonstrative metaphysics. This concern found a ready response in Germany and is partly why his reputation there never suffered the same fluctuations of fortune that it did in France. It also partly explains why Leibniz should appear both as a forerunner of the Enlightenment and as epitomising what it was against. If, however, the agreement of Hume and d'Alembert in rejecting systems is evidence of the international character of the Enlightenment, Leibniz's much better reception in Germany is evidence that it is confusing to think of the Enlightenment as a unified historical phenomenon.

NOTES

1 When I refer to 'French philosophy' I mean philosophy that was conducted in the French language. Descartes, by writing in French, made serious philosophy accessible to a wider readership, including aristocratic women, than formerly. But some French philosophers continued to write in Latin even in the late seventeenth century. And French became, in some measure, the language of the Cartesians, including those in Holland. Leibniz was untypically German in the trouble he took to learn French. In his own time Latin was the language in which German philosophers communicated with one another. Christian Wolff is usually credited with having made the German language a suitable one for philosophical transaction.

2 See Charles B. Schmitt's 'Towards a Reassessment of

Renaissance Aristotelianism', republished in his *Studies in Renaissance Philosophy and Science* (London: Variorum Reprints, 1981).

3 For some further details, see J.S. Spink's *French Free-Thought from Gassendi to Voltaire* (New York: Greenwood Press, 1969). 189 ff.

4 A letter written by Leibniz to his former teacher Jacob Thomasius in *1669* exemplifies this tendency to harmonise Scholastic and Modern philosophy. See *Philosophical Papers*, 93–103.

5 Malebranche proceeded by laying out the various possible ways in which external objects can be seen and by examining each in turn to discover which is 'the likeliest way'. His method was, in effect, one of exclusion. The implausibility of each of the rival accounts is appealed to in support of his own view that we see all things in God. It is what he called a 'proof' rather than a strict 'demonstration'. See *Search after Truth*, 219 ff.

6 Its fashionability was, of course, already made possible by the fact that a vernacular language was being used for philosophical communications. One sign of this was the increasing interest in metaphysics shown by women. Leibniz communicated in French with a number of aristocratic women, including Lady Masham and his own patroness, the Electress Sophie.

7 See Leroy E. Loemker's 'Notes and Documents relating to the origin of Leibniz's *Discourse* of 1686' *Journal of the History of Ideas*, 1946, 465.

8 For a fuller account of this, see Richard A. Watson's *The Downfall of Cartesianism 1673–1712* (The Hague: Nijhoff, 1966).

9 The view that the world is ultimately made up of simples or what Leibniz later called 'monads' betrays Leibniz's commitment to Platonism. See my Introduction to *Leibniz: Discourse on Metaphysics and Related Writings*, eds R.N.D. Martin and Stuart Brown (Manchester University Press, 1987).

10 In a separate correspondence, Leibniz had been accused by Antoine Arnauld of founding his requirement that substances be true unities on a definition made up contrary to common usage. His reply suggests Leibniz thought this requirement was founded on a tautology – that 'what is not truly *a* being is not truly a *being*'. (*Philosophische Schriften*, ii, 96). It is not clear whether Leibniz remained convinced of this spurious argument or what he finally thought the status of his 'view of unities' was.

11 The distinction is broadly that between the scepticism of the (Platonic) Academy, which Foucher claimed to have revived, and the tradition of Pyrrhonian scepticism to which Bayle evidently belongs. See Richard H. Popkin's Preface to his *A History of Scepticism from Erasmus to Descartes* (Assen: van Gorcum & Co., 1960).

12 Leibniz was lavish in his praise for Bayle as a critic. See *Philosophical Papers*, 582.

13 By Nicholas Jolley in his *Leibniz and Locke: A Study of the New Essays on Human Understanding* (Oxford University Press, 1984). Jolley brings out well how Leibniz read Locke's *Essay* as a defence of a rival system and not, as subsequent philosophers have done, as a critique of systems.

14 See my Introduction to *Leibniz: Discourse on Metaphysics and Related Writings*, op. cit.

15 In his *Theodicy*, Leibniz remarks by way of preliminary that in the primitive Church 'the ablest Christian authors adapted themselves to the ideas of the Platonists' but adds: 'Little by little Aristotle took the place of Plato, when the taste for systems began to prevail, and when theology itself became more systematic . . .' (76). This 'taste for systems' seems, from the context, to refer to the proneness to various heresies, such as Manicheanism, that bedevilled early Christianity and which Bayle liked to write about in his *Dictionary*. Leibniz does not contradict the common opinion that many of these heresies were inspired by Plato's philosophy. But he seems to have thought that it would have been better to systematise Plato than to try to accommodate Christianity to the already systematic Aristotle.

16 There seems to have been a good deal of confusion about the word 'system' in the late seventeenth century, arising partly from divergent views about the relations between theology, metaphysics and the natural sciences. There was no agreement about how to separate these subjects in Leibniz's time nor about how each might make use of the conclusions of the others, if at all. Conditions were ripe for attempts at stipulating what a proper 'system' should be like, a matter to which Leibniz began to give thought in the 1690s. Such a stipulation is implicit in Pierre–Sylvain Regis' claim that his *Système de Philosophie* (1690) was the first proper 'system' of philosophy to be produced. The fashion, however, was not for such demonstrative systems but for the more speculative explanatory systems offered by Malebranche and taken up by Bayle.

17 That Bayle was a fideist is convincingly argued by Elizabeth Labrousse in her 'Past Masters' book on *Bayle* (Oxford University Press, 1983). See especially 56 ff.

18 See, for instance his paper *De primae philosophiae emendatione* . . . ('On the Correction of Metaphysics . . .') of 1694, *Philosophical Papers*, 432 f.

19 See, for instance, Kant's *Prolegomena to Any Future Metaphysics Which Will Be Able To Come Forth as Science*, first published in 1783.

20 That Leibniz agreed with the Cartesians on this point and also on insisting (if for reasons of his own) on a *plenum* was

public knowledge. Leibniz had carried out a public correspondence with a disciple of Newton (Samuel Clarke) and his opposition to Newton may have been one reason for the hostility to Leibniz shown by the French Newtonians, such as Voltaire and d'Alembert.

21 For a detailed account of the French reception of Leibniz, see W.H. Barber's *Leibniz in France from Arnauld to Voltaire* (Oxford, Clarendon Press, 1955). Although this work is now in some respects dated, it has not been superceded.

SHORT BIBLIOGRAPHY

D'ALEMBERT, JEAN (1751) *Preliminary Discourse to the Encyclopaedia of Diderot*, ed. Richard Schwab. Indianapolis: Bobbs-Merrill, 1963.

BAYLE, PIERRE (1696) *Historical and Critical Dictionary – Selections*, eds R. Popkin and C. Brush. New York: Bobbs-Merrill, 1965.

BECK, LEWIS WHITE (1969) *Early German Philosophy*, Cambridge: Harvard University Press.

CONDILLAC, ETIENNE BONNOT DE 1746 *Traité des Systèmes*, trans. Franklin Philip, *Philosophical Writings of Etienne Bonnot. Abbé de Condillac*, Hillsdale, New Jersey: Lawrence Erlbaum, 1982.

HUME, DAVID (1751) *Enquiry Concerning the Principles of Morals*, in *Hume's Enquiries*, ed. L.A. Selby-Bigge. Oxford: Clarendon Press, 1902 and many impressions.

LEIBNIZ, GOTTFRIED 1875–90 *Philosophische Schriften*, ed. C.I. Gerhardt, 7 vols, Berlin. Reprinted Hildesheim: Olms, 1978.

——(1969) *Philosophical Papers and Letters*, ed. and trans. L.E. Loemker, 2nd edition. Dordrecht: D. Reidel.

——(1704) *New Essays on Human Understanding*, eds P. Remnant and J. Bennett. Cambridge University Press, 1981.

——(1710) *Theodicy: Essays on the Goodness of God, the Freedom of Man and the Origin of Evil*, ed. Austin Farrar, trans. E.M. Huggard. London: Routledge and Kegan Paul, 1951.

MALEBRANCHE, NICOLAS (1674–5) *The Search after Truth*, eds T.M. Lennon and P.J. Olscamp. Columbus: Ohio State University Press, 1980.

2

JOHN WILLIAMSON

Boyle and Locke on Material Substance

One of the achievements of Enlightenment thought was a co-operative result not due to any one person. It was to put chemistry in a relatively orderly state. Boyle is often described as the father of chemistry, but he seems a Neanderthal ancestor in comparison with late eighteenth century chemists such as Lavoisier, Priestley or Davy. This caricature aims to suggest a perspective, not to disparage, for Boyle undoubtedly had some role in the process, though it is hard to assess what it is. Relatively clear ideas emerged about the nature of material substances, and what system governs their changes, and it is difficult to describe exactly the original confusion regarding these ideas, and how it was overcome. The problem concerns the understanding of those changes in nature, vital to industrial society, in which different kinds of chemical substances come into existence or perish. It self-evidently requires some general conception of what constitutes identity of a material substance, and the conditions under which chemical identities begin or end.

A temporally parallel feature in pure philosophy is that theories about substance seem to have been regarded increasingly obsolete as major issues. Some might think this has only an accidental and verbal connection with the history of chemistry, on the ground that philosophers' substance theories were not about chemical substances. That is not clearly so. 'Substance' is notoriously ambiguous in the history of ideas. It is often hard to know what a particular writer means by it, and two different users of it might be referring to different things. In two important cases for the topic in hand, Aristotle and Locke, there was a keen and direct concern with what might now be called chemistry. The narrow theme of this paper is Locke's theory of substance. That his theory has this kind of scientific provenance is part of what I have to say about it. The reason for thinking so has in part to do with the relation of his philosophy to Boyle's, and the nature of what Boyle had to say about substance in, for example, *The Sceptical Chymist*. In recent years it has been well recognised that there are

significant affinities between Locke and Boyle, though not the
specific affinity I shall discuss.

The immediate problem which occasions this paper is exegetical.
It is that Locke in the *Essay Concerning Human Understanding*
does not sufficiently explain what he is talking about in the matter
of substance. He appears to say inconsistent things about it, and
he inherited a notoriously ambiguous terminology. The inconsistency does not seem unduly forbidding, but commentators have
not agreed on how to sort it out. My solution makes him out to
refer, in a marginal way, to a chemical theory now obsolete, so my
secondary theme is much broader. It is to reflect on the fate of
that theory, and on the fact that the death of 'substance theories'
in the Enlightenment as a debatable philosophical subject was
also, *inter alia*, the dropping by philosophers of that age of a
perfectly good subject, the philosophy of chemistry.

The apparent inconsistency appears in the first statement of
Locke's view in *EHU*, II. xii. 6 where he says that each idea of a
substance is a combination of simple ideas, plus the confused idea
of substance. He manifestly does not intend to say paradoxically
that some complex contains itself, and I assume he has a
consistent doctrine, badly expressed to modern ears. It is that
each idea of a particular thing or chemical substance is a complex
of simple ideas, plus the confused idea of a certain entity which is
in a certain sense theoretical, and sometimes called 'substratum'.
His examples are the idea of man (particular) and the idea of lead
(chemical substance). The problem is to know what this object of
reference is when using the word 'substratum'.

Locke's doctrine about this unidentified object seems quite
clear. That the substratum exists is not a perceived fact; it is
postulated to exist (II.xxiii. 1); we have no idea of it; (II.xiii.19,
xxiii.2–4); we do have an idea that two things are true of it;
namely (a) that the qualities that simple ideas are ideas of *belong* to
it (II.xxiii.3,37) and (b) *subsist* or *inhere* in it (II.xiii.19; II.xxiii3,
37) or are supported by it (II.xiii19, xxiii.4). There is some doubt
about Locke's own commitment to the existence of a substratum.
When he says 'we postulate it', does he include himself? Is the
idea that the qualities of lead inhere in a substratum, an idea that
we merely contemplate or entertain, or is it a belief, and in
particular a belief of Locke's?

There are three things to which he might be referring under the
name 'substratum', roughly describable as a kind of metaphysical
or logical entity; or as an epistemic entity; or as a chemical entity.
These names suggest perhaps more the reasons which he might

have had for postulating its existence, rather than its intrinsic nature. What the reasons were, and who else postulated the same, are conjectural matters.

The standard option seems to be the metaphysical version, though it is scarcely coherent, and there is no apparent reason why Locke should have held there to be such a thing. The substratum on this view is a secret real particular thing that underlies each apparent particular thing, a propertyless property bearer that 'stands under' the properties, and is the real thing itself behind the appearances. If to bear a property is to have it, there is a contradiction in saying that x has certain qualities; yet the real x has no such qualities, but only 'bears' them. In fact Locke explicitly says that the substratum owns or has the qualities, and he would be inconsistent to claim that a thing having qualities is identical with a thing that does not.

Combining the incompatibility of having qualities with standing under them is evidently inconsistent with the claim that there is also an identity. The identity claim has nothing to recommend it in modern eyes, nor apparently in Locke's. He mentions it in a footnote, referring to the Bishop of Worcester's comments on an earlier edition, without indicating his own view about it. He says that the substratum 'was looked upon as the thing itself' (II.xxiii.1, note). Who by? For what reason? It may be that he is purporting to give an account of the genesis of a universally held thesis, so that he himself holds the thesis too, but there is no indication that it is so. He may merely be indicating the views of others.

One way to avoid the inconsistency is to deny the identity, and to regard the underlying secret thing as real, and the appearance as unreal, a doctrine somewhat Platonic in spirit. Another recourse is to take the apparent object to *have* but not support the qualities, and the underlying reality to *support* but not have them. None of these is explicit in Locke's text, on the contrary, he takes the substratum to both have and support the qualities, so the identity needs no questioning. At least, this is so for material substance; mental substance is decidedly another matter, and it may very well be right to allege that Locke's account of mental substance fits ill with his account of material substance, as might well be said about Berkeley.

The postulation of a substratum is sometimes represented as a response to the obvious logical requirement, that a quality should belong to something. The smile needs the Cheshire Cat. Locke no doubt accepted that, for who does not? It is an unimportant point because there is no lack of an owner. The ordinary superficial horse is all that the qualities of the horse require. There is nothing missing that logic needs, so there is no basis relating to the logic for postulating any substratum.

It is a characteristic of this interpretation of substance that it focuses on individuals. The doctrine is about individuals, and if chemical substances come into the discussion, they do so as a minor special case, and it is about their pieces and portions, not about them *simpliciter*. The substratum is conceived as an individual underlying individuals. The two alternative views here considered both differ from this view; the first in saying that substratum is the real essence of a thing, and so is a class of qualities; the second in saying that substratum is a chemical substance, in much the sense in which that word is understood in contemporary speech.

What 'substratum' and 'real essence' undoubtedly have in common is that, according to Locke, we have no idea of that which either names. The reason in the case of real essence is epistemological. It could only be got by sense perception, and the senses are not adequate to see such very small things. The real essence of a thing is the constitution of its finer physical parts and imperceptible particles. It would presumably be completely specified by a true description of all qualities of all such parts.

The merit of this interpretation depends on what alternatives there might be, and I am inclined to think it better than the 'metaphysical' view. There is little positive otherwise, for Locke nowhere says that substratum is the real essence of anything, and does not bring the two into relation. Considering the circumstantial evidence, there are some strong objections. Some are reviewed by Alexander,[2] and I add some points. First, the doctrine about substratum is not on the face of it intelligible when taken to be also about real essences. This would explain his failure to advocate the doctrine, but not his tolerance of it. The two facts about substratum that we have an idea of are that it has the properties of whatever it underlies, and it also underlies them. The real essence of a thing might be supposed to underlie a thing, in some sense, but not to have its properties. It is a constitution, characterised by some composite description of various qualities of various parts of a thing, and such constitutions are not green, or pear shaped, and the like. A constitution is a set of facts about small bodies, and does not have the qualities of the macroscopic body the small bodies constitute.

A second difficulty is that Locke seems to suppose that there is some unique theoretical entity, the substratum, but there are many real essences, as many as there are different classes or chemical substances with a general name. Both theories so far discussed neglect this point, for they both suppose that when substratum is mentioned it is to be taken as relativised to some object. On the metaphysical view, we are to speak about the substratum of some individual; on the epistemic view, we are to speak about the substratum of a species or class; but Locke does not speak of it in that way. He refers to it as 'substance in general', or as 'substratum' in the singular, never in the plural form to be expected if there are many substrata, as there are many essences.

A third difficulty is that Locke claims that individuals have no essence, yet it would be absurd to claim that he held there to be no substratum underlying each material individual. Where this thesis is announced (III.vi.4), he does not distinguish for this purpose between real and nominal essence, so it might be conjectured, were there nothing else to go on, that it might only be true of nominal essences, that individuals have none. *Qua* member of a species, an individual has sundry nominal essences, in the sense that it has all those qualities, the ideas of which are part of that abstract idea of whatever several species it belongs to. There are several, because an individual belongs to many species at once, as a man may be a sailor, husband, Whig, hero and Welshman simultaneously. Might it be supposed that Locke thought, though he did not say it, that an individual has at least one real essence, and that when he said individuals have no essence, he thought the opposite, and only meant that they have no nominal essence?

It seems unlikely that Locke should have been so inept at saying what he thought. His account of real and nominal essences also shows that they are linked; if a thing has no nominal essence considered in a certain way, it has no real essence either in that way.

Here is a second doubt, this time over which qualities the real essence is postulated to explain the existence of. In III.vi.2 the real constitution of individuals is said to be that on which 'depends' the nominal essence and all the properties of that class. I take this reference to properties to be to the properties definitive of the class, or which are common to all its members (the same thing, for Locke); but one might conjecture that he refers to all the properties of every member of the class. The real essence, then, explains the possession of every quality of every member, not just the possession of those which belong to its nominal essence. It seems clarified in III.vi.6 where he is more explicit, and says the real essence is the 'foundation' of just those properties that are combined in the nominal essence. If the real

essence of a class is to be identified in terms of its nominal
essence, then if there is no nominal essence, there is no real
essence either. He adds that even in the sense of real essence,
essence relates to a sort, and supposes a species. So, when he says
that individuals have no essence, and makes no distinction at that
point between kinds of essence, the natural supposition – that he
means it of all kinds without distinction – is also the right
supposition. The objection therefore stands; individuals *per se*
have a substratum but no real essence, so substratum cannot be a
real essence.

The favoured third alternative is that Locke intended to refer
to what it would be harmless to call now underlying matter,
though it requires some explanation and qualification. The
suggestion has several components. First, what is being referred
to when Locke uses 'substance' in the now mystifying sense is, in
a certain unusual respect, a theoretical entity. Second, the theory
in question is not his invention. Third, it is scientific, and belongs
to physics, not to psychology or philosophy, so it is not part of his
subject matter to expound or defend it. In fact we only want to
know what the theory is in order to know what he was talking
about; what he says about it is clear enough. Fourth, a good deal
of the mystification is due to 'substance' being a mass term, to use
modern jargon, which does not refer to an individual, nor to a
species or class, but to a substance in the ordinary modern sense.
Fifth, the theory is obsolete. Locke's discussion is not a piece of
perennial philosophy that we may now debate on its intrinsic
merits, but a contribution to a transient matter in the philosophy
of science of his time, but not of ours. What made it transient is
not any development in philosophy, but the evolution of chemistry.
Sixth, the answer to the question posed earlier *en passant*, as to
who conjectured the existence of substratum, is not the man in
the street, and not any antique school of influential philosophy
that Locke was fighting against, but the men of science of his day.
He is reacting to learned scientific theory.

These points being granted, it becomes understandable, both
that he should not undertake to expound or defend the theory in
question, since it is not within his chosen science, so to speak; and
yet that he should also tolerate and go along with it, just as we all
now go along with standard accepted theories of our own day, by
and large, when not professionally involved. The pages of his text
are for the same reason not the best place to gain understanding of
the details of the theory, since he has no commitment to its
exposition. Boyle is the best author for that, not only on account
of his personal association with and doctrinal influence on Locke,

but because he was the principal chemical theorist of his day. Dominating his whole approach to the subject was a theory of substance and of underlying matter. Boyle has not been conspicuously honoured by historians of chemistry for that theory, and it was forgotten, perhaps by the time of Lavoisier, but it is not credible that contemporaries such as Locke were equally oblivious to it. There was no comparable rival theory, no comparably authoritative source, no alternative argued case.

Locke's conjecture that there is a substratum refers to the conjecture that there is a prime matter, *materia prima* or elementary matter, that underlies all the apparent chemical distinctions between substances such as water, lead, gold, mercury and so on. In one form or another, the idea is ancient, and pre-Socratics could be said to have dabbled in its crude forms, as when Thales says that everything is water. Almost all the ancient science is irrelevant in this context however. The term *materia prima* is often associated with medieval Aristotelean metaphysics, where the phrase presumably originated, but Boyle's theory is not medieval, not metaphysical and not Aristotelean. To borrow a term is not to join a school. It is no argument against the suggestion that Locke in speaking of underlying substance is referring to *materia prima*, that he was not an Aristotelean. It has recently been disputed, whether Aristotle had a doctrine of prime matter, but that, too, is beside the point.[3]

The oddity of Locke's usage of 'substance' is this. In modern use, it is a mass sortal, to coin a phrase. That is to say, it is a sortal noun used to signify classes whose members are not individuals but masses, which is to say those objects referred to by mass terms. For example, 'lead', 'water', oxygen' and 'flesh' are commonly now called mass terms; the masses they refer to are sundry chemical entities, materials, stuffs, commodities or substances. 'Material', 'stuff' and 'substance' are sortal terms signifying classes, and the class members are masses. This mass-class-denoting use of the word 'substance' is not of recent origin in English, and is, for example, Boyle's ordinary way of using the word. If, on the other hand, substance in the sense of 'substratum' refers to prime matter, it is being used as a mass term, not as a mass sortal. 'Prime matter' is a mass term, and prime matter is a mass, viz that substance which constitutes every material thing, unknown though that supposed fact may be to the man in the street; or to put it another way, unknown to the senses.

I will supply a little evidence in support of the point about Boyle's use of 'substance' as a mass sortal. In *The Sceptical Chymist* Boyle variously speaks of 'a certain saline substance I prepared'; 'a hard and brittle substance'; '. . . can resolve them into elementary substances . . .'; 'any substance simple enough to deserve the name of an element . . .'; 'some such distinct substances may be obtained from some concretes without fire'; 'the substances which chymists are wont to call the salts . . .'; 'he could dissolve metals, marchasites (etc) into their several similar substances'; 'in our own common analysis of a mixt body there remains a terrestrial and very fixt substance'. These examples and many more occur throughout the work.[4] Boyle thus habitually and frequently uses 'substance' as we now do, as a mass sortal.

The sense in which prime matter is a theoretical object is unusual. Electrons, quarks and the like are the usual modern examples, and these are imperceptible; whereas prime matter is not, for it is everywhere one looks. What escapes the senses is not prime matter, but the capacity to identify it as such. We can see it, but we cannot see that it exists, or that that is what we are seeing. It is the facts about it which are imperceptible, not itself.

A strange corollary of this connection with identity theory is that all the substances and chemical individuals that are the topic of chemistry are on this theory identical with one another, since they are all identical with prime matter. The identity here is not that of individuals, nor of classes, nor of any abstract things, but of substances or masses. Lead is the same substance as prime matter, and so is gold, so lead is the same substance as gold, in theory. It does not appear to be, and so the theory is about identity 'behind the appearances', so to speak, or underlying the apparent differences of materials.

The sense of identity cannot be that defined by Leibniz's law of 'absolute' identity, or as the law might be argued, the law of that sortal relative identity predicate expressed by 'is the same individual as'. That is to say, 'is the same substance as' is a kind of identity which does not coincide with perfect coincidence of properties, if the ordinary perceptible properties of substances are genuine properties. Gold is yellow, and lead is not, yet we are to entertain the idea of their identity. In this period of philosophy, it might be questioned which properties are real, and whether yellowness is a real property, for the theory of secondary properties was well entrenched, one way or another, and was accepted by Boyle and Locke. Still, coincidence of properties cannot be supposed to define this sense of identity, since it is a kind of sortal relative identity, expressed by 'is the same chemical substance as'. To show this: graphite is the same chemical substance as diamond; red phosphorus is the same chemical substance as white phosphorus; ice is the same chemical substance as steam; and so on. In each case, this kind of sameness by no means requires sameness of *all* properties, only of certain crucial properties.

It is a species of sortal relative identity, but distinctive in relating to mass sortals. 'Substance' is nearly always a mass sortal in Boyle's usage, but only occasionally in Locke's. Modern chemistry is rich in mass sortals, but not in Boyle's day. For example, graphite is the same element as, but not the same allotrope as, diamond. The term 'mass sortal' is best understood from its modern exemplars, such as 'acid', 'rare earth', 'gas', 'salt' alcohol' etc. Acids, I claim, are a class; 'acetic acid' is a mass term; acetic acid is a member of the class, and is in my terminology a mass; and acids are a class of masses. 'Substance' is now usually used as a mass sortal, but it is untypical in being exceptionally general. It is comparable to 'thing' or 'object' or 'entity' among individual sortals, and covers a much bigger class than words like 'acid.'

The sortal relative identity predicate 'is the same substance as' is therefore one of great generality, comparable in its broadness to 'is the same individual thing as', but differing entirely from it in its range of application, since it ranges over masses, not individuals.

The criteria of correct application of this relational predicate is therefore a question of comparable generality, and one might suppose of difficulty, to the question of the criteria of individual identity, and seems of similar theoretical interest to it in philosophy. It is also, however, in particular a question for chemical natural philosophy, for the conditions under which some substance loses its identity, and ceases to exist as such, is the same as the question of what chemical change consists of. It is therefore not quite an 'armchair' question, but central to pure chemistry. There is no reason why it should not also belong to philosophy and in Boyle's time philosophers could treat it as both, without having to change their trade union.

When sulphur burns, the sulphur ceases to exist, for sulphur dioxide is a different substance. Yet the sulphur exists 'in potentiality', for we can recover it from the oxide. In cases of evaporation, a substance may apparently disappear, but not really. The senses do not tell us which is which, and do not distinguish the cases where there is chemical change from where there is none. The unaided senses do not tell us when a substance, such as sulphur, ceases to exist, and so the criteria of identity of substance are not entirely sensible, but a matter for theory. How to distinguish chemical change from non-change was therefore, understandably for the end of the alchemical era, acutely problematic. When wax melts, the substance seems to change into a different substance, yet it does not; that this is so is a modern theory, not determined by the perceptible facts about wax.

The problematic nature of theories of this kind has an additional interest where there is a financial interest, as in the case of gold. When gold dissolves in mercury, it does not cease to exist; when it dissolves in acid, it does. The appearance of cessation of existence is the same in each case, for the gold vanishes in both. The difference between chemical change and physical change is determined by the criteria of sameness of substance, and coincides with the distinction between events where a substance stays the same substance, and those where it ceases to exist. Change of properties may occur in both, and the substance may disappear to the senses in both cases.

Ancient atomism bequeathed a theory of chemical identity, in outline, and updated by Bacon, in the form of a theory of textures. The characteristic or even definitive properties of various substances could be attributed to their having fine particles of a certain texture, i.e. a certain (perhaps average) shape and size of particle, having certain spatial relations. It is this, along with the accompanying doctrine of primary and secondary qualities that Boyle alludes to in remarking, for example, that the three principles of the world as it now is are matter, motion and rest, whereas 'colours, odours, tastes, fluidity and solidity, and those other qualities that diversify and denominate bodies may intelligibly be deduced from these three'. My suggestion is that 'and denominate' here may be read as 'and determine the chemical identity of', since 'denominate' refers to names, and names go with identities.

The idea of a universal of prime matter arises from this, for if to have a certain identity (as for example salt, or sugar) is to have a certain form, pattern or texture because the corpuscles have certain characteristic shapes, sizes and motions, it follows that the corpuscles themselves do not have that same chemical identity. They have no texture whatever, since they lack any finer corpuscles. For the same reason, they cannot change their chemical identity; they cannot be created or destroyed by chemical action. Chemical change is change of chemical identity, and is to change from the texture characteristic of one substance to that of another. It is change of form, not change of matter, if by 'matter' is meant that of which the pieces of a thing are made, for all things are made of the same unique and uniform universal substance.

Eighteenth-century critics of earlier doctrines of material substance, such as Berkeley and Hume, made a big feature of the uncertain meaning of 'inherence' or its converse 'underlying', and if one disregards technical theorising, it is hard to understand. In what way does universal matter underlie matter? The theory that takes Locke's substratum to be real essences would make it like the theoretical entities of modern science, i.e. it is just a question of being imperceptible. The alternative I propose differs from that, for prime matter is just as perceptible as secondary matter, since it is the same substance as every substance.

Berkeley and others assumed that the relation of underlying holds between an individual and its qualities. The individual therefore becomes mysterious, for if qualities inhere in the individual, and 'underlie' is the converse relation, the individual underlies its own qualities. On the theory of prime matter as a chemical entity, the relations hold between masses, so no such mystery arises. Prime matter underlies secondary matter, and 'underlying' refers to a relation between mass term referents. Prime matter is that undistinguished uniform substance which underlies all the distinctions we make between apparently different substances under names such as 'iron', 'sulphur', 'water' and the like. They are 'apparently' different in that they differ to the senses, supposedly because of the differences in the textures of their minute parts. Some might say that they are unreal differences, but that is not the language of Boyle or Locke. They are secondary differences rather as secondary qualities are secondary, in depending on relations they have to perceiving beings, and hence having a kind of subjective dependence on the existence of perceivers.

Prime matter is referred to at the beginning of 'The Sceptical Chymist as universal matter, in Proposition 1 and subsequently. Eleutherius remarks that 'according to Aristotle, and I think according to truth, there is but one common mass of all things, which he has been pleased to call *materia prima* . . .' Carneades is usually regarded as more properly the mouthpiece of Boyle's opinions, and he soon after takes it up.

> I consider, that there being but one universal matter of things, as 'tis known that the Aristoteleans themselves acknowledge, who call it *materia prima* . . . the portions of this matter seem to differ from one another, but in certain qualities or accidents . . . upon whose account the corporeal substance they belong to receives its denomination, and is referred to this or that particular sort of bodies; so that if it come to lose . . . those qualities, though it ceases not to be a body, yet it ceases from being that kind of body . . . (SC, 87).

In *The Origin of Forms and Qualities* he remarks that 'there is one universal matter, common to all bodies, an extended, divisible, and impenetrable substance . . . This matter being in its own nature but one, the diversity in bodies must necessarily arise from somewhat else'. One little habit of vocabulary to notice is that Boyle often uses 'body' to mean 'substance', so that this passage may be very naturally read as dealing with chemical substances. Locke's usage is quite distinct. For him, a body is always a spatially specific individual.

In the context of the last quoted passage, Boyle goes on 'when oil takes fire, the oil is not said to be altered but corrupted or destroyed, and fire generated; (but) nothing substantial either in this or any other kind of corruption is destroyed'. This deductively implies that oil is not substantial. The reference to corruption indicates the generalisability of this remark to any case of chemical change, which is to say, to any case where some apparent chemical substance ceases to exist and is replaced by a different substance. The general implication is that no chemical substance of the kinds we ordinarily give names to, such as 'oil' 'water' and the like, is substantial. The one universal matter is the only substantial thing, the only material substance. It is intelligible grammar to use 'substance' in the singular, as Locke does.

Mass terms answer the question 'what is this thing made of?' The usual answers are in some way secondary, since all things consist of the same substance, the 'one catholic or universal matter common to all bodies'. The diversity we see in bodies must necessarily arise from somewhat else than the matter they consist of (OFQ, 18). This somewhat else is their corpuscular texture, which determines chemical identity to appearances.

> If it be true, as 'tis probable, that compounded bodies differ from one another but in the various textures resulting from the bigness, shape, motion and contrivance of their small parts, it will not be irrational to conceive that one and the same parcel of universal matter may by various alterations and contextures be brought to deserve the name, sometimes of a terrene, or aqeous body . . . (SC, 64).

Further on, he repeats, 'by a change of texture . . . the same parcel of matter may acquire or lose such accidents as may suffice to denominate it salt, or sulphur, or earth . . . (SC, 199). The transmutation of base metals into gold is feasible; it is a kind of engineering problem, of how to crunch up the pieces to give the right texture to make it fit the human description 'gold' instead of that of 'lead'. Whether it is transmutation of an element is an open question, for it is open whether there are any elements. What *The Sceptical Chemist* was sceptical about was primarily whether there is any determinate number of elements, so it is a question whether there are any at all. The fundamental theory does not require their existence. Boyle criticised older views of elements such as those of Paracelsus, but he did not replace them with any modern alternative.

One idea which has survived, and was a notable innovation, was his suggestion that chemical identity and change are a matter of clusters, rather than of separate corpuscles. In the ancient theories, macroscopic properties such as the viscosity of butter and water, to take an example from Lucretius, were postulated to result from the different shapes of the atoms: what hooks and protuberances they have. Boyle's overall conception of corpuscles is much like the antique, but his theory of clusters appears new. By the time of Lavoisier, that chemical identity is associated with stable and characteristic molecules seems well established, and certainly of course in Dalton's time. The interim history of that idea in the Enlightenment seems of some interest.

It does not belong to the history of philosophy in that period, and Locke's discussion of material substance closes a chapter, if I am right in thinking that it had anything to do with it at all. The concept of chemical identity and its relation to change had been among the accepted topics of philosophy before Locke and Boyle, and I think it was still so for them, but it has not appeared in philosophy since. It is one aspect of the beginning of the divorce between science and philosophy. The disappearance during the Enlightenment of theories of substance has come to seem the dropping of muddled and mystifying and unnecessary obsessions. No doubt in part it was, and good riddance, but along with it went a package of real problems about identity.

The narrow central question this paper treats of is exegetical. Locke says two principal things about substance 'in general'; that we have no idea of it, except the idea that certain things are true of it; and that it underlies, or stands under, the perceptible features of things. The problem is to know what he is talking about. The suggested answer is that he speaks ambiguously, because his predecessors did so, but as Boyle is one of them, one thing among others Locke ought to be referring to is *materia prima*, if he is merely taking the term as he finds it. If he is, what he says about it makes good sense, which helps to confirm that it is what he had in mind.

If substratum is prime matter, universal matter, *materia prima* or catholic matter, all these being mass terms signifying the same thing, Locke's doctrine is that we have no idea of prime matter, and that prime matter underlies the perceptible features of the material world. Underlyingness is not taken to imply imperceptibility in any ordinary sense, since if everything is constituted by prime matter, and we can perceive, say, iron, then since iron is prime matter as well as iron, we perceive portions and pieces of prime matter, Perceptibility is not a straightforward matter for masses in general, however. Do we perceive nitrogen, for example? Well, if we can perceive air, perhaps we can, but obviously we cannot tell from the sensory experience alone that that is what we are doing, nor can we distinguish seeing nitrogen from seeing oxygen which is also in the air.

If prime matter is perceptible, we must have sensory impressions of it, according to the general Lockean psychology of ideas. Locke evidently thinks that mass terms of chemistry signify an abstract idea as well, also referred to as a nominal essence. His lists of sorts often include a mass term or two, such as 'gold' or 'lead', as well as class sortals such as 'horse' or 'man'. The nominal essence of gold is the central example in his discussion of the thesis that different people have different nominal essences attached to the word 'gold'. In his terminology, 'the idea of X' is usually the abstract idea or nominal essence of X. If so, the thesis that we have no idea of prime matter is the thesis that prime matter has no nominal essence. It is therefore anomalous among masses.

A rationale for the thesis is afforded by his general doctrine of abstract ideas, considering the nature of the special case. The nominal essence of mass terms is the idea of all those qualities common to all examples or instances of that mass. It is also the complex idea whose constituents are the ideas of those qualities definitive of the name of that substance. In the case of gold, it is, for the average person, the idea of a certain colour, and certain degree of weight, malleability, fusibility, electrical conductivity, shine, and so on. There could be no such set of constituents in the idea, if there were one, of prime matter, because every substance is prime matter, and substances differ comprehensively. Gold is yellow, so those specimens of prime matter which are also gold are yellow; but mercury is not yellow, and it too is a bit of prime matter, so yellow is not common to all specimens. The same goes for any quality belonging to the nominal essence of any substance; you can always find some other substance that has not got it. So there are no properties common to all specimens of prime matter, hence it has no nominal essence.

If there is no idea of prime matter, prime matter has no essence, so no attribute is essential to it. I differ over this point from Alexander, whose interpretation of Locke is otherwise similar. He regards Locke as holding that solidity is the essential attribute of substance in general, so that Locke must be inconsistent on his account, but not on mine. He says: 'My suggestion is that (that matter is a solid stuff and in bodies is qualified by specific shapes, sizes and motions) is what Locke meant by substance in general for material things', and he adds that 'solidity is its essential characteristic although it is not a quality.[5]

The point is fine. We agree, I think, that substratum is prime matter, but not that it is appropriate to simply talk here about matter, for prime matter is a technical term, and there is also matter in the commonly understood sense. Prime matter is matter, but the two concepts are not to be identified in Locke's usage of 'matter'. Solidity may be an essential property of matter in the vulgar sense, but that precludes the identity of matter in that sense with substratum. Locke is scrupulous on this point. '*Body* stands for (the idea of) a solid extended figured substance, whereof *matter* is . . . used for the substance and solidity of body (EHU, III,x,15). My reading of this takes Locke to be saying that the 'partial and confused conception' of matter, and hence its nominal essence, is a complex of two components, the idea of solidity and of prime matter (which is imperfect). Alexander's reading takes it to say that the idea of substance is used for the substance and solidity of body. This takes it to be crudely circular, and saddles Locke with the inconsistency of saying that substance is essentially solid, and yet we have no clear idea of it, so it has no nominal essence, and hence no essential properties at all. My reading may not be right, but it is more charitable to Locke.

Locke's other main thesis, that prime matter underlies perceptible nature, has a straightforward sense if 'underlying' is taken to refer to the imperceptibility, not of prime matter, but of the *facts* about its identity relations. Each piece of sulphur is the same chemical substance as a piece of prime matter, but this a theoretical, not a perceptible fact. Prime matter underlies an individual such as a horse in the sense that each horse is *inter alia* a piece of horseflesh, and this in turn is, unknown to the senses, also a class of pieces of prime matter. Substratum underlies a quality such as being yellow, in the sense that the property is a property of a class of pieces of prime matter, though again this is a theoretical, not a perceptible fact.

Boyle's theory is obsolete in this way. The fundamental mass-sortal-relative identity predicate 'is the same substance as' enters into the definition of a battery of basic chemical ideas: purity, chemical versus physical change; the distinction between synthesis and analysis. To be sure of purity is to know the difference in a given case between one substance and several in some given location. Chemical change is the end of existence of one substance and the beginning of another, whereas in physical change there is uninterrupted identity. Synthesis is to form one substance from several; analysis is, roughly, the reverse. Elements are the limits of decomposition. The problem for the alchemists was to know when you had decomposition and when you did not, a matter of criteria of identity of substance. The crucial idea of modern theory is perhaps the association between chemical identity and gravity. Elements are the lightest by weight of all the substances in which they occur, and a fixed weight of an element will never form a smaller weight of something else from which it can later be recovered. The complete clarification of at least the basic relations between chemical change and weight change was available by the time of Dalton's publication of his revision of the atomic or corpuscularian theory. The beginnings occur in Lavoisier's work, I guess, but not in Boyle's. He was working with the old theory that 'is the same substance as' coincides with 'has the same texture of corpuscles as'. This texture was supposed describable, not by humans, but from a sufficiently godlike worm's eye view of the minuscule particles in terms of properties essential to their being bodies (that at least is Locke's idea), i.e. their shapes, motions and spatial relations. This is not only inaccessible to humans, but crosscuts the connection with weight. Dalton implicitly killed off the theory of textures. Some related matters that fell in consequence into neglect, among scientists, if not among philosophers of the Enlightenment, were primary and secondary matter, and the supposed role of primary and secondary qualities in explaining that distinction.

NOTES

1 I use the abbreviations EHU for Locke's *Essay Concerning Human Understanding* (1690), SC for Boyle's *The Sceptical Chemist* (1661, and OFQ, for 'The Origins of Forms and Qualities'. Page references are to the Everyman edition of SC, and for OFQ to *Selected Philosophical Papers of Robert Boyle*, ed. M.A. Stewart (Manchester University Press, 1979).

2 P. Alexander, Ideas, Qualities and Corpuscles (Cambridge University Press, 1985).

3 The dispute is documented in Alexander, chapter 2, note 9.

4 These examples occur in SC, 30–50.

5 Alexander, op. cit., 224.

STEPHEN CLARK

Soft as the Rustle of a Reed from Cloyne

I

George Berkeley's contribution to British philosophy, as it is studied in most universities, consists of *The Principles of Human Understanding* I (1710), *Three Dialogues between Hylas and Philonous* (1713), and perhaps *A New Theory of Vision* (1709) and its *Vindication* (1733). Students are expected to answer questions on Berkeley in papers entitled 'The British Empiricists' or perhaps 'Early Modern Epistemology', and the usual assumption is that he occupies an uneasy interval between John Locke and David Hume – the original 'Englishman, Irishman and Scotsman'! That he is usually also entitled 'Bishop Berkeley' (although all the aforementioned works – except the Vindication – were written in his twenties, while he was, in effect, a struggling research fellow) is only intended to convey that his churchmanship left him without the courage to carry his sceptical principles far enough. Even if no one can refute him, as James Boswell remarked (1963, 333), we are all quite sure that he was wrong in what he is supposed to have concluded, although quite correct in his misapplied methodology. The properly enlightened student is simultaneously convinced that materialistic science offers a true account of life, the universe and everything, and that there can be no known truths in matters metaphysical.

Berkeley – so the story goes – accepted the rule that we could only have knowledge of what was presented to our senses, and that such percepts depended for their quality on the state of our sense-organs. Colours, smells and raw feels were what we could grasp at once: anything more than these were merely theoretical entities which we had no epistemological right to posit. Indeed, we could not even understand what it would be to posit them, since all our concepts were merely remembered, and categorised, percepts. Whereas John Locke agreed with the Aristotelian thesis that we had several ways of sensing size, for example, or speed or number (so that these were not intrinsically linked, as sound or colour were, to one particular sense), Berkeley pointed out in *A New Theory of Vision* that our visual experience of size, speed, number and the rest were strictly of different things than we experienced through touch: we learnt by experience to associate certain visual signals with tactile or auditory expectations. John Locke had supposed that these 'primary' qualities (as they could exist for us in any of a number of sensory modalities) could also exist unperceived, as the material substrate or explanation of all our experience. Berkeley insisted that these properties were no less features of our experience, and unimaginable outside a perceiving mind. Nothing that was not a matter of immediate experience could be known, and there could be no point applying concepts drawn from experience to something that was by definition wholly inexperienceable. 'Matter' or 'material substance' was a quite incomprehensible and useless postulate: all we had were phenomena. Hume completed the sceptic's task by pointing out that we had no better right to postulate spiritual substances 'behind' the phenomena. If matter was an unnecessary hypothesis, so were God and the human soul.

On this view Berkeley was a minor member of the Enlightenment, where that is understood to mean the project conceived in the seventeenth century of rebuilding the edifice of human knowledge from the ground up, dispensing with the archaic and ill-founded theses of older philosophy. Modern philosophy is supposed to have begun with Descartes, but there is a case for saying, with Wolfson (1948, II, 457ff.), that it was Spinoza who really took the decisive, and dreadful step of defining his own terms and arguing without any attempt to make his conclusions compatible with accepted, and religious, doctrine. The self-image of modern philosophers, heirs of the Enlightenment, requires them to 'think for themselves', in such terms as any rational inquirer could think of for himself, and without relying on received opinion. More objective commentators might suspect that such 'free-thinking' merely amounts to the credulous acceptance of fashionable dogma – and that was indeed Berkeley's opinion.

For Berkeley did not suppose himself to be a 'free-thinker' or a sceptic: his strategy was to begin from sceptical principles in order to subvert them, as Philonous declares to Hylas. 'The same principles which at first view lead to scepticism, pursued to a certain point, bring men back to common sense' (*Dialogues*: 2, p.263). William Blake had the same optimistic thought: 'if the fool would persist in his folly he would become wise' (Blake 1966, 151). The minute philosophers, as he jestingly named 'free-thinkers' in *Alciphron* (1732: one of the great philosophical dialogues, written on Rhode Island during his American adventure),

had denied us any right to believe doctrines that could not be
directly demonstrated (to men of fashion) from self-evident
principle or from immediate sensory experience. Berkeley pointed
out that since they also believed that our immediate experience
was not of things in themselves, they were therefore committed to
a denial of all extra-experiential reality. As he put it in a passage of
the *Philosophical Commentaries* (1707–8) which he later rejected
(as not representing his own opinion): 'nothing properly but
persons i.e. conscious things do exist, all other things are not so
much existences as manners of the existence of persons' (24: 1,
p.10). He was similarly inclined to point out the oddities of
contemporary mathematical and physical theory, as embodying
contradictions and indemonstrable principles of a kind that were
regularly criticised in theological or moral discourses. 'That
philosopher is not free from bias and prejudice who shall maintain
the doctrine of force and reject that of grace, who shall admit the
abstract idea of a triangle, and at the same time ridicule the Holy
Trinity!' (*Alciphron*, 7:8: 3, p.296). And again: 'With what
appearance of reason shall any man presume to say that mysteries
may not be objects of faith, at the same time that he himself
admits such obscure mysteries to be the objects of science?' (*The
Analyst*, 1734: 4, p.69).

Normal empiricists had insisted that although our ideas, the
phenomenal impressions of sights, sounds, and smells, were not
the real things posited by scientific intellect, yet they could be
'like' those real things. The image to which I attend when I seek
to attend to my left hand is at least like my left hand in having five
fingers, being to one side of my right hand, having a ring on, and
so on. Or at least it has five of something, and has something on,
which are in turn like other real things discernible or hypothesis-
able by scientific intellect. It was Berkeley's crucial revelation
(*Commentaries* 379: 1, p.46) that nothing could be like an idea
except another idea, and that 'neither our ideas nor any thing like
our ideas can possibly be in an unperceiving thing'.

The Lockean and Cartesian division between what was immediately and indubitably present to our senses, and the real
material objects that were thought to cause our ideas, is sometimes rejected nowadays by people with no interest in accepting
Berkeley's conclusion. It is therefore worth spelling out exactly
why the division was and is so plausible. If I were to have the job
of guiding a robot about a distant place, I should be able to do so
with the aid of regularly updated information about its position
and condition, its immediate environment and the likely behaviour
of other mobile units in the vicinity. This information might be

presented to me in visual form, on a television monitor, or in the form of graphs, colour coded symbols, modulated tones or suitably ordered smells. As long as I could understand the code, it would not much matter what sensory modality was used. I might even be able to receive mere mathematical formulae and respond appropriately. At no stage would I have to suppose (and I would indeed be wrong to suppose) that the information was identical with the robot and its locality, nor that it was structurally similar to the robot and its locality, any more than the English sentence 'the cat sat on the mat' is structurally similar to the bare reality of cat and mat. The information would be accurate just if it enabled me to cope with the situation, to guide the robot around in accordance with my wishes. To say that the cause of my receiving the information must be something that was 'like' the information would be merely confused, even if we added that the 'likeness' was of course merely 'formal'. But how does the thought-experiment differ from our present experience? My visual, auditory, olfactory, tactile data may be more or less helpful, but there is no need to think that what causes them is 'like' them.

Locke of course insisted that a square visual datum was 'like' a square tactile datum, and hypothetically 'like' the real material object. Berkeley observed that the 'likeness' even between visual and tactile element was notional, something that we had to learn about, not something that we directly 'sensed'. Things 'look square' in an endless variety of ways (try tipping the square). The relationship was really that between a symbol and what it symbolises: a word in a language and the thing the word embraces. 'Bird' is not much like a bird; nor is the endless variety of ways of 'looking like a bird' like a bird, or like 'what it is to be a bird'. We can of course reply, verbally and pedantically, that how a bird looks to us is exactly what a bird looks like (to us). But how a bird looks is not a bird (i.e. does not have the same or structurally similar properties), if the bird is something more than a bundle of ideas.

> How do you know but ev'ry Bird that cuts the airy way,
> is an immense world of delight, clos'd by your senses five?
> (Blake 1966, 150)

Berkeley himself seems to have held, sometimes, that 'we see the Horse itself, the Church itself; it being an idea and nothing more' (*Commentaries* 428: 1, p.53), whereas we never see a person (i.e. a conscious being) just as such (*Alciphron*: 3, p.147). The ordinary materialist or dualist would usually insist that there must be something 'there', in the world beyond sight and sense, that causes our ideas of the bird or horse or church, and can properly be spoken of with concepts drawn from our everyday experience. But can we form any real concept of what this would be? We can pretend to ourselves that we are imagining what would exist if there were no one at all to perceive it – but to do so is merely to imagine what we would see if we were there to perceive it (*Dialogues*: 2, p.200). This argument is usually taken to involve a fallacy: the claim being that we cannot imagine something that is simultaneously not being imagined, whereas we can imagine something that is not being perceived. Berkeley, it is said, simply confused the meanings of 'perceive' and 'imagine'.

It is true that Berkeley did indeed believe that imagination and perception were not different in kind, and that all objects of private imagination as well as of perception, were to that minimal extent entirely real (*Commentaries* 472f: 1, p.59). But I do not myself think that his argument here is fallacious, nor that it depends on any equivocation between 'imagine' and 'perceive'. The tree I imagine existing unperceived cannot be the tree as it is in itself, since all that I can imagine is simply the set of ideas I would have were I to perceive the tree. If those ideas are not the tree itself, but information about it and my future experience, then it is pointless to suggest that I can explain what it would be for something 'like' that information to exist outside a perceiving mind merely by imagining myself in receipt of the information in question.

So if the sensory experience I perceive is caused by anything other than my own imagination (and it seems very plausible to insist that it is, simply because I cannot recall it at will: *Principles* 29f: 2, p.53), and if it is about anything other than the next batch of information to come my way (and it seems very plausible to insist that I do not, pace certain recent literary critics, live in a mere sea of human discourse), then what causes my ideas at least cannot be said to be like those ideas. What then is it? What concepts do we have that can either be drawn from experience or from mathematical logic that will serve to say what it is for things to exist unperceived?

Berkeley's reply was that to exist was either 'percipi or percipere (or velle i.e. agere)' (*Commentaries* 429: 1, p.53). All that experience or right reason can show us are objects and subjects, items of information and the wills or spirits that contemplate and originate that information. Those spirits are not 'spiritual substances', as inscrutable as 'material substances': they have their existence in will, action and intellection, and do not exist at all if they have no objects of perception. But such spirits are not simply bundles of the ideas we have of them, nor was Dr Johnson being more than wittily malicious when he prayed that one who had defended Berkeley should not leave the assembled company, 'for we may perhaps forget to think of you, and then you will cease to exist!' (Boswell 1963, 1085). They are real subjects of experience, as are we ourselves.

Berkeley's own analysis of what it was to be a subject was lost, if it was ever wholly formulated, when volume II of the *Principles* was lost during his tour of Italy (2, 282). But he was in no danger of ending his days as a solipsistic phenomenalist, unable to conceive of any phenomena than those immediately present to his own senses, though it may be true of him – as it was of the youthful Newman – that there were for him 'two and two only absolute and luminously self-evident beings, [him]self and [his] Creator' (Newman 1967, 4). On the contrary, he emphasises the obvious truth that none of us can construct the edifice of human knowledge on the basis merely of our own sensations (Berkeley, 1948 3, p.143; 6, p.206). 'So swift is our passage from the womb to the grave' that no one could learn much by his own experience (7, p.14). Where the 'minute philosophers' pretend to an ahistorical grasp of truth, enabling them to reject traditional belief and practice on the grounds that they and their friends managed not to see the world in traditional categories, Berkeley reckoned that we should begin not from our own experience, at the most banal, but from the testimony and enthusiasm of the ages. We must begin from testimony, and distrust it only when obvious contradictions emerge. In an early piece of philosophical science fiction, Berkeley imagines the effect of philosophical snuff: Ulysses Cosmopolita thereby investigates the subjective experience of a deracinated free-thinker, and finds it populated by terrors entirely of his own devising (7, pp.188f). Blake borrowed the motif in *The Marriage of Heaven and Hell*: 'My Angel, surprised, asked me how I escaped [from the infinite Abyss, fiery as the smoke of a burning city]? I answer'd: All that we saw was owing to your metaphysics; for when you ran away, I found myself on a bank by moonlight hearing a harper' (Blake 1966, 156).

It is the common sense of humankind that provides us with a beginning, even if our eventual conclusions seem distant from such common sense. 'There is a vast Majority on the side of Imagination or Spiritual Sensation' (Blake 1966, 794). Just so a later Anglo-Irishman 'began telling people that one should believe whatever had been believed in all countries and periods, and only reject any part of it after much evidence, instead of starting all over afresh and only believing what one could prove' (Yeats 1955, 78; see Newman 1979, 286). Doctrines that require us to deny our common experience, and say, for example, 'the Wall is not white, the fire is not hot & c' are at a disadvantage – 'we Irishmen cannot attain to these truths' (*Commentaries* 392: 1, p.47; see *Dialogues*: 2, p.183 on the claim that 'real sounds are never heard') – but our present and past experience does not embrace the universe. 'If the doors of perception were cleansed every thing would appear to man as it is, infinite' (Blake 1966, 154). The unseen worlds of glory that surround us only wait for our eyes to open. The believer may expect

> a happyness large as our desires, & those desires not stinted to ye few objects we at present receive from some dull inlets of perception, but proportionate to wt our faculties shall be wn God has given the finishing touches to our natures & made us fit inhabitants for heaven. (Sermon 1708: 7, p.12)

Enlightenment thought, then and now, also makes assumptions about the proper emotional style of empirical enquiry, as if those experiences that are borne in on us when we remain distant and uninvolved are more 'reliable' than those made manifest to a loving delight in God's universe. But Berkeley reckoned that it was what we were inclined to say enthusiastically, and what preserved in us the proper spirit of obedient faith, that was most reliable. Objective reality was not the narrow sphere of the value-neutral scientist (supposing any such creature ever existed), but the realm manifested to that life which is God's presence in us. It is those who enjoy a landscape that truly possess it (7, p.195), and to describe it aright we must describe it with the sort of affection that does not seek to keep its object only for itself. 'The same atheistical narrow spirit centering all our cares upon private interest and contracting all our hopes within the enjoyment of this present life equally produceth a neglect of what we owe to God and our country' ('Essay toward preventing the ruin of Great Britain', 1721: 6, p.79). The test of truth – or at least one important test of truth – is the extent to which it is edifying (3, p.60). 'A fool sees not the same tree that a wise man sees' (Blake 1966, 151). 'The tree which moves some to tears of joy is in the Eyes of others only a Green thing that stands in the way . . . To the Eyes of the Man of Imagination, Nature is Imagination itself' (Blake 1966, 793).

In other words, Berkeley did not agree that we could speak meaningfully only of those things that we had ourselves experienced, or even those things that humankind at large had experienced. His 'empiricism' was not that of Hume, who found he had nothing to say about causality, identity, substance or moral duty beyond what could be found in the mere impressions foisted on our senses. Causal efficacy was not something that could be identified in the impressions: if there were such an impression, it would only be one further phenomenal feature, whose interior link with what was supposed to be an effect would still be a matter merely of regular (or supposedly regular) concurrence. Berkeley too observed that ideas did not cause ideas, but did not conclude that causality was a nullity, or a mere habit of our associative minds. He concluded instead that causality lay always at the level of spirit, that we knew from within what it was to cause something, and that we did so not by noticing any special internal impression (as the sensation of effort, or a preliminary unease, as Locke had suggested: *Commentaries*, 653: 1, p.80; see 145a: 1, p.21), but immediately. To will something is not to have a special sensation (though people frequently behave as if 'willing' was a matter of clenching one's teeth) but to operate as what one essentially is, a free spirit. 'We have no idea annext to the word Will' (*Commentaries* 665: 1, p.81).

Berkeley's notions of cause, of spirit, of identity are 'empirical' in a sense. We have no 'ideas' of them, any more than we have ideas of virtues and vices (*Commentaries* 660: 1, p.79), but they are those notions that we find we require to speak about what we immediately know ourselves to be. Unlike later empiricists, he did not endorse the view that words only have meaning in so far as they symbolise or evoke ideas – a view he considered and rejected (*Commentaries* 637: 1, p.78). If 'the meaning is the use' there are many uses of language, and many ways of making sense. Berkeleian notions of cause, spirit, virtue or identity are not 'empirical' in the sense that they are to be identified with anything that can be an object of experience. But our understanding of such terms is grounded in what we immediately experience ourselves to be, not as objects but as subjects. 'The only original true notions that we have of freedom, agent or action are obtained by reflecting on ourselves, and the operation of our own minds' (3, p.318). From this Berkeley concluded, like Gregory of Nyssa (Sorabji 1983, 287ff), that if there were a cause of phenomena, it could only be the sort of active will we found ourselves to be. To cause can only be to will successfully.

Which is where God comes in. The popular view of Berkeley's argument is that he first eliminated any reason to believe that fires or churches or chairs existed in the absence of a conscious observer, and then concluded that God must exist because otherwise such objects would cease to exist when we stopped observing them. It is immediately replied that we either have reason to think that they exist when we do not perceive them or we do not: if we do, then we have reason to believe that they can exist unperceived; if we do not, we have no reason to believe that God observes them either. It is true that once God is admitted to the story Berkeley has a way of acknowledging the strong intuitive pressure to believe that there are no real gaps in the world, that the patches of perceived reality are joined together (as we imagine them to be) by a divinely perceived reality. 'For to have an idea is all one as to perceive: that therefore wherein colour, figure, and the like qualities exist, must perceive them; hence it is clear there can be no unthinking substance or substratum of those ideas' (*Principles* 7: 2, p.43). All that can 'stand under' the perceived qualities is Understanding itself (see *Dialogues*: 2, pp.198, 212). But Berkeley's argument is more complex than that. God, 'a watchful, active, intelligent, free Spirit with whom we have to do, and in whom we live and move and have our being' (*Theory of Vision Vindicated* 2: 1, p.251), is the source of the information we commonly receive. We are assured of His existence in just the same way as we are assured of anyone else's existence, that there are communications from Him of a kind that strike home as orderly and well-informed (3, pp.148ff). It is because the phenomena are orderly, informative and compelling that we are driven to postulate a single cause (which is to say, an agency).

Whether that Spirit is to be understood to be acquainting us with the very ideas (some of the ideas) that He eternally possesses, or to be forming ideas in us that bear a merely derivative relationship to divine archetypes or intellectually discriminable blueprints, is not a matter on which Berkeley offers a definitive opinion (*Principles* 45: 2, p.59). In the *Commentaries* he declares only that 'bodies do exist even when not perceived they being powers in the active being' (52: 1, p.48). In his correspondence with the American divine, Samuel Johnson, he says that he does not much mind whether God has the very ideas we have, or only plans to produce them in us (2, p.292). It may none the less be better to suppose that it is the former account that fits the Berkeleian thesis. If God is Spirit then He too has ideas (since subject and object are discriminable only in thought). If they are merely archetypical ideas, then Berkeley has admitted the existence of concrete (not abstract) universals of a kind that neo-Platonists hypothesised. If 'Art & Science cannot exist but in minutely organized Particulars and not in generalizing Demonstrations of the Rational Power' ('Jerusalem' 55, 62: Blake 1966, 687), as Berkeley taught Blake to believe, perhaps we had better suppose that God holds all particular ideas in place. If the other,

archetypical account were preferred, it must still be that God does
have immediate access to the ideas we have (though 'without
being in any degree pained thereby', *Commentaries* 675: 1, p.82),
or else there could be no content in the notion that they are
copies. Creation, as Moses describes it, can only be His revelation
to created spirits of what was real before. 'The act of creation
consists in God's willing that those things be perceptible to other
spirits which before were known only to Himself' (Letter to
Percival, 6.9.1710: Rand 1914, 84.) That what we call creation
was really manifestation is a doctrine that Berkeley (*Siris*: 5,
p.325) finds in the Hermetic Corpus (Poimander 5.11) – a
reminder that his philosophical ancestry lies with the thinkers
that the Enlightenment scorned.

II

Berkeley had arguments for his position, but it may indeed be
true that they were also a product of his temperament. John
Henry Newman described his own childhood views as follows:

> I thought life might be a dream, or I an angel, and all this
> world a deception, my fellow angels by a playful device
> concealing themselves from me and deceiving me with the
> semblance of a material world. (Newman 1967, 105f)

Newman was wrong, on Berkeleian terms, only in thinking
that there might have been a 'material' world even if there was
actually none. In so far as the concept 'material' has any real
content, it is indubitable that many things are material, but also
clear to any exact analysis that such materiality is an element that
cannot be abstracted from the realm of experience. If matter were
what materialists imagine, it would be something that we could
never detect or understand, since we could never say of any item
in our experience that it was itself material. Theists above all can
hardly allow any content to the notion of a 'material stuff' that
would continue to exist even if God wholly withdrew His
attention from it.

Newman and Berkeley reached very similar conclusions, but
expressed them, temperamentally, in opposite ways. For Newman
– and for W.B. Yeats – the phenomenal world was a dream, and
truth lay in what was borne in upon the soul when she allowed the
spirit of prayerful obedience to arise in her. Berkeley accepted
much the same criteria of tradition and saving faith: the doctrine
of the Trinity, for example, is correctly maintained if 'it makes
proper impressions on the mind, producing therein love, hope,
gratitude and obedience, and thereby becomes a lively operative

principle, influencing his life and actions, agreeably to the notion of saving faith which is required in a Christian' (*Alciphron*: 3, p.297). But the conclusion was not, in Berkeleian terms, that this phenomenal world was exactly a dream.

When Yeats spoke of 'Goldsmith and the Dean, Berkeley and Burke' as 'four great minds that hated Whiggery' (Yeats 1950, 272), and as four travellers on his 'ancestral stair' he identified Berkeley as

> God-appointed Berkeley that proved all things a dream,
> that this pragmatical, preposterous pig of a world, its farrow
>   that so solid seem,
> must vanish on the instant if the mind but change its theme.
> (Yeats 1950, 268)

It is easy to conclude that Yeats must have misunderstood. The eminent Berkeleian scholar, A.A. Luce, was always incensed by the suggestion that Berkeley was a limp-wristed visionary mooning after the infinite (see Berman 1985). On the contrary, Berkeley was adamant that all the common things of life were real and present only on his view of them, that it was the Lockean materialists who had turned the world of common day into a drifting illusion, that it was they who imagined that 'reality' must be forever hypothetical. Berkeley also scorned those who neglected common duties and loyalties and preferred their private whims and fantasies to the good of the commonwealth (see Clark 1985). He was not caught away from common sense and common goods to live in fairyland. 'Whatever the world thinks', he wrote in *Siris* (1744: 5, p.350), 'he who hath not much meditated upon God, the human mind and the summum bonum, may possibly make a thriving earthworm, but will most indubitably make a sorry patriot and a sorry statesman.' That last work, we should note, was both a meditation on existence, and an attempt to popularise the virtues of tar-water (not the crazy delusion of a 'hypochondriacal recluse', but an entirely reasonable plea for a drink at least more healthy than contaminated water and small beer).

Yeats misjudged the Bishop and the practical reformer, but if we remember that for Yeats a dream was not absolute or constant unreality, and that 'the mind' does not mean only the individual, waking mind, we can understand and endorse his point. We can even agree with Yeats's judgement that Berkeley was, at least in his youth, a mischievous and rebellious spirit, though rejecting Yeats's misapprehension that he grew up to be an episcopal humbug. 'I am young, I am an upstart, I am a pretender, I am vain, very well' (*Commentaries* 465: 1, p.58). But he did also seriously intend to be a good believing Christian. His proofs of immaterialism were weapons in a war against what he perceived as a narrow, egotistical spirit that had forgotten the wider realms of God's creation, and our duties in it.

Because Berkeley conceived himself as something more than an academic philosopher, it is worth recalling the extent to which Yeats too conceived his immaterialism as part of a project for national and personal revival. Where undergraduate courses connect Berkeley, Locke and Hume, it would, for many purposes be better to group him with Blake, Newman and Yeats. We might then begin to understand that all these thinkers were themselves much better philosophers than has been realised. On this occasion I shall concentrate on Yeats. Both Yeats and Berkeley saw themselves as Irishmen, but not as Catholics. Both sought to arouse their nation to a proper independence of mind and manners as, they thought, Great Britain sank lower into being, not merely wicked, but wicked on principle (6, pp.53, 84). Yeats, of course, lent his – qualified – support to rebellion, whereas Berkeley, knowing how such rebellion must usually increase the very evils against which it acts (see 6, pp.41ff.), urged the duty of passive obedience. 'The ills of rebellion are certain, but the event doubtful' (6, p.55). The spirit of rebellion, of 'laughing ecstatic destruction', grows as 'a religious fear and awe of God, the centre that unites and the cement that connects all human society' (6, p.219) declines or is rooted out. Yeats hoped for a new revelation as that rebellious spirit, the 'rough beast slouching toward Bethlehem to be born' (Yeats 1950, 211), took concrete shape in the next age of the world. Berkeley, perhaps with greater realism, thought that 'the prevailing notions of order, virtue, duty and Providence' were what made the world habitable (6, p.202), and that in the general decay of manners, 'the Age of Monsters was not far off' (6, p.221). 'A general corruption of manners never faileth to draw after it some heavy judgement of war, famine or pestilence' (6, p.79).

These are genuine and vital differences, but Yeats did not worship destruction for its own sake, nor Berkeley worship order. Both saw currently fashionable society as the product of an unimaginative, grasping mentality, and put their hope in what was currently despised: old-fashioned faith and virtue. 'The finger of God will unravel all our vain projects' (6, p.71), unless through architecture, sculpture, painting (and literature) we fill men's minds with great ideas, 'spiriting them up to an emulation of worthy actions' (6, p.82). Both believed that it was by recalling their fellow citizens to traditional wisdom that they would best serve the commonwealth. Both believed that the world of humane endeavour and imaginative excellence was not simply a human fiction, a drama played out against an intrinsically unmeaning universe, but rather reality itself, accommodated to our finite view.

The editor of Yeats's and Sturge Moore's correspondence (Bridge 1953, xvii) seems to have taken it for granted that Yeats was philosophically naïve, that Sturge Moore, as G.E. Moore's brother and defender against Yeats' criticisms, 'had the greater philosophical bent' and was justified in laughing at Yeats's 'unscientific ways'. My own view is that the long, confused, vitriolic and often very amusing debate between Yeats and Moore (especially Bridge 1953, 59–154) ended in victory for Yeats. G.E. Moore's argument for the 'reality' of what was commonly perceived and 'known' does indeed imply that any shared and stable percept was just as real, just as much a something different from the mere perceiving of it (as Berkeley also had believed). In so far as such empiricists insist upon the existence of hands, people and past time, and deny or ignore the existence of visionary experience and its objects, they betray a dogmatic ignorance. Idealists of Yeats's kind need not deny (as Sturge Moore imagined) that there are people and relations between people: the question is, what is it that people are? Neither Yeats nor Berkeley answered, 'Spiritual substances' (as Sturge Moore supposed: Bridge 1953, 71). Where they agreed was in saying that percepts, the more 'real' the more they are shared (i.e. the more they are the percepts of a wider mind than our individual being), could have their being only in the sea of experience. Yeats explicitly endorsed Blake's aphorism that 'God only acts or is in existing beings or men' (Bridge 1953, 80), whereas Berkeley, putting the same point the other way round, described God as that 'watchful, active, intelligent, free Spirit in whom we live and move and have our being' (1, p.251: see Clark 1988). What percepts we encounter, what regions of the infinite realm of experience we visit, depends on the direction or character of our will. 'Actions leading to heaven are in my power if I will them, therefore I will will them' (*Commentaries* 160: 1, p.22). That he later rejected this dictum (to judge from the marginal note) is perhaps a mark of his growing realisation of the real weakness and moral ambiguity of our desires. 'Strange impotence of men. Man without God. Wretcheder than a stone or tree, he having only the power to be miserable by his unperformed wills, these having no power at all' (*Commentaries* 107: 1, p.18: also obelised).

Berkeley's ambivalence here, his uncertainty whether a human will could effect anything, is the moral and religious aspect of the

problem on which, it may be, the second volume of his *Principles*
foundered. We are conscious of ourselves as naked wills, not
determined to act by any idea or uneasiness. 'We move our legs or
selves. Tis we that will their movement' (*Commentaries* 548: 1,
p.69). It is from that interior knowledge of our own willing that
we are able to grasp that there is a divine agency at work: 'What
means cause as distinguished from occasion? Nothing but a Being
which wills [better, a Will: 499a] when the effect follows the
volition. Those things that happen from without we are not the
Cause of therefore there is some other Cause of them i.e. there is a
being that wills these perceptions in us' (*Commentaries* 499: 1,
p.63). But we must now acknowledge that the shared perception
of my leg's motion that follows after my will to move my leg is
itself something that happens 'from without'. My will is efficacious
in the wider world just if God wills (*Principles* 147: 2, p.108): do I
then have any real experience of willing as a sole determining
cause, and can I find any way out of the conclusion that volition
too is only an occasion, that I know nothing of the inner
determinant of actions?

The only available answer seems to be that we do experience
direct causality when willing an imagined motion: the relation
between my imagining a chimera and there being an imagined
chimera is not extrinsic and occasional. My imagining a chimera
and there being a chimera visible to more than one created spirit
is occasional, and depends on the infinite free Spirit's (that
'contains' all the contents of our individual wills) making it
present to others. Such shared imaginations, over and above those
we are licensed to expect by the regular course of nature, are
attested by visionaries, and by Yeats. Yeats was consciously
unorthodox in his belief that the spiritual realm was best conceived
in its multiplicity, that it might be an infinite realm of complex
hierarchies of magicians, without any single source or final unity.
Berkeley had higher hopes, but he too recognised the multifarious
nature of phenomenal reality, the extent to which shared visions
or narrow interests might condition what we can grasp of the
infinite. Yeats was right after all to see in Berkeley a 'mind that
hated Whiggery':

> But what is is Whiggery?
> A levelling, rancorous, rational sort of mind
> that never looked out of the eye of a saint
> or out of a drunkard's eye. All's Whiggery now,
> but we old men are massed aganst the world . . . ('The Seven
> Sages': Yeats 1950, 272)

Berkeley's voice was one

soft as the rustle of a reed from Cloyne
that gathers volume; now a thunder-clap.

Goldsmith and Burke, Swift and Berkeley, so Yeats said, all
'understood that wisdom comes of beggary'. At first sight it is not
a judgement that Berkeley – who spent his episcopate in schemes
to raise the expectations and desires of the Irish peasantry that
they might escape from beggary – would have quite accepted. But
Yeats perhaps had in mind the 'poor in spirit', whose is the
kingdom of heaven (Matthew 5.3). If so, he caught Berkeley's
drift: the failure of the minute philosophers was not that they
were ruled by base desires (as traditional philosophy might have
argued), but that their desires and expectations were too feeble.
'Faith is not an indolent perception, but an operative persuasion'
(*Alciphron*: 3, p.301), and the way to lay hold upon that saving
faith is to awaken one's imaginative and loving involvement in
'that purple sky, those wild but sweet notes of birds, the fragrant
bloom upon the trees and flowers, the gentle influence of the
rising sun . . . and a thousand nameless beauties of nature [that]
inspire the soul with secret transports' (*Dialogues*: 2, p.171).
'Sensual pleasure is the summum Bonum' (*Commentaries* 769: 1,
p.93), and it is 'by an improvement of sensual enjoyment' that
'the whole creation will be consumed and appear infinite and holy
. . . whereas it now appears finite and corrupt' (Blake 1966, 154).

That wisdom is not the province of the complacent rich, that
reality is discernible, and is to be found in the whole realm of
experience and not one narrow province (whether that be the
world of the scientific materialist or of the fashionable libertine),
that we shall know the truth when we have embraced our duty to
God and the city, are doctrines Berkeley emphatically endorsed.
'I do not pretend', he wrote to the American divine, 'that my
books can teach truth. All I hope for is, that they may be an
occasion to inquisitive men of discovering truth, by consulting
their own minds, and looking into their own thoughts' (2, p.282).
This is not an Enlightenment aphorism, but a reminder of what,
on ancient testimony, is the ground and true enlightener of our
fragmentary and corruptible reason. 'I know now that revelation
is from the self, but from that age-long memoried self that shapes
the elaborate shell of the mollusc and the child in the womb, that
teaches the birds to make their nest; and that genius is a crisis that
joins that buried self for certain moments to our trivial daily
mind' (Yeats 1955, 272).

BIBLIOGRAPHY

BERKELEY, G. (1948) *Collected Works*, eds A.A. Luce & T.E.

Jessop. Edinburgh: Thomas Nelson.

BERMAN, D. (1985) 'George Berkeley: pictures by Goldsmith, Yeats and Luce'. *Hermathena*, 139, 1985, 9–23.

BLAKE, W. (1966) *Collected Works*, ed. G. Keynes. Oxford: Clarendon Press.

BOSWELL, J. *Life of Johnson*, London: O.U.P.

BRIDGE, U. (1953) ed., *W.B. Yeats and T. Sturge Moore: Their Correspondence 1901–1937*. London: Routledge & Kegan Paul.

CLARK, S.R.L. (1984) *From Athens to Jerusalem*. Oxford: Clarendon Press.

——(1985) 'God-appointed Berkeley and the General Good' in J. Foster & H. Robinson, eds, *Essays on Berkeley*. Oxford: Clarendon Press, 233–53.

——(1986) *The Mysteries of Religion*. Oxford: Blackwells.

——(1988) 'Cupitt and the Divine Imagining', *Modern Theology*, 5, 45–60.

NEWMAN, J.H. (1967) *Apologia pro Vita Sua*, ed., M.J. Svaglic. Oxford: Clarendon Press.

——(1979) *An Essay in aid of a Grammar of Assent*. Indiana: University of Notre Dame Press, 1st ed. 1870.

SORABJI, R. (1983) *Time, Creation and Necessity*, London: Duckworth.

WOLFSON, H.B. (1948) *Philo*. Cambridge: Harvard University Press.

YEATS, W.B. (1950) *Collected Poems*. London: Macmillan, 2nd ed.

——(1955) *Autobiographies*. London: Macmillan.

4

ANGUS J. MCKAY

David Hume

David Hume is typical of a number of important thinkers in that he both determined to some extent the characteristics of his age and also reflected them. He was a product of previous thinkers, sharing with them some of the Enlightenment enthusiasms of the times, although he also shared with some, such as Kant and Voltaire, the desire to deflate certain aspects of its optimism. His interest in the place and scope of religion in society, in the nature of morality, but above all in our attempts to understand the workings of our own minds and our relation to the world we take ourselves to be a part of, are all part of mainstream philosophical thinking as well as themes of the Enlightenment. That human beings are essentially a part of the natural world was to a great extent the thrust of Hume's philosophy.

Hume was in one sense, if a restricted one, a system-builder in philosophy. He was what Strawson has termed a descriptive metaphysician (Strawson, 1959), in that he wanted to turn from so-called 'speculative' accounts of human thinking and its objects, which can be characterised briefly by its attempts to begin with what its author wishes to claim we know, and then produce a scheme within which these claims can be justified. Hume's desire was to provide an account of what does go on in our thinking and one which took as its starting point what we are most entitled to claim we are aware of in empirical awareness. Unlike, for instance, Kant, Hume did not have a great passion for exhibiting his philosophy as a system within which every interconnecting link is demonstrated; but he saw and tackled philosophical problems as a unity, and his philosophy is one which tries to present answers to questions in terms of one overriding theory.

For Hume, the theory in question was a highly developed version of empiricism, a tradition already well-established in British philosophy by Locke and Berkeley. More than either of these two philosophers, Hume's philosophy begins and ends in the claim that what we are entitled to say we know is based on what we experience through the senses. And Hume accepted

Locke's starting point that the mind is blank until written upon by the senses, while almost immediately modifying the explanation given by Locke of the details of what this involves.

Hume stands in the long line of thinkers both before and after him who had the ambition to become what is often referred to as 'the Newton of the moral sciences', and perhaps more than anyone else up till then pursued that ambition. Just as Isaac Newton had apparently brought some sense of order to, and the hope of understanding the puzzling ways of, the inanimate part of the universe by showing that the natural sciences could explain its behaviour in terms of 'laws of nature' so it seemed to many that this task could in principle be undertaken for the science of human nature (the moral sciences). The acclaim that would accompany the discovery of such fundamental laws, which could lay bare the way in which the human mind worked, was a powerful lure. So Hume wanted both to say that human nature was susceptible of such a treatment, rather than being an ineradicably mysterious matter concerning which we could at best speculate, and also to exhibit what the essential manner of its working was. This first task, that of establishing that the mind can properly be seen as a fit object of science in that it has 'workings', was never in any detail argued for by Hume, although it had been by some of his predecessors. Thomas Hobbes, for instance, had attempted to explain the workings of society in terms of its constituent parts which, when seen as a connecting whole, would exhibit the manner of its operation (at least as Hobbes took it to be operating). And for Hobbes, this operation of society was itself the result of the manner in which individuals, the constituent parts of society, were composed, and how they in turn worked. While his philosophical preoccupations involved Hobbes in reflecting on that issue, there is in Hume no detailed working out of any such positions; just for this reason it is sometimes difficult to be clear about the extent to which Hume has a fully worked out view of the matter. It is clear, however, that he belongs amongst the thinkers for whom this was a preoccupation, and that whatever difficulties he was or was not aware of in the project, it was a project of exhibiting the manner in which our cognitive processes work.

In this connection, the sub-title of the most important of Hume's works, the *Treatise on Human Nature* (Hume, 1739–40, described in the sub-title as 'An Attempt to Introduce the Experimental Method of Reasoning into Moral Subjects', reflects Hume's ambitions. The experimental method was, for Newton, the manner by which truths about the material world were to be established. To find out how the world actually works – what the relevant laws are – we need to observe what actually happens by designing and performing experiments which test and establish our views (hypotheses) about what might be going on. And the Newtonian natural philosophy appeared to have established by its very success the credentials of this method.

For Hume, the way to find out about human nature (how to go about doing the science of morals) is similar to the Newtonian model. Rather than speculate about what might be possible and then attempt to square it with the facts, Hume insisted that there could be a science of human nature which would consist in looking at the facts about human beings and their cognitive processes, and finding the explanation which best fits them; those of his conclusions which seemed to his contemporaries the most unbelievable or outrageous are usually the result in part of sticking rigorously to this method. They are also those conclusions which are philosophically the most troublesome, in that they create tensions within Hume's overall account or appear for other reasons to be unsatisfactory.

One of the best examples of the application by Hume of the experimental method is to be found in the structure of his well-known attempt to show that the Hobbesian theory usually referred to as psychological egoism is false, and indeed absurdly so. In *Leviathan* (1651), Hobbes had argued that all human motivation is the result of an individual's desire for particular future states of that individual, a view often referred to by Hume as 'the selfish theory' (Hume, 1777). It is a consequence of this theory, and was so intended by Hobbes, that there cannot be such a thing as what we ordinarily call 'altruistic' human behaviour; we do not have desires to help other people, however close they may be to us. Rather, we have desires for things for ourselves, and apparent desires to help other people, or sympathetic concern for them, are to be seen according to Hobbes in a different light. For Hobbes, the mechanism of sympathy is a basic part of the human constitution, and is so arranged as to result in our ability to perform actions which at first sight may appear to be the product of a desire to help others, but are in fact the result of desires for something for ourselves. 'Sympathy' for Hobbes is a technical notion, which refers strictly to our ability to put ourselves in the place of another and to create in ourselves the experience which they are having. In this way, what we may refer to as compassion, for instance, is, for Hobbes, the result of the sympathy mechanism. My apparently selfless action in sending a cheque to Oxfam is the result of being moved by consideration of the plight of those less

fortunate than myself, according to the 'altruistic' account. For
Hobbes, it is the result of a desire created within me to do
something about a situation which is causing me distress. Having
put myself in the place of others and having experienced something
of what I take to be their feelings, I now have a desire to do
something, but for Hobbes this desire is to help myself, since I
have put myself in the place of another.

Of course, such explanations of individual conduct have always
been common, as are other theories which cast doubt on what
may appear to be a person's motives. And we may well agree with
Hobbes that people sometimes, perhaps often, disguise their own
interests as what they refer to as 'genuine concern for others'
without agreeing with his theory. For this theory holds not only
that people are often deceived about the true character of their
apparently selfless actions, but that there are and can be no other
such actions than those which are motivated by a desire for
something for ourselves. It was this view which Hume attacked,
and in doing so applied 'the experimental method'.

For Hume, the way to approach Hobbe's theory is to ask the
question 'how well does the "selfish hypothesis" represent the
facts that we all know about?' His answer to this is that it does
not, and that if the theory were true, the facts that we would
observe would be very different from those that we do in fact
observe. Thus, Hume argues, Hobbes' account is actually a very
odd one. For if it were true, people behaving as Hobbes tells us
they behave would do sorts of things that only sometimes occur.
Hobbes's account thus disguises rather than clarifies, for it tends
to obscure real differences between people.

Hume wanted to reply to Hobbes that there are such things as
benevolent actions; there is a difference between wanting to do
something for someone else and wanting to do it for myself. It is
true that we can give an account of human motivation which by
stretching credulity will be able to say something about those
cases that do not apparently fit the Hobbesian hypothesis; we can
invent secret, hidden interests in the mind of someone who is
apparently acting for other motives, and in this way hypothesise
that such motives exist. But for Hume, to do this is to get the
order of explanation wrong: the conclusion is erroneous and was
likely to be so precisely because the way it was arrived at was the
wrong way.

'The most obvious objection to the selfish hypothesis is, that,
as it is contrary to common feeling and our most unprejudiced
notions, there is required the highest stretch of philosophy to
establish so extraordinary a paradox' (Hume 1777, 298). According

to Hume, Hobbes's mistake arises 'entirely from that love of simplicity which has been the source of much false reasoning in philosophy' (Ibid.). The point being made here is as follows. If we start off by looking at the facts, what we see is that some actions are apparently selfish, and some are not. Hobbes, as a result, according to Hume, of his 'love of simplicity', insists that in fact all actions are at root motivated by selfish concerns. Hume insists that there is an alternative hypothesis which is consistent with the facts, once we allow that Hobbes's account is not the only possible account. Indeed, it is not the best account at all. For, according to Hume, Hobbes's hypothesis demands that we do some extraordinary things with the facts, and twist their most obvious interpretation. The only reason for doing that is to save Hobbes's interpretation from being shown to be false. The needs of Hobbes's theory are then being given priority over a dispassionate view of the facts; and it is this that Hume is objecting to when he says that such notions are prejudiced – they are so in that they force us to abandon 'impartiality' in order to come to Hobbes' conclusion.

The same methodology is to be seen in Hume's epistemology, or theory of knowledge. The project of setting out the way in which the human mind operates involves for Hume dealing with issues in one of the oldest areas of philosophical enquiry, which concerns questions about how we come by the kinds of knowledge that we can claim to have. And Hume stands as the most celebrated example of the tradition of British Empiricism, a tradition which located the answer to these questions in the view that knowledge, and indeed all the contents of the mind, are the result of sense experience. For Hume, the business of what goes on when we think, or when a process involving the acquisition of experience occurs, is a process, and furthermore it is one which occurs according to identifiable and discoverable rules or laws, which are to be found out by the experimental method. Hume went further than his predecessors in this matter precisely by explicitly introducing such a method. Examples of this can be seen in his treatment of our idea of the self, and in his account of causality.

For Hume, the 'contents of the mind' – everything we can be at any time aware of, that can be present to our mind as a thought or as the object of a thought or as any kind of feeling – are referred to as 'perceptions'. And perceptions, according to Hume, are of two kinds, which he called impressions and ideas. Although it is notorious that he failed ever to make clear exactly how the two kinds of perceptions were to be distinguished from each other,

Hume's main criterion was that impressions were those perceptions which were the more 'lively'. Further, ideas were conceived by Hume to be copies of impressions, which latter were the source of ideas about 'matters of fact'. Since ideas are 'derived from' impressions, any content of an idea must have previously been present to the mind as an impression. It follows, Hume thinks, that we can show that nothing is present to the mind if we can show that there is not nor could be any impression from which it might be derived. And for Hume, we find out about our impressions by a process similar to that which would today be called introspection; he takes it for granted (as do nearly all empiricists) that there is nothing essentially problematic about the task of reviewing or inspecting what is present to our minds, and that we can therefore, by considering those perceptions which are impressions, examine the raw data of our experience.

Reflection on his own difficulties in clearly distinguishing impressions from ideas might have been sufficient to make him think twice about this. Hume certainly thought, however, that despite the difficulties of the account, he could show that all our sense experience which resulted in impressions was the source of any knowledge we had about matters of fact.

When he considered traditional claims to knowledge in various areas, or when he came to justify the conclusions he drew from his own position, conclusions which frequently involved the claim that we do not have knowledge of the kinds which previous thinkers had claimed on our behalf, Hume applied what is sometimes known as 'Hume's Fork'. This is essentially the tactic referred to above: requiring that an impression be produced which corresponds to the idea that we are supposed to have. Examples of this tactic are to be found in Hume's treatment of the 'force' or 'power' which we take to be at work in causal connections, when we say that an effect, B, is made to happen because of a cause, A. (Hume, 1739–40, Bk 1, pt 3). According to Hume, we have the idea that A and B are connected not only by the regularity' by which A is followed by B, but also by there being some necessity about this, which we express by saying something to the effect that 'if A happens, then B must follow'. What, Hume asks, is the meaning of 'must' in this respect? We are inclined to say that we know that B must happen, and justify this by saying that B will happen as a result of the force or power which A possesses to make B happen. But, says Hume, when we consider in detail what we actually experience when we observe an example of a causal connection, what we can at most claim to be aware of is, for instance, that my depressing the switch is regularly followed by the light coming on. If I say that the one 'makes' the other happen, Hume replies that I have in fact no idea what this supposed 'making' consists in. For I am never presented with an impression of 'making' or of the force alleged to be at work, no matter how many times I may have switched the light on, and no matter how long I pay attention to what I am aware of. Since there is no impression, and since all ideas about what is going on in the world at any level are copies of sense impressions, it follows for Hume that we do not have any idea corresponding to the force or power we have supposed to be at work in the relation between what we call cause and what we call effect.

There is of course an answer to the question 'so why do we have this idea, confused as it may be, and why do we speak as if we are aware of the connection between the two events as being one in which some kind of making is involved?' But for Hume, that answer does not involve the admission that we have any knowledge via an impression of any such thing as the force or power allegedly present.

Hume's treatment of causality is certainly not the last word; but whatever its merits, it is an example of the experimental method at work. And if the results of this method are at variance with our previous beliefs about the world, or (as is often the case with Hume) with what 'common sense' tells us, then it is our previous beliefs which go by the board in the interests of upholding the experimental method, which here requires us to point to the impression of 'necessary connection' if we are to have a rightful claim to it. So a careful examination of the contents of our awareness (the 'experiment') results in a hypothesis which will be in line with what is observed, and in not going beyond that, is more justified than that which may be the more entrenched.

In fact, Hume is not beyond making inconsistent claims on behalf of the experimental method, and in one passage in the *Second Enquiry* he claims that it is to be distinguished from the experimental method as seen at work in the natural sciences. Having argued, as we saw above, against Hobbes's 'selfish hypothesis', because according to Hume it arises from an inappropriate love of simplicity, Hume almost immediately thereafter claims that, in the case of the natural sciences,

> 'Many a hypothesis . . . contrary to first appearances, has been found, on more accurate scrutiny, solid and satisfactory . . . But the presumption always lies on the other side, in all enquiries concerning the origin of our passions, and of the internal operations of the human mind. The simplest and

most obvious cause which can there be assigned for any phenomenon, is probably the true one. (Hume, 1777, 299). This passage seems inconsistent with Hume's claim that Hobbes's mistake arises from an illegitimate desire for simplicity, although Hume could certainly claim here that what he says is true of his own account of human motivation, since he has argued that his account, while more complex than that of Hobbes, is the better representation of the facts as we experience them. (And indeed he does claim that his has the greater 'simplicity'.) But it is certainly less obvious that this is true than of some of Hume's other philosophical views. This may be the result of his not having thought through exactly what he wants to claim on behalf of the experimental method, which even if it guarantees simplicity of a kind, cannot be said to guarantee that the explanation given will be in line with 'first appearances'.

As we have already seen, Hume's account of causality in terms of 'constant conjunction' (his term for the regularity which we observe between cause and effect) is an account which reflects all that which on the basis of experience we are entitled to say that we discover. But it cannot be said that it is the most simple explanation, any more than it can be said that it is an explanation most in line with first appearances. For the answer given by Hume to the question 'what is the origin of the belief in causal necessity?' is that we, the observers, impose on the world (falsely) the view that there is some kind of necessity between A and B as a result of our regularly associating the two. The 'necessity' however, originates in our mind, and is not a fact that we experience or observe in the world.

Whether satisfactory or not, Hume's account does not preserve the claim that in the case of the moral sciences, as opposed to the natural sciences, the simplest explanation is the best. This can also be seen to be the case with Hume's account of the self (Hume, 1739–40, Bk 1 pt 4).

For Hume, there is a difficulty in explaining what we refer to when we talk of ourselves as distinct or unitary beings existing through time. This is because we have no impression of such a being and, Hume argues, we could not have such an impression. We cannot experience this self which we claim to underlie and be the unifying substance behind our various perceptions, since by introspection we can attend only to the particular experiences we have. This can only reveal the experience (impression) which we are having at that particular time, and on any other occasion the same will be true. There is no such impression as that of the self as such, merely impressions of particular separate and discrete kinds. Another way to put this is that the self which we suppose to be the recipient of our experiences is not given to us in experience at all. What is given is the experiences.

Again, this account is the result of the experimental method, which in this case yields the surprising conclusion just mentioned. The passage previously referred to, in which Hume contrasts the experimental method in the natural and moral sciences, contains the claim that in the natural sciences the simplest explanation is not necessarily to be preferred. But whatever is the case about the science of human nature, it has for a long time been an accepted view in the natural sciences that what is known as 'Occam's Razor' applies. In other words, that the explanation of any phenomenon which is the most economical, in that it requires the least postulation of entities not directly observed, is to be preferred. This may be a good enough reason for Hume's dismissal of Hobbes's insistence that there must be all sorts of hidden selfish motives constantly at work in human nature, but it might also have seemed to Hume a good enough reason, taken in conjunction with what he says about first appearances, to rethink his account of the self (although he admitted himself that it was unsatisfactory). It would appear to be the case that in his treatment of our idea of the self he is prepared to accept an account which, by insisting on the priority of all and only that which we experience, is paradoxical, and which cannot be said to be the simplest, since it results in the view that the mind which is the recipient of our experiences is itself unknown to us. Indeed, as we will see, Hume was not beyond invoking theoretical and unobserved entities, in order to save his own theories.

It seems likely that Hume did not have a clearly worked out view of precisely what the experimental method entailed, or of the relation between its application in the natural and in the moral sciences. And perhaps the best known case in which Hume is willing to allow a hypothesis to assume priority over what we can directly experience is in the uses to which he puts the so-called 'law of the association of ideas', which is an essential part of his explanation of such topics as causality.

For Hume, ideas are often associated for a number of reasons; the most common reasons being that they resemble one another, or that they occur frequently together in time and space. Thus our insistence on the causal connection between two events has much to do with the fact that because they constantly occur in succession, we associate the one with the other. It is some kind of 'law' that the mind will do this with ideas which occur together, and one which is inferred from the evidence, in the same manner that Newton inferred physical laws from the evidence. Now this principle or law was for Hume, though not his own invention or discovery, of crucial importance. It was seen by him as analogous to principles in the natural sciences, such as attraction, in the importance it had for explaining phenomena. And yet, of course, such principles are hypotheses, even if they are correct. We observe the results of magnetism; it refers in the first place to behaviour, not to a theory or a 'scientific law'. Similarly, for Hume, what we observe is an idea, or a number of ideas; we cannot directly observe such a thing as the association of ideas, but rather conjecture that it must occur. The association of ideas is in Hume the answer to how the mind does many things: causality, abstraction from particular to general, our belief in the continued and distinct existence of the external world, and our belief in the distinct existence of the self, are all explained by Hume partly by reference to the association of ideas. But this explanation is invariably produced when there is no further 'experimental observation' which could produce an explanation, and also when its production will produce a theory which is least in accordance with simplicity, and sometimes not in accordance with the first appearances to which, as we have seen, Hume wanted to give such pride of place.

It was, as previously remarked, precisely those features of Hume's system which appeared to many of his readers to have results at variance with what we ordinarily believe, that produced a philosophy regarded by some as one of extreme scepticism. And there swiftly came about the so-called 'commonsense' reaction against Hume, which objected to the perceived sceptical conclusions.

In fact, there are at least some respects in which it can be said that the reaction against Hume's views, like many such occurrences in the history of ideas, contained and accepted far more of his ideas than was thought to be the case. For Thomas Reid, who was the immediate and most important critic of Hume, does in fact retain some of the more important aspects of his Philosophy. While he criticised the form in which he took Hume to have cast the theory of ideas, first set out by Locke, and insisted that it is not ideas but objects (which ideas were meant to represent or copy) which are immediately present to the mind, he none the less accepted without question a great deal of what was behind British empiricism; in particular, he appears to have accepted that what philosophy has to start from is precisely whatever we are immediately most aware of. In this respect, his philosophy is at one with Hume's in accepting the essence of the experimental method.

And indeed, Reid's view that the dictates of 'commonsense' are sanctioned by the fact that they ultimately deliver what the human constitution can deliver, that their authority lies in the fact that they reveal how we actually and must work, is itself an acceptance of Hume's own views that the study of the mind is a science.

BIBLIOGRAPHY

HOBBES, THOMAS (1651) *Leviathan*, ed. J. Plamenatz. London: Fontana, 1962.

HUME, DAVID (1739–40) *A Treatise on Human Nature*, ed. L.A. Selby-Bigge, 2nd edition. Oxford: Clarendon Press, 1978.

——(1777) *An Enquiry Concerning Human Understanding*, ed. L.A. Selby-Bigge. Oxford, Clarendon Press, 1902.

STRAWSON, P.F. (1959) *Individuals*, London: Methuen, 1959.

5

R.F. STALLEY

Common Sense and Enlightenment:
the Philosophy of Thomas Reid

I

Almost all the thinkers we regard as most representative of the Enlightenment shared the belief that the way to release mankind from prejudice and superstition was by applying to the study of human nature the systematic and rational methods of enquiry characteristic of the new science. Their thought might be regarded as élitist, in the sense that they claimed an insight into human affairs that was not available to the common man, and also as subversive, in the sense that it tended to criticise established beliefs in religion and politics. It may therefore seem perverse to suggest that one of the more significant figures of the Enlightenment was a Scottish minister who sought to combat scepticism and defend orthodox religion by means of an appeal to common sense. I shall nevertheless argue that this is the case.

Thomas Reid was born in the manse of Strachan in Kincardineshire in 1710. He was educated at Marischal College Aberdeen under George Turnbull, and after a period as librarian of the College was presented in 1737 to the parish of New Machar, Aberdeenshire. In 1752 he became Regent and Professor of Philosophy at King's College Aberdeen, and in 1764 moved to Glasgow to succeed Adam Smith in the chair of Moral Philosophy. He retired from teaching in 1780 and died in Glasgow in 1796.

From the philosophical point of view, the most important event in Reid's life was his reading of Hume's *Treatise*, which he seems to have acquired soon after its publication in 1739. By Reid's own account he had until then accepted the Berkeleian doctrine he had learnt from Turnbull, but his reading of Hume convinced him that the premises which had been taken for granted by virtually all philosophers since Descartes led inevitably to a total scepticism, not only about the existence of the external world but even about that of our minds. Reid set himself to refute Hume, and almost all his philosophical work is directly or indirectly related to this task. His first book, the *Inquiry into the Human Mind on the Principles of*

Common Sense, was published in 1764 shortly before he left Aberdeen. It contains an examination of each of the five senses and is designed to refute scepticism by defending the common-sense view that we do genuinely perceive external objects. In some ways it is Reid's best work but it is, of course, limited in its scope. For a fuller statement of his philosophy we have to look to the two much lengthier volumes which he prepared for publication after his retirement from the Glasgow chair. The *Essays on the Intellectual Powers of Man* considers in turn perception, memory, conception, abstraction, judgement and taste. A main aim is once again to refute the scepticism which Reid took to be inherent in the work of his predecessors. The primary aim of the *Essays on the Active Powers* is to demolish the necessitarianism of Hume and Priestley, but it includes substantial discussion of the notions of power and causality, of the will, of motivation and of morality. The two works thus constitute a more-or-less complete survey of what Reid would call the 'operations' of the human mind.

While he was still at Aberdeen, Reid's ideas were taken up by his colleagues Oswald and Beattie. The latter scored a remarkable literary triumph with his *Essay on Truth*, which went through many editions earning its author a royal pension and an honorary doctorate from Oxford. But Beattie was no philosopher and the *Essay* is nothing more than a violent diatribe against the irreligious scepticism of Hume, in which Beattie shows little grasp of the real issues. A more important figure was Reid's pupil Dugald Stewart, who held the chair of Moral Philosophy in Edinburgh from 1785 to 1811. Partly through Stewart's influence, Reid's ideas came to dominate Scottish thought in the early part of the nineteenth century. The Common Sense school became known as 'the Scottish philosophy'. But even in Scotland Reid always had his critics, the most significant of whom was Thomas Brown, Stewart's colleague and successor at Edinburgh. Eventually, with the spread of Kantian and Hegelian ideas, interest in the Common Sense school dwindled, though most British philosophers in the second half of the nineteenth century still found its ideas worth discussing. Meanwhile Reid's influence spread to America, largely because many of the professors in American colleges, notably McCosh of Princeton, came from Scotland. Some of the recent revival of interest in Reid's work stems from the interest of American scholars in their own intellectual roots.

In France, Reid's ideas were taken up by Royer-Collard, who saw it as an antidote to the sensationalism of Condillac. The appointment of Victor Cousin, another follower of Reid, as minister of public instruction ensured that the common sense philosophy was for much of the nineteenth century the official doctrine in the schools and left an enduring mark on French thought.

II

Reid's account of the aims and methods of his philosophy is closely modelled on the introduction to Hume's *Treatise* – itself a classic statement of Enlightenment ideals. In particular, Reid agrees with Hume on the following four points.

(1) The task of the philosopher is to describe the nature and mode of operation of the human mind. It is thus parallel to the task of the natural philosopher, who describes the nature and behaviour of the material world.

(2) The study of the human mind is of vital importance, not only because of its intrinsic interest but also because an understanding of the scope and limits of our knowledge is an essential prerequisite for progress in most other fields.

(3) The method to be followed in the science of the mind is substantially the same as that used in natural philosophy – it must follow the inductive method first described by Bacon, and successfully used by Newton in discovering the fundamental laws of the material world.

(4) Little has so far been achieved in the science of mind because philosophers have either failed to use the Newtonian method or have applied it improperly. In particular they have based their conclusions on hypotheses or conjectures with no adequate basis in experience.

Unlike most of his contemporaries and most of us who now write about the Enlightenment, Reid did not need to rely on a half-understood popular account of Newton's work. He had taught natural philosophy at both Aberdeen and Glasgow and had the mathematical and scientific capacity to read and understand Newton's original texts. His first published paper, although prompted by Hutcheson's attempt to introduce quantitative methods into moral philosophy, was largely taken up with a discussion of the dispute between the followers of Newton and those of Leibniz about the measure of force. He carried on a lively scientific correspondence with friends such as David Skene, James Gregory, and Lord Kames, and in Glasgow showed a close interest in the work of men such as Joseph Black and James Watt.

Reid's active involvement in the science of his day partly explains the difference between his Newtonianism and that of Hume. Hume frequently refers to the need to follow the method of experiment and observation, but in practice he seems to have been chiefly impressed by the simplicity of Newton's fundamental laws. Just as Newton had accounted for a wide variety of different physical phenomena by showing them to result from the effect of gravitation on material bodies, so Hume hoped to explain the phenomena of the mind as the effects of association on ideas and impressions. Reid, on the other hand, was primarily impressed by the Baconian method which he believed Newton to have followed. He calls this inductive method 'the master key to the knowledge of nature' and contrasts its success with the sterility of the old method of deduction (*I.P.* V.vi,402; *Brief Account of Aristotle's Logic*, VI.ii.712a).[1]

> The art of syllogism produced numberless disputes and numberless sects . . . but did nothing considerable for the benefit of human life. The art of induction, first delineated by Lord Bacon, produced numberless laboratories and observatories, in which nature has been put to question by thousands of experiments, and forced to confess many of her secrets that before were hid from mortals: and, by these, arts have been improved, and human knowledge wonderfully increased. (*Brief Account*, VI,ii,712a)

It is not surprising, therefore, that Reid, in his account of the mind, is greatly concerned with the investigation of particular phenomena and is much less eager than Hume to subsume all these under some relatively simple theory. Indeed, associationists such as Priestley criticised Reid precisely for the complexity of his views – that is for postulating far too many ultimate principles.[2]

This methodological Newtonianism proved to be one of the most influential features of Reid thought. His popularity in nineteenth-century France, for example, stemmed largely from the prospect which his philosophy seemed to offer of establishing a genuinely empirical science of the mind. As his translator, Jouffroy, saw it, the Scots had established once and for all the idea that there is an observational science which can discover laws of the mind in the same way that physicists discover laws of matter.[3] In Britain, Reid seems to have been the main source from which nineteenth-century philosophers such as Whewell and Mill derived their conception of an inductive scientific method.[4]

The most distinctive feature of Reid's philosophy is, of course, his appeal to Common Sense. He takes this to refer to certain principles 'which the constitution of our nature leads us to believe, and which we are under a necessity to take for granted in the common concerns of life.' (*Inquiry*, II,vi,108b) In other words, the principles of common sense are implanted in our natures and cannot be doubted in practice, however sceptical one is in theory. Reid's many examples of such principles include the beliefs 'that those things do really exist which we distinctly perceive by the senses', 'that those we converse with are living intelligent beings', 'that those things did really happen which we distinctly remember', 'that we continue the same identical persons' and 'that we have some degree of power over our actions and the determinations of our will' (*I.P.* VI.v,441a–452; *A.P.*. IV.iv,618b).

Reid denies that there can be any real opposition between common sense and reason. In the *Inquiry*, he argues that since both are the work of God there must be order and consistency among them. In fact Reason needs Common Sense to provide self evident premises. 'All reasoning must be from first principles; and for first principles no other reason can be given but this, that, by the constitution of our nature we are under the necessity of assenting to them . . .' (*Inquiry*, V.vii,130a).

Reid's commitment to common sense is thus fully consonant with his admiration of Newton, for Newtonian science depends on the acceptance of certain methodological assumptions for which no justification can be given. Reid argues, with some plausibility, that these are simply applications of the common-sense principles by which we govern our ordinary lives:

> The man who first discovered that cold freezes water, and that heat turns it into vapour, proceeded on the same general principles, and in the same method, by which Newton discovered the law of gravitation and the properties of light. His *regulae philosophandi* are maxims of common sense, and are practised everyday in common life; and he who philosophises by other rules, either concerning the material system or concerning the mind, mistakes his aim. *Inquiry*, I.1,97)

In the *Essays on the Intellectual Powers*, Reid identifies Common Sense with reason in its role as the faculty which discovers necessary truths:

> We ascribe to reason two offices, or two degrees. The first is to judge things self-evident; the second to draw conclusions that are not self-evident from those that are. The first of these is the province, and the sole province of common sense; and, therefore it coincides with reasoning in its whole extent, and is only another name for one branch or one degree of reason. (*I.P.* VI.ii,425b)

Here Reid appears to align himself with the rationalist tradition of eighteenth-century thought. But this is misleading. The rationalists saw the truths of reason as necessary truths, independent of the particular facts of human nature and the human situation. Reid, on the other hand, explicitly categorises many of his first principles as contingent. We are obliged to believe them not because they must hold in any possible world but simply because God has made us that way.

Reid makes two main uses of these beliefs in his philosophy. In the first place, common sense provides a criterion or standard against which philosophical theories may be tested. If philosophy purports to cast doubt on 'principles which irresistibly govern the belief and the conduct of all mankind in the common concerns of life', then it is philosophy which must be rejected. 'In this unequal contest betwixt Common Sense and Philosophy, the latter will always come off both with dishonour and loss; nor can she ever thrive till this rivalship is dropt, these encroachments given up, and a cordial friendship established' (*Inquiry* I.v,101a–b).

Common sense thus has a regulative role, in that it sets the boundaries within which philosophy must confine itself on pain of absurdity. Its province is, as Reid puts it, 'more extensive in refutation than in confirmation' (*I.P.* VI.ii,425–6). Reid's point is, of course, that the theories of his predecessors, particularly Hume, must be rejected since they imply the falsehood of principles which in reality we cannot help believing.

The second major use Reid makes of his principles of common sense is in his accounts of the different kinds of mental activity. Characteristically, he argues that certain very fundamental beliefs are presupposed in ordinary experience. For example, he argues that perception involves a belief in the existence both of the subject perceived and of oneself as a perceiving object. His analysis of human action is likewise based on the claim that all our voluntary activity presupposes the common-sense belief that we are the agents and causes of our own actions. I shall say more on this aspect of Reid's doctrine of common sense in section IV below.

III

The close association of Reid's Newtonianism and his theory of common sense is apparent in his criticisms of his predecessors. He argues that the principal source of error is the failure to take seriously Newton's warnings against the adoption of 'hypotheses' or 'conjectures', that is, assumptions which are not derived from observation or experiment. Newton, in Reid's view, took care 'to distinguish his doctrines, which he pretended to prove by just induction, from his conjectures, which were to stand or fall as future experiments and observations should establish or refute them' (*I.P.* II.iii,249a). But the trouble with most previous writers on the mind is that they have based their theories on claims which, whether they admit it or not, are in fact no more than 'the reveries of vain and fanciful men, whose pride makes them conceive themselves able to unfold the mysteries of nature by the force of their genius'. Reid therefore lays it down as a 'fundamental principle' of his enquiries 'that no regard is due to such conjectures and hypotheses'. We must accustom ourselves to 'try every opinion by the touchstone of fact and experience' (*I.P.* I,iii,236a).

Another source of error in writings on the mind is the improper use of analogy. Because we are not used to paying much attention to mental operations, we describe these in terms borrowed from our talk about material objects. We are then tempted to take this language literally. In particular, since material bodies can act on one another only by contact, we are misled into supposing that the mind can be affected only by things with which it is in direct contact. This leads to the erroneous theory that the objects of a mental act must be something within the mind.

Reid argues that these mistakes have vitiated the work of virtually all his recent predecessors from Descartes onwards, including, of course, Locke, Berkeley and Hume. The false analogy with the material world has encouraged philosophers to suppose that we can never directly perceive an external object but only a 'representative image' or 'idea' within the mind (*I.P.* II.viii,274a). They have made this assumption the basis of their entire philosophy of the mind.

Reid argues firstly that this theory of ideas is 'a mere fiction and hypothesis', for which no solid proof has ever been advanced (*Inquiry*, II.iii,106a), and secondly that it inevitably leads to scepticism about the external world and even about the existence of our own minds. Descartes and Locke tried hard to avoid these sceptical conclusions – to show that, even though, according to the ideal theory, we never perceive external objects, we still have good reason for believing in their existence. This struggle was in vain. Berkeley, on Reid's interpretation, showed that if we cannot directly perceive external objects, we have no grounds for believing in them. He thought that he had

> demonstrated by a variety of arguments, grounded on the principles of philosophy universally received, that there is no such thing as matter in the universe; that sun and moon, earth and sea, our own bodies and those of our friends, are nothing but ideas in the minds of those who think of them, and that they have no existence when they are not the object

of thought; that all that is in the universe may be reduced to two categories, to wit, minds and ideas in the minds. (*I.P.* II.x,281a)

He hoped that by doing so he might at least 'secure the world of spirits'. But Hume went one step further, and brought out the full implications of the ideal theory. He showed that if all we are aware of is ideas, then there can be no good reasons for believing in the existence of anything else at all, not even in our own minds. All that is left is a succession of ideas. As Reid puts it: 'He adopts the theory of ideas in its full extent; and in consequence, shows that there is neither matter nor mind in the universe; nothing but impressions and ideas. What we call a body is only a bundle of sensations; and what we call the mind is only a bundle of thoughts, passions and emotions, without any subject' (*I.P.* II.xii,293a). Hume's theory, as Reid understood it, was thus one of total scepticism. Reid did not in any sense accept this scepticism – he was particularly troubled by Hume's apparent dissolution of the mind – nor did he think that anyone else could seriously believe it. Nevertheless he did consider that Hume had argued correctly from his premises. In doing so he had done a great service: he had shown that total scepticism is the logical outcome of the theory of ideas.

It has been argued, notably by Thomas Brown, that the theory of ideas which Reid claimed to have refuted had not seriously been held by any significant philosopher. Reid's mistake, according to Brown, was to assume that his predecessors meant to be taken literally when they spoke of ideas as images within the mind, when in fact this language is purely figurative. By 'idea' they did not mean some distinct mental object but 'the mind affected in a certain way' or, in other words to 'the mind existing in a certain state'.[5] An essentially similar line of criticism has been pursued quite recently by John Yolton, who argues that ideas were not meant to be entities or proxy objects but as 'the psychic contents of awareness'.[6]

These philosophers are undoubtedly correct in arguing that ideas need not be understood as images, but it is unlikely that Reid would have regarded this point as a serious criticism of his own position. Even if thinkers of the quality of Locke, Berkeley and Hume were not confused when they wrote as though ideas were mental likenesses, many of the lesser figures certainly were and Reid did a real service in pointing out the dangers. More importantly, Reid's key arguments do not depend on the assumption that ideas are to be taken in this way. Hume, the opponent whom Reid has principally in mind, officially at least, maintains that all the phenomena of the mind may be analysed in terms of impressions and ideas which follow one another in accordance with regular laws of association. Impressions are defined to include 'all our sensations, passions and emotions, as they make their first appearance in the soul' and ideas are simply 'the faint images of these in thinking and reasoning' (*Treatise*, 1).[7] Hume sees that, on this theory, the self can be no more than 'a heap or collection of different perceptions united together by certain relations and suppos'd, tho' falsely, to be endow'd with a perfect simplicity or identity' (*Treatise*, 207). His theory creates a similar problem about how we can make sense of the idea of a material body. When we take ourselves to be observing the same body at different times and in different contexts, we are in fact aware only of perceptions, so 'the notion of external existence when taken for something specifically different from our perceptions' is absurd' (*Treatise*, 188). Our idea of external body arises because we confuse the coherence of perceptions with continuity, and their constancy or resemblance with identity. We thus *fallaciously* ascribe a continued existence to sensible objects and perceptions, though philosophy tells us this is absurd.

Reid is clearly right in suggesting that these Humean conclusions run counter to common sense, for common sense insists both that perceptions are the acts of a mind that perceives, and that normally they have an object which exists independently of the mind. Although Reid spends a good deal of time attacking the conception of ideas as mental images, he does not need this conception in order to make good the two key claims (a) that Hume's theory conflicts with common sense and (b) that it is the logical outcome of the theory of ideas. The fundamental failure is not the suggestion that ideas are images, but a grossly over-simplified theory of the mind which attempts to analyse virtually all mental activity as the having of ideas.

Brown also pointed out, quite correctly, that Reid and Hume had more in common than one might suppose. They both accept (a) that the existence of the external world cannot be proved by argument and (b) that the belief in the external world is nevertheless irresistible. Brown saw the difference between the two philosophers on these matters as one of emphasis rather than substance.

> The creed of each, on this point, is composed of two propositions, and of the same two propositions; the first of which is that the existence of a system of things, such as we understand when we speak of an external world, cannot be proved by argument; and the second, that the belief of it is of

a force that is paramount to that of argument, and absolutely irresistible. The difference, and the only difference is, that, in asserting the same two propositions, the sceptic pronounces the first in a loud tone of voice and the second in a whisper, – while his supposed antagonist passes rapidly over the first and dwells on the second with a tone of confidence. (*Lectures on the Human Mind*, chap. XXVIII,177)

Here again, the point Brown scores is not in any sense fundamental. Although Hume did not expect his readers to abandon their everyday beliefs in the existence of their own minds and in that of the external world, he did hold that such beliefs cannot be justified philosophically. Reid, on the other hand, holds that if the conclusions of a philosophical or scientific argument conflict with common sense, philosophy must give way – that is, there must be something wrong either with the argument itself or with the premisses on which it is based. So in his view, the fact that Hume's philosophical conclusions cannot be reconciled with common sense shows that Hume has gone astray. His main mistake was to have accepted the unjustified hypothesis of ideas instead of carrying out a genuinely empirical inductive investigation of the mind.

IV

The main difficulty in following an inductive method in the study of the mind is, of course, that of finding suitable observations or experiments from which to begin. Here Reid recommends the use of what he calls 'reflection' – we would call it 'introspection'. By this method a man may, he believes, reach 'a clear and certain knowledge of the operations of his own mind' (*I.P.* I,ii). Such reflection is 'the chief and proper source of this branch of knowledge' (*I.P.* I.v,238b). But, although we are all conscious of the operations of our minds, it is not easy to make them the objects of our attention. Reid claims that he has himself worked hard to acquire the capacity to do this. As he put it, 'I claim no other merit than that of having given great attention to the operations of my own mind, and having expressed with all the perspicuity I was able, what I conceive every man who gives the same attention will feel and perceive' (*Inquiry*, Dedication, 96a–b).

Reid also recognises two other methods which he regards as 'subservient' to the method of reflection. The first consists in taking note of features common to all languages. These must have some common cause and must therefore result from 'some common notion or sentiment of the human mind'. For example, the fact that all languages, according to Reid, have plural forms shows that 'all men have notions, not of individual things only, but of attributes, or things which are common to many individuals' (*I.P.* I.v,238b). Similarly, he takes the 'fact' that all languages incorporate a distinction between the active and the passive voices to show that we are all conscious of the distinction between active power and mere passivity (*A.P.* I.11,515a–518b). The second method consists in paying attention to the ways in which people behave, for our actions are the effects of our sentiments, passions and affections, and we are often able to 'form a judgment of the cause from the effect'. Men's opinions too may cast light on the structure of their minds, for these are the effects of the intellectual in the same way that actions are the effects of the active powers (ibid.). In actual fact, Reid makes more use of these 'subservient' methods than he seems prepared to admit. His use of linguistic and behavioural criteria means that the style and method of his work in the philosophy of mind often resembles that of Gilbert Ryle and like-minded twentieth-century thinkers.

Whatever one makes of Reid's claims about introspection, there is little doubt that much of the interest in his philosophy lies in his detailed examinations of different mental phenomena. He tries hard and with some success to consider the particular cases before he makes generalisations – a method most apparent in the *Inquiry*, where he treats in turn each of the five senses, beginning with smell, which he takes to be the simplest, and ending with sight, which he takes to be the most complex. Other philosophers, by contrast, have concentrated on sight and have treated the other senses peripherally. Reid is right to think that this has distorted their discussions of perception, for sight differs in many respects from the other senses.

Reid, as we have seen, took it for granted that his predecessors regarded the ideas which are the immediate objects of our perception as images within our minds. On Locke's theory, these inner images would be likenesses of things which really exist in the external world. When I see a house or a tree, I have a visual image which in certain respects resembles an object which really exists somewhere in front of me. When I merely imagine the house or the tree, I have a similar image but this time there is no external reality to which it corresponds. Berkeley and Hume, as Reid understood them, modified this picture by denying the existence of anything external, and regarded the images within the mind as the only objects of perception. Whether or not this is an accurate picture of the views really held by these philosophers,

the model does have some plausibility as long as we stick to sight,
But, as Reid shows, this plausibility vanishes as soon as one
concentrates on the other senses, such as that of touch. Philosophical orthodoxy maintained, not unreasonably, that through
touch we can acquire ideas of hot and cold, hardness and softness,
extension in space and the like. Reid asks his readers to reflect on
what it is actually like to touch a hard object. If we do this with
sufficient attention, we will see that there certainly is a distinct
sensation. But this sensation is in no sense similar to hardness or
to our concept of hardness. Thus to have the sensation of
hardness is clearly a quite different kind of phenomenon from
thinking about hardness, or having the concept of hardness. The
same, Reid suggests, goes for all other sensations and the
concepts we acquire by means of them. They are no more alike
than a pain is like the point of a sword which causes it.

This argument points to a key theme in Reid's treatment of
perception: his insistence on the distinction between perception
and sensation. In his view, the approach of his predecessors had
tended to erode this distinction and even to deny it altogether. If
all mental activity is a matter of having ideas, seeing a table,
imagining one, remembering one and believing that there will be
one in the same place tomorrow, must all be analysed in fundamentally the same kind of way. For a representative theorist like
Locke, the difference between these states of mind lies largely in
the way which they are related to an external reality, but Berkeley
and Hume saw that if ideas are the only direct objects of
perception, there can be no sense in talking about such a reality.
This leaves them with the problem of explaining the difference
between different mental states or acts of mind, all of which have
the same object. Hume notoriously relied on the notion of
vivacity to make these distinctions. Taken literally, it implies that
the perception of the sun rising, the memory of its rising
yesterday, the belief in its rising tomorrow, and the imagination
of its rising are all simply livelier or fainter instances of the same
idea. Reid has no difficulty in showing that this approach is
inadequate to the point of absurdity (*Inquiry* VI.xxiv,198b–199a).

The trouble with Hume's view is that he emphasises the
content, the idea, that different mental acts have in common but
has little to say about how those mental acts differ. Reid, on the
other hand, emphasises that acts of mind such as believing,
conceiving, imagining and willing differ in kind from one another.
Although familiar to us all, they are too simple in their nature to
be defined. In other words, Reid treats them as primitive.
Hume's treatment of the cases just discussed leaves out the

elements of judgement and conception. Seeing a table, for example, is not merely a matter of having a certain visual sensation. It also involves having some conception of what one sees and a judgement that it is really there. As Reid puts it, 'the perception of an object implies both a conception of its form, and a belief of its present existence (*Inquiry* VI.xx,183a). Similarly, if one remembers seeing a table, one does not simply have an image or idea of the table but must have some conception of it and must judge that one has seen it. Imagining a table, on the other hand, involves only what Reid calls 'simple apprehension'. There need be no belief as to its present, past or future existence.

In this way, Reid argues that to have a sensation, whether it be visual, auditory or of any other kind is not to perceive something. Perception involves sensation but it also involves belief. This is not a fully worked out theory of perception, but it does at least provide the beginnings of an answer to the key problem 'How can we be said to perceive external objects, as distinct from mere ideas within our own minds?' The beliefs we form in perception are beliefs about external objects, the beliefs we form in memory are beliefs about past events and so on. There is thus a sense in which external objects can be said to be the immediate objects of perception, and in which past events can be said to be the immediate objects of memory. Ideas no longer create a barrier between us and the outer world.

This of course, raises the question of how sensation and belief relate to one another in perception. Reid's answer is summed up in his claim that sensation is a 'principle of belief'. The human mind is so constituted that sensations naturally lead us to believe in the existence of the corresponding objects. For example, when I get a sensation like the one I have when I press my finger against the table, I inevitably acquire a belief in the existence of something hard. The acquisition of this belief is not the result of inference, for there is no way in which one can argue logically from one's awareness of a sensation to the existence of a table. The point is simply that, human nature being what it is, the belief inevitably ensues. There are various ways in which Reid tries to elucidate this passage from sensation to belief. Sometimes he says that the sensation 'suggests' the existence of the external object, in the same kind of way that the hearing of a certain sound suggests that a coach is passing. He also uses analogies with language. The sensation is a sign of the external thing just as a word is a sign of the thing it stands for. When I hear the word, I immediately form a conception of what it refers to. In the same way the sensation leads me to conceive the object. Reid claims that we instinctively tend to trust what is said to us. Similarly we by nature trust our senses. That is, we treat them as truthful signs of the external world.

V

Reid was not, of course, the only important philosopher who reacted strongly to his reading of Hume. As is well known, Kant also claimed that Hume had aroused him from his 'dogmatic slumber'. So far as one can tell, Reid had no knowledge at all of Kant. Kant knew of Reid only indirectly, through Beattie, and through the very hostile and uncomprehending account of him in Priestley's *Examination*. Not surprisingly, Kant was unimpressed by the idea of a common-sense philosophy:

> To appeal to common sense when insight and science fail, and no sooner – this is one of the subtle discoveries of modern times, by means of which the most superficial ranter can safely enter the lists with the most thorough thinker and safely hold his own. But as long as a particle of insight remains, no one would think of having recourse to this subterfuge. Seen clearly, it is but an appeal to the opinion of the multitude, of whose applause the philosopher is ashamed, while the popular charlatan glories and boasts in it.[8]

Kant's ignorance of Reid is manifest – by no stretch of the imagination could the latter be described as a ranter – but the issues raised in this passage remain pertinent. How can a thinker base his philosophy on an appeal to common sense without sacrificing the commitment to systematic rational enquiry, which is the hallmark of the Enlightenment?

There are, I think, two separate charges to consider here. The first is that the philosophy of common sense is little more than appeal to the prejudices of the masses. The key point here is surely that Reid does not regard every widely held belief as a deliverance of common sense. Genuine principles of common sense are ones which human nature cannot avoid accepting, and Reid tells us a good deal about the criteria by which these genuine principles may be distinguished from those that are spurious. Genuine principles of common sense are universally accepted. They may be denied by sceptical philosophers but, even if such scepticisms cannot be refuted, in practice they die way. The behaviour even of sceptical philosophers in their everyday lives shows that they accept the principles of Common Sense. These principles are implicit in the structure of all languages. They appear in the mind too early to be due to education or false reasoning (*I.P.* VI.iv,437b–441a). To deny them is to fall not merely into falsehood but into absurdity. Much of Reid's philosophy consists in a detailed working out of these points. Characteristically, he attempts to show not only that the principles of common sense are genuinely believed but that they are presupposed in all our everyday thought and practice or, as Reid would put it, in all 'the operations of the mind'. We have already seen how Reid argues this in the case of the belief in the existence of the objects of perception. His point is that we do not first have the perceptual experience, and then infer from that the existence of an object which is perceived. Rather, a belief in the existence of the object is implicit in the experience. Similarly, one central contention of the *Essays on the Active Powers* is that our experience of voluntary action in ourselves and in others presupposes the belief that we have 'some degree of active power', i.e. that we are agents who can cause things to happen in the world.

Not all of Reid's principles of Common Sense are as plausible or as well defended as these. Although Reid's method is not, and does not claim to be, infallible, it is, I think fundamentally sound. It offers a genuinely empirical way of deciding which principles are to be included as principles of Common Sense and which may not. Honestly and consistently applied, it can avoid the danger of investing the prejudices of a particular age or creed with the title and dignity of 'self evident first principles'.

The second charge implicit in Kant's comments is more fundamental, and was indeed used by many nineteenth-century authors as a standard objection to the common-sense philosophy. Reid explicitly describes the principles of common sense as principles of human nature, i.e. the reason why we are bound to believe them is simply that we are made that way. The obvious reply is that this does nothing to show that those beliefs are true. It is conceivable that we are made with a propensity to accept a picture of the world which simply does not correspond with reality. G.H. Lewes, perhaps the most scathing of Reid's nineteenth-century critics, put the point as follows:

> To say that the belief in objective existence is a Fundamental Law, is simply saying that *we are so constituted* that we are forced to attribute external reality to our sensations. As well say that we are so constituted that fire applied to our bodies will give us pain. We *are* so constituted. What then? Does this advance us one step? Not one. We have still to seek some proof of the *laws of our constitution* being the measure of the laws of other existence – still to seek how what is true of the subjective must necessarily be true of the objective.[9]

Lewes is undoubtedly right here, but his argument does not, I think, constitute a serious criticism of Reid. He assumes that Reid meant to use the fact that everyone believes in the reality of the external world as a proof of the existence of such a world. This, of course, overlooks Reid's claim, mentioned above, that common sense is more effective in refuting than in establishing philosophical theories, an oversight which seriously distorts the form of Reid's argument. As Reid sees it, the conflict between common sense and the conclusions implicit in the theories of his predecessors shows that there must be something wrong with the theories. His aim is to discover the source of the error, and to offer an alternative account of the mind consistent with common sense. In other words, the main thrust of his argument is not to prove the existence of the external world, or even of our own minds, but rather to refute a particular kind of argument for scepticism. It is thus beside the point to object that he fails to prove that there is an external reality.

Reid himself believed that his 'refutation' of the theory of ideas was his most important contribution to philosophy. As we have seen, his attempt to bring a scientific method into philosophy was at least as important. But the ideal of a common-sense philosophy has in itself a perennial attraction. Whenever philosophy seems to have lost its way, as it did to Reid in the eighteenth century, the obvious move is to attempt to recall it to the world of ordinary experience and to the beliefs which structure our ordinary lives. It is this, as much as anything, that has led to the revival of interest in Reid in recent years. Modern philosophers may see our most fundamental beliefs as implicit in our language rather than as part of the constitution of human nature, but many still find inspiration in Reid's careful common-sense empiricism.

NOTES

1. References are to *The Works of Thomas Reid*, ed. Sir William Hamilton, 6th edn (Edinburgh, 1863). The titles of the *Essays on the Intellectual Powers of Man* and the *Essays on the Active Powers of Man* are abbreviated respectively to *I.P.* and *A.P.*

2 Joseph Priestley, *An Examination of Dr Reid's Inquiry into the human mind. . . . Dr Beattie's Essay on the nature and immutability of truth, and Dr. Oswald's Appeal to common sense on behalf of religion* (London, 1771).

3 *Oeuvres completes de Thomas Reid* (Paris, 1836), vol. I,viii.

4 See L. Laudan, 'Thomas Reid and the Newtonian turn of British methodological thought', in eds R.E. Butts and J.W.

Davis, *The Methodological Heritage of Newton* (Oxford, 1970).

5 Thomas Brown, *Lectures on the Human Mind*, 13th edn, (Edinburgh, 1842), Lecture XXV,156.

6 John Yolton, *Perceptual Acquaintance from Descartes to Reid* (Oxford, 1984), 73.

7 Hume references are to David Hume, *A Treatise on Human Nature*, ed. L.A. Selby-Bigge, revised P.H. Nidditch (Oxford, 1978).

8 I. Kant, *Prolegomena to any Future Metaphysic*, trans. P. Carus (Indianapolis: Library of Liberal Arts, 1950), 8.

9 G.H. Lewes, *History of Philosophy* (London, 1867), vol. II,383.

MURRAY MACBEATH

Kant

Enlightenment of the masses is the public instruction of the people in its duties and rights vis-à-vis the state to which they belong. Since only natural rights and rights arising out of the common human understanding are concerned here, then the natural heralds and expositors of these among the people are not officially appointed by the state but are free professors of law, that is philosophers who, precisely because this freedom is allowed to them, are objectionable to the state, which always desires to rule alone; and they are decried, under the name of enlighteners, as persons dangerous to the state . . .[1]*

Kant was self-consciously an Enlightenment philosopher, and his view of the fate of such figures, to be regarded as 'persons dangerous to the state', was born out of his own experience. He had been obliged by Frederick William II, the less tolerant successor of Frederick the Great, to promise that he would 'abstain entirely from all public lectures on religious topics, whether on natural or revealed religion, and not only from lectures but also from publications'.[2]

While Frederick the Great had been alive, Kant had written, in an essay entitled 'What is Enlightenment?':

If we are asked, 'Do we now live in an *enlightened age?*' the answer is, 'No,' but we do live in an *age of enlightenment*. As things now stand, much is lacking which prevents men from being, or easily becoming, capable of correctly using their own reason in religious matters with assurance and free from outside direction. But, on the other hand, we have clear indications that the field has now been opened wherein men may freely deal with these things and that the obstacles to general enlightenment or the release from self-imposed tutelage are gradually being reduced. In this respect, this is the age of enlightenment, or the century of Frederick.[3]

A page later, still speaking of Frederick the Great, Kant says:

only one who is himself enlightened is not afraid of shadows,

and who has a numerous and well-disciplined army to assure
public peace, can say: 'Argue as much as you will, and about
what you will, only obey!' A republic could not dare say such
a thing.[4]

The year was 1784. By the time, more than a dozen years later,
Kant came to write the work from which my opening quotation
was taken, the clear indications of an age of enlightenment in
Prussia had faded. None the less, despite the bitter tone of its
remarks about the state's opposition to philosophy, this later
work as a whole is optimistic: for, if the German sky had clouded
over, momentous events had been taking place in France.

The title of the work is 'An Old Question Raised Again: Is the
Human Race Constantly Progressing?', and in it Kant argues that
the old question cannot be answered 'directly through experience',
that is, simply by examining the history of the human race to
date. For, he says, there can be no guarantee that the progress
which we might find to have prevailed hitherto will not be
reversed at any moment. This remark comes from the philosopher
who so firmly believed, in opposition to Hume, that reason makes
possible the discovery of laws of nature, and thus licenses the
belief that the future will be like the past. Why does the study of
human history not enable us to predict the future of our race?
Because, says Kant, 'we are dealing with beings that act freely,
to whom, it is true, what they ought to do may be dictated in
advance, but of whom it may not be predicted what they will
do.'[5] So we cannot argue directly from past progress to future
progress. However it is possible, Kant thinks, to find in recent
history a clue as to the moral character of the human race, and to
see, in the character thus disclosed, reason to believe that human
history does involve 'progress toward the better'. The clue is
provided, not by the French Revolution itself, but by the
response to it: 'this revolution . . . finds in the hearts of all
spectators (who are not engaged in this game themselves) a
wishful participation that borders closely on enthusiasm'.[6] (When
Kant says 'borders closely on', he means it, for enthusiasm itself,
'the passionate participation in the good', is 'not to be wholly
esteemed, since passion as such deserves censure'.[7] The disinter-
ested sympathy felt by observers of events in France 'can have no
other cause than a moral predisposition in the human race'.[8] Two
moral principles inform this sympathy:

> first, that of the *right*, that a nation must not be hindered in
> providing itself with a civil constitution, which appears good
> to the people themselves: and second, that of the *end* (which is,
> at the same time, a duty), that that same national constitution

alone be just and morally good in itself, created in such a way as to avoid, by its very nature, principles permitting offensive war. It can be no other than a republican constitution, republican at least in essence . . .[9]

Kant makes it clear, however, that he is not advocating revolution in Prussia: progress toward the better can be expected, he says. 'not by the movement of things *from bottom to top*, but *from top to bottom*',[10] principally by means of an education system involving 'the public instruction of the people in its duties and rights'. What benefits will this bring? 'Not an ever-growing quantity of morality with regard to intention, but an increase of the products of legality in dutiful actions whatever their motives.'[11]

The works which make Kant a central figure in the history of western philosophy, the works of his so-called Critical period, began to appear in 1781, when he was already fifty-seven. He turned his attention successively in the following years to problems of epistemology and metaphysics, of ethics, of aesthetics, of religion, and of politics and history. Twentieth-century philosophers write about Kant as though this chronological order also constituted order of importance, or as though Kant's writings had declined in insight as he moved into old age. 'An Old Question Raised Again' is one of the last pieces that Kant published. I have taken it as my starting point, not as a protest against contemporary wisdom, but because in it Kant sets out his views on enlightenment, in the process drawing on some central doctrines of his Critical philosophy.

The freedom of human beings, which makes it impossible to predict what they will do, is a consequence of their rationality. 'Everything in nature', says Kant in the *Groundwork of the Metaphysic of Morals*, 'works in accordance with laws. Only a rational being has the power to act *in accordance with his idea* of laws – that is, in accordance with principles . . .'[12] Only of a rational being can we ask 'What was her reason for doing that?', and the question implies that she chose to do what she did, and could have chosen to do otherwise. This suggests that the actions of human beings are not governed by laws of nature, or scientific laws, that, unlike everything else in nature, human beings escape the otherwise merciless clutches of causal determinism. But this is not Kant's official position: the official position is that, despite the freedom which we must ascribe to them, the behaviour of human beings is as causally determined as anything else. Hume, of course, had declared that there was no incompatibility between liberty (or freedom) and necessity (or determinism), and had argued that I act freely when the determining causes of my behaviour lie within my own character; but Kant treats with contempt Hume's claim that close attention to the meanings of the words 'liberty' and 'necessity' will simply dissolve the problem:

> With this manner of argument many allow themselves to be put off and believe that with a little quibbling they have found the solution to the difficult problem which centuries have sought in vain and which could hardly be expected to be found so completely on the surface.[13]

If the only freedom we possessed were that which Hume allows us, 'it would in essence be no better than the freedom of a turnspit, which when once wound up also carries out its motions of itself'.[14] Empiricists like Hume try to find a place for freedom within a deterministic causal nexus; Kant too wished to preserve intact the causal nexus, but thinks that the only freedom worth having has to be located outside it, a transcendental freedom.

To see how Kant's proposed accommodation works – an accommodation between freedom and determinism radically different in spirit from Hume's, we should first ask why Kant is a determinist. The answer is, that for us to have experience of an objective world in which events occur at identifiable times or in a specifiable order, there must be a principle of connection among events; and the principle in question is that of causality. The truth of determinism is not for Kant, as it is for Hume, a conclusion at which we arrive after much experience of seeing things constantly conjoined; rather, it can be known *a priori*, since it is a precondition of our having the kind of orderly experience which would enable us even to notice constant conjunctions.

Whether or not Kant is right about this, he sees it as an important implication of his view that the justified application of the principle of causality extends only to the objects of experience, to things *as they appear to us*. But it is possible at least to think of things *as they are in themselves*. The contrast Kant has in mind is not between the way things look, under odd lighting conditions perhaps, and the way they really are. It is more like the contrast, due mainly to Locke, between primary and secondary qualities, between, on the one hand, those qualities of things, like size and shape, which are as they appear to us, and on the other hand, those qualities of things which cause us to perceive them as blue or red, sweet or sour, though colours and flavours are not themselves qualities of things. But Kant's contrast is vastly more far-reaching than Locke's:

> the things which we intuit [or are aware of] are not in themselves what we intuit them as being . . . if the subject, or even only the subjective constitution of the senses in

general be removed, the whole constitution and all the
relations of objects in space and time, nay space and time
themselves, would vanish.[15]

It is clear that, in Kant's view, to think away the features of things
that belong to those things only as they appear to us is to think
away far more than their colours and flavours: it is to think away
all their spatio-temporal properties, indeed everything that enables
us to identify things as the things they are. Given how much has
to be thought away, it is not surprising to find Kant conclude that
we can have no knowledge of things as they are in themselves.

Our most basic beliefs about the world had been declared by
Hume to be incapable of philosophical justification; rather, Hume
thought, the aim of the student of human nature should be to
show that these are *natural* beliefs, capable of explanation perhaps,
but not of justification. Where Hume naturalises, Kant trans-
cendentalises. Our basic beliefs about the spatio-temporal structure and causal organisation of the world that we experience,
can, according to Kant, be justified, by showing that, were they
false, there would be no world of experience. Kant's transcen-
dentalism takes the form of transcendental *idealism*: that is to say,
he thinks that the general structural and organisational features of
the world of experience are mind-dependent. Space and time are
forms of human sensibility; causality is one of the categories of
human understanding. But Kant insists that transcendental idealism does not commit him to maintaining, with Berkeley, that the
material objects which we encounter in experience are not real:
Kant proclaims himself to be, not only a transcendental idealist,
but also an empirical realist. Whereas Berkeley holds that 'esse est
percipi', that a thing exists only in so far as it is the object of
awareness, Kant insists that 'our mode of intuition [or awareness]
is dependent upon the existence of the object, and is therefore
possible only if the subject's faculty of representation is affected
by that object'.[16]

Kant is a determinist because he thinks that the events of
experience have to be systematically connected, and that causality
constitutes the principle of connection. But it is only to the
objects of our experience, to things as they appear to us, that we
are bound to apply the principle of causality. There is no reason
why we should regard things as they are in themselves as subject
to causal laws. Now, if I look at my watch, and put to myself the
question 'What might this watch be like in itself, independently
of how it appears to me?', why should I not raise the same
question about myself as I raise about the watch? I know myself
to be of average height and a fair complexion (these features being

determined largely by genetic factors), to be indecisive and pedantic (these features being, I suppose, determined largely by the nature of my upbringing). But I can at least raise the question 'What am I like, considered not in terms of my empirically observable properties, but as I am in myself?'

What point is there in asking this question when, as we have already seen, there is no prospect of an answer, since we can have no knowledge of things in themselves? Kant does not help himself to the supposition that, in my own case, I have some kind of privileged access to what I am like in myself: 'I have no *knowledge* of myself as I am but merely as I appear to myself.'[17] So why consider the question 'what I am like in myself?' Because, though we cannot answer it, we can say this much: unlike myself as I appear to myself (or to others), there is no necessity to regard myself as I am in myself as being subject to causal laws. There is a point of view that I can adopt towards myself which does not constrain me to see myself as being enmeshed in the toils of causality.

The compatibility of freedom and determinism is thus, in Kant's view, a matter of there being two standpoints from which a human being can consider himself or herself. Now the world-view of science encourages us to adopt the standpoint from which our thought and behaviour are seen as governed by causal laws; but what, other than the desperate desire to think of ourselves as free, could lead us to adopt the other standpoint? The short answer is 'morality'. A slightly less short version of the same answer would run as follows. When I say to myself 'You ought not to have done that', what I say to myself implies that I could have refrained from doing what I did, that I was free to act otherwise. In general, since 'ought' implies 'can', for me to regard a person (whether myself or anyone else) as a proper target for moral advice or appraisal is for me to regard that person as free.

Kant saw his own epistemological and metaphysical theories as an attempt to reconcile rationalism and empiricism; but his moral philosophy is unreservedly rationalist.

> Every one must admit that a law has to carry with it absolute necessity if it is to be valid morally – valid, that is, as a ground of obligation; that the command 'Thou shalt not lie' could not hold merely for men, other rational beings having no obligation to abide by it – and similarly with all other genuine moral laws; that here consequently the ground of obligation must be looked for, not in the nature of man nor in the circumstances of the world in which he is placed, but solely *a priori* in the concepts of pure reason; and that every

other precept based on principles of mere experience – and even a precept that may in a certain sense be considered universal, so far as it rests in its slightest part, perhaps only in its motive, on empirical grounds – can indeed be called a practical rule, but never a moral law.[18]

That morality addresses itself to all rational beings simply in virtue of their rationality, Kant takes for granted: he will have nothing to do with a view like Hume's, which holds that moral considerations only move me in so far as I am capable of being sympathetically affected by the pains and pleasures of others. The second basic tenet of Kant's moral philosophy has two halves: first – and here Kant agrees with Hume – the moral worth of an action depends on the motive from which it is performed; second – and here Kant and Hume are once more in marked disagreement – the only motive which can bestow moral worth on an action is a sense of duty, or respect for the moral law: to have moral worth an action must be performed, not just in accordance with duty, but from duty. When the two tenets are put together, according to Kant, we must conclude that the will of a person acting morally is influenced by 'nothing . . . but the conformity of actions to universal law as such, and this alone must serve the will as its principle'.[19] This conclusion constitutes an expression of Kant's famous doctrine that the moral law confronts us with a categorical imperative, and it also foreshadows the first formulation that Kant offers of the categorical imperative: 'Act only on that maxim through which you can at the same time will that it should become a universal law.'[20] It is not, I think, foreign to the spirit of what Kant means by this to suggest that he is proposing that, when considering the morality of an action, we should ask ourselves 'What if everyone did the same?' This question, though much asked of passengers and parasites, is not self-evidently a rational one to ask. For while it may be perverse to reply, with Yossarian, the hero of *Catch-22*, 'Then I'd certainly be a damned fool to act any other way', it is not manifestly absurd to reply 'But everyone won't do the same, so why suppose that they will?'. Classical utilitarians, who pride themselves on their realism, might well make this latter reply. And even if the question 'What if everyone did the same?' is considered an admissible one to ask, its interpretation remains problematic. Why, for example, when your daughter says 'I've been thinking about how best I can be of use to the community, and I've decided to become a surgeon', would it be absurd to say 'You should really think again; what if everyone became a surgeon?'? A moral philosopher who believes in the rationality of the question 'What if everyone did the same?'

has to offer an account of what it is to 'do the same'. Kant has such an account: he would say that two people do the same if they act on the same maxim, or the same principle. This appeal to the principle on which I act is what would enable Kant to deal with the problem posed by the case of the would-be surgeon. Asking 'What if everyone became a surgeon?' will produce the unwelcome response 'Chaos', but it is the wrong question to ask; rather, we should ask 'What if everyone decided what career to follow on the basis of considering how best they can serve the community?'. There is thus a stress, in Kant's moral theory, on the inward dimension of morality, a stress not just on what one does, but on why one does it. This aspect of Kant's theory, when taken together with his views on the inscrutability of freedom, yields the conclusion that we can never know whether someone has acted morally: indeed, Kant confesses that he finds it possible, in his darker moments, 'to become doubtful whether any genuine virtue is actually to be encountered in the world'.[21] In any case, the fact that we can never penetrate to the free heart of another person's action makes it impossible to base morality on examples: 'every example . . . presented to me must first be judged by moral principles in order to decide if it is fit to serve as an original example – that is, as a model',[22] even if the proposed example is 'the Holy One of the gospel'. The idea that the moral life might consist in an imitation of Christ is summarily dismissed: 'imitation has no place in morality'.[23] The same goes for the view that the moral life might consist in an attempt to live in accordance with commands laid down by God. Kant does not agonise, like Kierkegaard, over the obedience of Abraham. Because his doctrine of the categorical imperative precludes any 'teleological suspension of the ethical', Kant's verdict is uncompromising: he leave us in no doubt that Abraham behaved 'unconscientiously' in showing himself prepared 'to slaughter his own son like a sheep'.[24]

Kant's arguments against any attempt to base morality on religion are part of his rejection of any appeal to authority in settling moral questions. This is not to say that, in his view, the state has no right to tell me what to do; but every citizen, he thinks, has 'the lawful freedom to obey no law other than one to which he has given his consent'.[25] As it stands, this sounds too liberal to be workable, and indeed Kant does not mean it to be taken at face value: the consent he has in mind is rational consent. The assumption underlying the idea of rational consent is that, while you and I may want very different things from life, in so far as we think rationally about how life ought to be lived, we will be in full agreement. So Kant is able to portray every rational being as consenting to, indeed as making, the laws to which he or she is subject. In the political sphere, Kant declares, 'a citizen must always be regarded as a colegislative member of the state (that is, not merely as a means, but at the same time as an end in himself)'[26] In the larger moral sphere, Kant declares that man 'is subject only to *laws which are made by himself* and yet are *universal*', [27] and that this idea of 'the autonomy of the will' constitutes 'the supreme principle of morality'.[28] Thus Kant's moral theory is both individualist and universalist, the two strands being held together by his enormous faith in reason.

Kant's affirmation that every citizen is to be regarded 'not merely as a means, but at the same time as an end in himself' echoes what is usually numbered as the second formulation of the categorical imperative: 'Act in such a way that you always treat humanity, whether in your own person or in the person of any other, never simply as a means, but always at the same time as an end.'[29] This celebrated principle is the best expression of the humanist element in Kant's moral philosophy; though it should be pointed out that Kant's humanism also has its less acceptable face:

> But so far as animals are concerned, we have no direct duties. Animals are not self-conscious and are there merely as a means to an end. That end is man . . . Our duties towards animals are merely indirect duties toward humanity . . . for he who is cruel to animals becomes hard also in his dealings with men.[30]

Kant thinks that this principle of treating people as ends, not means, is equivalent to the universal law principle. But that earlier formulation of the categorical imperative seemed to appeal to a notion of fairness: acting immorally takes the form of disobeying a law by making an exception in one's own favour at the expense of those who obey. Kant's favourite example is of the false promise, the maker of which relies on others to maintain by their honesty, or at least by their conformity, the institution of promising, the existence of which is essential for the success of the lie. And here the question 'What if everyone did the same?' is at home, bringing out the unfairness of those who break to those who abide by the rules. But if we try to apply Kant's universal law test to rape, it would seem that what is wrong with the action is that the rapist is acting unfairly towards those who hold their sexual appetites in check, whereas it hardly needs saying that rape is worse than unfair, and that the rapist wrongs, not law-abiding men, but the woman who is his victim. If the rapist does not see what is wrong with what he has done, my asking him 'What if everyone did the same?' is not going to help. Kant's second formulation of the categorical imperative, with its prohibition on treating people merely as means, does conspicuously better at capturing what is wrong with rape. But it is not obvious what the positive part of that formulation amounts to, the injunction that people be treated as ends in themselves; and it is, indeed, significant that when Kant comes to apply the categorical imperative to concrete moral problems, he makes a much more plausible job of negative than of positive duties.

The negative element in Kant's moral theory is made more prominent by two unfortunate confusions which run through his work. First, holding that moral rules must be universal laws, not admitting of exceptions, Kant failed to distinguish between making an exception in my own favour, which does involve a denial of the universality of the law, and making a principled exception in cases of a certain kind, which preserves the universality of the law while restricting the range of cases to which it applies. Thus Kant is prepared to argue that, since 'I can by no means will a universal law of lying',[31] it is always wrong to tell a lie, even in order to save a life. Second, he failed to distinguish between an action motivated by desire or inclination and an action motivated by self-love or self-interest, and, seeing morality as directly opposed to self-interest, concluded that desire has no part to play in moral motivation. Behind this second confusion lies a pernicious philosophical doctrine, the hedonistic theory of desire, which says that my desires aim at my pleasure. If you hold such a theory, you will naturally think of all action that is motivated by desire as being prompted by considerations of self-love, but you can only hold the theory if you are prepared to see all our genuinely unselfish desires, for the welfare of our friends, or for an end to hostilities between two countries on the far side of the globe, distorted into desires for the pleasure which we expect to feel on hearing good news of our friends or on hearing of the announcement of a cease-fire. The gulf which Kant fixes between duty and desire leads him to deny all moral significance to our desires, to what we care about; or worse, to say, when talking about 'passionate participation in the good', that 'passion as such deserves censure', or to say of inclinations that 'it must . . . be the universal wish of every rational being to be wholly free from them'.[32] When Kant says that 'reason despises these impulsions and is able gradually to become their master',[33] he is strikingly at odds with Hume's famous claim in the *Treatise* (which Kant probably had not read) that 'reason is, and ought only to be the slave of the passions'.[34] But, strangely enough, the divergence

between Hume and Kant is as sharp as it is because of an
assumption that they share, namely, that only desire can give
direct rise to action. Hume concludes that, since reason cannot
give rise to desire, reason cannot prompt our actions. Kant, on
the other hand, concludes that, since reason can prompt our
actions, reason must be capable of giving rise to desire, and
therefore, given the hedonistic theory of desire, of *'infusing a
feeling of pleasure* or satisfaction in the fulfilment of duty'.[35] How
it does this is, in Kant's view, a mystery: 'It is, however, wholly
impossible to comprehend . . . how a mere thought containing
nothing sensible in itself can bring about a sensation of pleasure
or displeasure'.[36] Hume, of course, might have said exactly the
same, and concluded that the thing is impossible; but Kant's view
is that the thing must be possible, for if I am to think of myself as
bound by a moral law which bids me disregard my inclinations, I
must think of myself as not determined by them, as capable of
being determined by reason alone. Here we stand at 'the extreme
limit of moral enquiry'.[37] the point where explanation must come
to an end, since any successful explanation of a free act would
undermine its claim to be free. So Kant ends the *Groundwork of
the Metaphysic of Morals* with these words:

> And thus, while we do not comprehend the practical uncon-
> ditioned necessity of the moral imperative, we do comprehend
> its *incomprehensibility*. This is all that can fairly be asked of a
> philosophy which presses forward in its principles to the very
> limit of human reason.[38]

The two-standpoints argument is intended by Kant to provide a
way of reconciling determinism and freedom. But he repeatedly
slips into assertions which imply that, if we are free, then
determinism is false. Here is Kant's official line on determinism:
'if we could exhaustively investigate all the appearances of men's
wills, there would not be found a single human action which we
could not predict with certainty, and recognise as proceeding
necessarily from its antecedent conditions.'[39] But within a few
pages he has slipped: 'Our blame is based on a law of reason
whereby we regard reason as a cause that irrespective of all the
above-mentioned empirical conditions could have determined,
and ought to have determined, the agent to act otherwise.'[40] So
when Kant says, in 'An Old Question Raised Again', that 'we are
dealing with beings that act freely . . . of whom it may not be
predicted what they will do', however plausible his remark may
be, its invocation of freedom at the expense of determinism is not
his official position: indeed, one implication of the official position
is that, if the two were incompatible, it is determinism that would

have to be maintained at the expense of freedom, since we know the truth of determinism, whereas freedom is the object of faith not of knowledge. Speaking not only of freedom, but also of God and immortality, Kant says, in the preface to the second edition of the *Critique of Pure Reason*, 'I have . . . found it necessary to deny *knowledge*, in order to make room for *faith*.'[41] Once again Hume might have said the same – for example, when discussing miracles; but Kant says it quite without any of Hume's irony. Faith, in Kant's view, is not what is left for those who will not listen to reason: it is a step that reason itself requires us to take, because reason requires us to pursue morality, and morality can only be pursued by someone who holds, as an article of faith, that he or she is free.

It is far from obvious that the pursuit of morality similarly requires faith in God or in immortality. As far as God is concerned, the thrust of Kant's Critical philosophy, as I have outlined it so far, is wholly negative. First, as regards knowledge, we can know nothing of things that lie beyond the bounds of possible experience. Indeed, Kant sets out systematically to demolish all possible speculative proofs of the existence of God. For example, he argues that the attempt to prove that the world has a first cause is a misuse of 'the principle of causality, which is only valid within the field of experience, and outside this field has no application, nay, is indeed meaningless'.[42] Second, as regards morality, the moral law cannot be based on God's commands, since any alleged divine command has to be submitted to the test of independent moral judgement before it can be taken to require our obedience. God, it seems, is redundant both for our understanding of the world and for our working out of what we ought to do. But at this point, with the credentials of religion at a low ebb, the tide begins to turn. The argument that Kant uses to show that morality requires faith in God is perhaps less important than the fact that he advances such an argument at all. For the argument does not grow naturally out of Kant's moral theory, and it carries little conviction, yet he seizes upon it as the key to a 'religion within the limits of reason alone', a religion that would commend itself to people to whom the ideas of authority and of the supernatural were both suspect.

The argument goes like this. Morality enjoins the pursuit of the highest good. Moral virtue is, of course, an ingredient in the highest good, but only one ingredient, for a world of thoroughly virtuous but thoroughly miserable beings would still be some way from being an ideal world. Happiness, therefore, is the other ingredient, and the two, virtue and happiness, must be in proportion, for it is still not an ideal world in which some beings are either happier or less happy than they deserve. Now if morality enjoins us to pursue the highest good, this highest good, of virtue and happiness in proportion, must be attainable. However, there is no natural congruence between the two, so if we are to believe that they will be brought into proportion, we must believe that there is something capable of achieving this result. Whatever this something is, it will need to be possessed of great insight, in order to penetrate into people's motives and to establish what they deserve; and it will have to be possessed of great power, in order to secure the virtuous against misery and the wicked against happiness, to ensure that people receive what they deserve. Kant now cuts the final corner, in a way that he himself criticised when discussing the traditional theistic arguments, and says that the something must be omniscient and omnipotent, 'the cause (and consequently the author) of nature through understanding and will, i.e., God'.[43]

Kant set great store by this argument, and advanced it in several works, calling it, in the *Critique of Judgment*, a 'moral proof of the existence of God'.[44] But the name is misleading, for the conclusion of Kant's argument is, not 'God exists', but 'We must believe that God exists', or, in Kant's words, 'Therefore, it is morally necessary to assume the existence of God'.[45] This last wording too could be misleading, for it could be taken to mean that we have a duty to believe in God, whereas what Kant means is that it would be irrational for us not to believe in God while acknowledging our duty to pursue the highest good. The amoralist may say to Kant 'You have given *me* no reason to believe in God'; but Kant would reply that the amoralist is already in an irrational position in failing to recognise the moral demands of pure practical reason. The atheist may say to Kant 'Your argument implies that, if there is no God, morality is an illusion, so how can you persuade *me* that I ought to recognise the moral demands of pure practical reason?'; but Kant would reply that the atheist professes to know something that cannot be known, that there is no God. The doctrine of the categorical imperative, then, bars the attempt to escape from theism by denying any moral convictions; and the doctrine of the limits of knowledge bars the attempt to escape from morality by denying any theistic convictions.

Nevertheless, the argument fails to convince. First, it is suspicious that the idea of the highest good makes its appearance in Kant's moral philosophy only when he wants to establish the necessity of belief in God. Second, and more seriously, in claiming that if the highest good ought to be pursued, it must be achievable, Kant is relying on his belief that 'ought' implies 'can' (a belief that he never expresses quite so succinctly); but 'the highest good ought to be pursued' implies only 'the highest good can be pursued', not 'the highest good can be achieved'. Third, and most seriously, the only way in which I can pursue the highest good is by seeking to tread the path of virtue; and while this may involve my punishing some evil deeds or rewarding some good ones, in my capacity, say, as parent or magistrate, it involves no systematic attempt on my part to bring happiness into proportion with virtue; so all that my duty to pursue the highest good can amount to is the pursuit of virtue, and it is possible for me to pursue virtue whether or not I believe that virtue will ever be suitably rewarded. Kant flirts with the suggestion that the pursuit of morality could not be *sustained* unless one believed in a final justice, but this suggestion is so at odds with everything that Kant says elsewhere about moral motivation that it need not be taken seriously. It is, in any case, manifestly false.

Kant's argument is, in my view and that of the many commentators who either treat it as a historical curiosity or else ignore it altogether, a failure. Nevertheless, it is the foundation stone of his attempt to build an account of a rational religion. The rationality involved is that of pure practical, or moral, reason, not that of theoretical reason, which can tell us nothing about things beyond the bounds of experience; and the significance of religion is moral significance. Kant defines religion thus: 'Religion is (subjectively regarded) the recognition of all duties as divine commands.'[46] But what does it add to my seeing a task as my duty that I also recognise the carrying out of the task to be commanded by God? Will it make me conscious of a more strict obligation to perform the task? How can it, when, given that the task is my duty, I am already under a categorical imperative to carry it out? Is it that recognising my duty as a divine command provides me with extra motivation for performing the task – the fear of punishment, or the desire to please God? To the extent that my action is motivated by fear of the consequences, says Kant, it is prompted by self-interest and lacks moral worth; and the only actions that I have any reason to believe will be pleasing to God are those that are performed from duty, not those prompted by the desire to please him. This does not mean that Kant can find no place in his religion for either the fear of God or the love of God:

> *Godliness* comprises two determinations of the moral disposi-
> tion in relation to God: *fear* of God is this disposition in
> obedience to His commands from *bounden* duty (the duty of a
> subject), *i.e.*, from respect for the law; *love* of God, on the

other hand, is the disposition to obedience from one's own *free choice* and from approval of the law (the duty of a son).[47]

In the process of defining the fear and love of God, however, Kant appears to have allowed God to drop out of the picture, to be replaced by the moral law as the object of our respect and of our free obedience. We might begin to wonder, as we read Kant's account of godliness, how the religious life differs from the moral life. It might be thought that, if we follow Kant's argument and are led from reflection on the nature of morality to a belief in God, we will find that new duties emerge, duties to God or duties to do with specifically religious observances. But Kant denies that we can have duties to God: 'the duty of religion, namely that "of recognizing all our duties as . . . divine commands". . . is not the consciousness of a duty to God'; rather, 'to have religion can be asserted to be a duty of man to himself'. As for religious observances, here is what Kant has to say about the central ritual of the Christian faith:

> The oft-repeated ceremony (*communion*) of a *renewal, contin-uation, and propagation of this churchly community* under the laws of *equality*, a ceremony which indeed can be performed, after the example of the Founder of such a church (and, at the same time, in memory of him), through the formality of a common partaking at the same table, contains within itself something great, expanding the narrow, selfish, and un-sociable cast of mind among men, especially in matters of religion, towards the idea of a cosmopolitan *moral community*; and it is a good means of enlivening a community to the moral disposition of brotherly love which it represents. But to assert that God has attached special favors to the celebration of this solemnity, and to incorporate among the articles of faith the proposition that this ceremony, which is after all but a churchly act, is, in addition, a *means of grace* – this is a religious illusion which can do naught but work counter to the spirit of religion.[48]

Such significance as Kant will allow to this ceremony is moral significance; and, from what he has to say about that significance, he might as well be talking about a Rotary Club lunch.

I have been arguing that Kant reduces religion to morality, that there is nothing to his rational religion over and above morality. Kant would deny this: he would perhaps respond to my claim that, in his account of godliness, God drops out of the picture, by pointing out that in the very next sentence after his account of godliness, he had gone on to say that both the fear and the love of God

involve, . . . over and above morality, the concept of a
supersensible Being provided with the attributes which are
requisite to the carrying out of that highest good which is
aimed at by morality but which transcends our powers.[49]

Well, I have been unfair to Kant, but only marginally: there is
more, in his view, to religion than morality, but that more
consists, on examination, of nothing but belief in the existence of
'a supersensible Being', in the immortality of the soul, and in a
final justice. It may be thought that this concession of mine is still
unfair: surely Kant talks about more than these bare beliefs –
about worship, for example? Yes, he does; but what worship of
God consists in, for Kant, is 'endeavour towards a good course of
life': anyone who regards *rituals* of worship

> as being necessary to religion, and regards this obedience not
> merely as a means to the moral disposition but as the
> objective condition of becoming immediately well-pleasing
> to God . . . transforms the service of God into a mere
> *fetishism* and practises a pseudo-service which is subversive
> to all endeavours toward true religion.[50]

Moral action, itself, Kant says, is of intrinsic value; rituals, on the
other hand, have only conditional value, that is, they have value
only in so far as they serve a moral purpose, is so far as we have
purely moral reasons for engaging in them, independently of any
religious connotations they may have. 'True *enlightenment* lies in
this very distinction; therein the service of God becomes first and
foremost a free and hence a moral service.'[51]

I have been suggesting that God has only a walk-on part in
Kant's account of religion. Now Kant's rational religion owes a
considerable debt to Christianity; indeed, he thinks that 'of all the
public religions which have ever existed, the Christian alone is
moral'.[52] But the Christianity which Kant respects is not the
gospel of God's intervention in human history to save sinful men
and women through Christ's atoning death:

> it must be inculcated painstakingly and repeatedly that true
> religion is to consist not in the knowing or considering of
> what God does or has done for our salvation but in what we
> must do to become worthy of it. This last can never be
> anything but what possesses in itself undoubted and *uncon-
> ditional* worth, what therefore can alone make us well-
> pleasing to God, and of whose necessity every man can
> become wholly certain without any Scriptural learning what-
> soever.[53]

Kant goes further: just as Galileo had argued that the scientist can
tell the theologian that certain passages in scripture have to be

interpreted metaphorically, Kant claims that the sacred narrative 'must at all times be taught and expounded in the interest of morality'.[54] In the spirit of this remark, he offers a purely moral interpretation of the Christian doctrine of the atonement, an interpretation in which the central figure is, not the historical Jesus, but 'the personified idea of the good principle'.[55] It is an intriguing question why Kant thought it worth labouring so hard to create a place in his religion within the limits of reason alone for that most un-Kantian of doctrines, that one becomes a new man when the Son of God 'bears as *vicarious substitute* the guilt of sin for him',[56] to make of it a truth that can be known 'without any Scriptural learning whatever', simply by the exercise of pure practical reason.

Kant, I have said, almost entirely reduces religion to morality. But some readers of Kant might feel that a more accurate way of making the point would be to say that he elevates morality to a religion, and might cite passages like the following:

> Duty! Thou sublime and mighty name that dost embrace nothing charming or insinuating but requirest submission and yet seekest not to move the will by threatening aught that would arouse natural aversion or terror, but only holdest forth a law which of itself finds entrance into the mind and yet gains reluctant reverence . . . what origin is worthy of thee . . .?
>
> It cannot be less than something which elevates man above himself as a part of the world of sense, something which connects him with an order of things which only the understanding can think . . . It is nothing else than personality, . . so that the person as belonging to the world of sense is subject to his own personality so far as he belongs to the intelligible world. For it is then not to be wondered at that man, as belonging to two worlds, must regard his own being in relation to his second and higher vocation with reverence and the laws of this vocation with the deepest respect.[57]

In Psalm 19, the psalmist celebrates first God's heavens ('The heavens declare the glory of God . . .') and then God's law ('The law of the Lord is perfect . . .'). The underlying suggestion is surely that contemplation of the heavens and of the law leads to a deeper appreciation of the majesty and justice of God. At the end of the *Critique of Practical Reason* Kant echoes Psalm 19, but to very different effect:

> Two things fill the mind with ever new and increasing admiration and awe, the oftener and more steadily we reflect on them: the starry heavens above me and the moral law

within me. . . . The former view of a countless multitude of worlds annihilates, as it were, my importance as an animal creature, which must give back to the planet (a mere speck in the universe) the matter from which it came, the matter which is for a little time provided with vital force, we know not how. The latter, on the contrary, infinitely raises my worth as that of an intelligence by my personality, in which the moral law reveals a life independent of all animality and even of the whole world of sense – at least so far as it may be inferred from the purposive destination assigned to my existence by this law, a destination which is not restricted to the conditions and limits of this life but reaches into the infinite.[58]

The object of Kant's secular worship is what he calls 'personality'. As we ordinarily use that word, it refers to what makes each human being unique; but Kant uses it, as we might use the word 'personhood', to refer to what we have in common, our rational nature. Kant places a high value on each individual human being, but not on human individuality.

Kant's stress on autonomy is what most clearly marks him out as an Enlightenment thinker. It is in defence of the autonomy of the individual that he argues for both religious and political freedom. During the reign of Frederick the Great, as we have seen, he thought that the hallmark of enlightenment was religious freedom, the denial of which 'prevents men from being, or easily becoming, capable of correctly using their own reason in religious matters with assurance and free from outside direction'. Later, when an enlightened monarch was succeeded by one less enlightened, and there resulted a withdrawal of religious freedom, Kant perhaps began to think that political freedom was the more fundamental requirement. Now political advances promise less than religious advances: religion, at least as understood by Kant, promises to make human beings morally better, whereas political progress, as Kant pointed out in 'An Old Question Raised Again', promises 'not an ever-growing quantity of morality . . . but an increase of the products of legality in dutiful actions whatever their motives'. That is to say, political progress guarantees not that more actions will be performed from duty, but only that more actions will be performed in accordance with duty. This latter gain is not to be despised, however, for more widespread obedience to laws will bring an increase in civil peace; and, what is more, Kant thinks that if every nation had a republican constitution, wars between nations would be much less likely, and there would be a prospect of perpetual international peace:

If it is a duty to make real (even if only through approximation in endless progress) the state of public law, and if there is well-grounded hope that this can actually be done, then perpetual peace . . . is not an empty idea.[59]

That kings should philosophize or philosophers become kings is not to be expected. Nor is it to be wished, since the possession of power inevitably corrupts. But kings or king-like peoples which rule themselves under laws of equality should not suffer the class of philosophers to disappear or to be silent, but should let them speak openly. This is indispensable to the enlightenment of the business of government, and since the class of philosophers is by nature incapable of plotting and lobbying, it is above suspicion of being made up of propagandists.[60]

In not many universities, I suspect, would one find that a majority of academics thought the claims of this last sentence to be borne out by their own experience. Why is Kant so starry-eyed about the integrity of philosophers? I would suggest that the answer is not that he thinks philosophers to be people of an extraordinary moral and psychological constitution: rather, what he thinks marks them out is their extraordinary vocation, which is to follow the guidance of 'the untrammelled judgment of reason'. If I am right, Kant is not so much expressing his faith in philosophers as affirming his confidence in the integrity of reason itself. I spoke earlier of Kant's 'enormous faith in reason', meaning then his faith in its ability to provide a single and unequivocal guiding light to every rational being in his or her attempts to answer the practical question 'What ought I to do?'. Kant would protest, of course, that his faith in reason was the very opposite of uncritical: had he not devoted much time and energy to the writing of critical examinations (critiques) of reason in both its theoretical and its practical employment? Philosophers, as custodians of that flame which is the source of 'the light of reason', are, of course, expected to defend the rational approach to resolving problems; but Kant would surely add that they are also entitled to defend it, for, having studied the claims of reason, they know its light to be trustworthy, indeed to be the only light which can yield true enlightenment.

NOTES

*References to Kant's works are given in the following form: first, an abbreviated title of the work (a key to abbreviations will be found in the bibliography); then a (volume and) page reference to the standard German edition; and finally a page reference to the English translation I have used (these too are listed in the bibliography), this last reference being preceded by the translator's or editor's name. For all Kant's works except the *Critique of Pure Reason*, the standard German edition is in the multi-volume edition of Kant's collected works (the so-called 'Academy edition') originally published by the Royal Prussian Academy of Sciences from 1902 onwards, and now published by Walter de Gruyter (Berlin). References to the German text of the *Critique of Pure Reason* are standardly made to (A) the first edition and (B) the second edition of the work, published in Riga by Hartknoch in 1781 and 1787 respectively.

Thus '*CrPrR* 5 97; Beck 100' refers to a passage from the *Critique of Practical Reason*, Academy edition, volume 5, p.97; a passage to be found on p.100 of Beck's translation. '*CrPuR* A 176=B 218; Kemp Smith 208' refers to a passage from the *Critique of Pure Reason*, first edition, p.176, or second edition, p.218; a passage to be found on p.208 of Kemp Smith's translation.

1 *AOQ* 7 89; Beck 148.
2 *PC* 11 530; Zweig 220.
3 *WiE* 8 40; Beck 8–9.
4 *WiE* 8 41; Beck 10.
5 *AOQ* 7 83; Beck 141.
6 *AOQ* 7 85; Beck 144.
7 *AOQ* 7 86; Beck 145.
8 *AOQ* 7 85; Beck 144.
9 *AOQ* 7 85–86; Beck 144.
10 *AOQ* 7 92; Beck 152.
11 *AOQ* 7 91; Beck 151.
12 *GMM* 4 412; Paton 76.
13 *CrPrR* 5 96; Beck 99.
14 *CrPrR* 5 97; Beck 100–101.
15 *CrPuR* A 42=B 59;
   Kemp Smith 82.
16 *CrPuR* B 72; Kemp Smith
   90.
17 *CrPuR* B 158; Kemp Smith
   169.
18 *GMM* 4 389; Paton 55.
19 *GMM* 4 402; Paton 67.
20 *GMM* 4 421; Paton 84.
21 *GMM* 4 407; Paton 72.

22 *GMM* 4 408; Paton 73.
23 *GMM* 4 408; Paton 73.
24 *Rel* 6 187; Greene &
   Hudson 175.
25 *MoM* 6 314; Ladd 78.
26 *MoM* 6 345; Ladd 118.
27 *GMM* 4 432; Paton 94.
28 *GMM* 4 440; Paton 101.
29 *GMM* 4 429; Paton 91.
30 *LoE* 27.1 458–459; Infield
   239–240.
31 *GMM* 4 403; Paton 68.
32 *GMM* 4 428; Paton 90.
33 *GMM* 4 411; Paton 75.
34 Hume: *Treatise* II.iii.3
   (Selby-Bigge edn, p.415).
35 *GMM* 4 460; Paton 120.
36 *GMM* 4 460; Paton 120.
37 *GMM* 4 462; Paton 122.
38 *GMM* 4 463; Paton 123.
39 *CrPuR* A 550=B 578;
   Kemp Smith 474.
40 *CrPuR* A 555=B 583;
   Kemp Smith 477.

41 *CrPuR* B xxx; Kemp Smith 29.

42 *CrPuR* A 636=B 664; Kemp Smith 528.

43 *CrPrR* 5 125; Beck 130.

44 *CJ* 5 447; Meredith II.114.

45 *CrPrR* 5 125; Beck 130.

46 *Rel* 6 153; Greene & Hudson 142.

47 *Rel* 6 182; Greene & Hudson 170.

48 *Rel* 6 199–200; Greene & Hudson 187–188.

49 *Rel* 6 182; Greene & Hudson 170.

50 *Rel* 6 178–179; Greene & Hudson 166–167.

51 *Rel* 6 179; Greene & Hudson 167.

52 *Rel* 6 51–52; Greene & Hudson 47.

53 *Rel* 6 133; Greene & Hudson 123.

54 *Rel* 6 132; Greene & Hudson 123.

55 *Rel* 6 60; Greene & Hudson 54.

56 *Rel* 6 74; Greene & Hudson 69.

57 *CrPrR* 5 86–87; Beck 89–90.

58 *CrPrR* 5 161–162; Beck 166.

59 *PP* 8 386; Beck 135.

60 *PP* 8 369; Beck 116.

BIBLIOGRAPHY

AOQ   'An Old Question Raised Again: Is the Human Race Constantly Progressing?', trans. Robert E. Anchor, in Kant: *On History*, ed. Lewis White Beck. Indianapolis: Bobbs-Merrill, 1963.

CJ   *Critique of Judgment*, trans. James Creed Meredith. Oxford: Clarendon Press, 1962.

CrPrR   *Critique of Practical Reason*, trans. Lewis White Beck. Indianapolis: Bobbs-Merrill, 1956.

CrPuR   *Critique of Pure Reason*, trans. Norman Kemp Smith. London: Macmillan, 1929.

GMM   *Groundwork of the Metaphysic of Morals*, trans. H.J. Paton, in Paton: *The Moral Law*. London: Hutchinson, 1948, rev. 1953.

LoE   *Lectures on Ethics*, trans. Louis Infield. New York: Harper & Row, 1963.

MoM   *Metaphysic of Morals*, Part I, trans. John Ladd as *The Metaphysical Elements of Justice*. Indianapolis: Bobbs-Merrill, 1965.

PC   *Philosophical Correspondence 1759–99*, trans. Arnulf Zweig. Chicago: University of Chicago Press, 1967.

PP   *Perpetual Peace*, trans. Lewis White Beck, in *On History* (see *AOQ*).

Rel   *Religion within the Limits of Reason Alone*, trans.

Theodore M. Greene & Hoyt H. Hudson. New York: Harper & Row, 1960.

WiE   'What is Enlightenment?', trans. Lewis White Beck, in *On History* (see *AOQ*).

7

CHRISTOPHER J. BERRY

Adam Smith: Commerce, Liberty and Modernity

Adam Smith in his lectures at the University of Glasgow is reported to have professed that 'opulence and freedom' were 'the two greatest blessings men can possess' (*LJ*, 185).* Smith here couples together what many have held asunder as contraries. One such thinker, with whose thought Smith was well acquainted, was Rousseau. He reviewed Rousseau's *Discourse on Inequality* for the second edition of the short-lived *Edinburgh Review* of 1755/6 and, as was characteristic of eighteenth-century reviews, Smith's account contained lengthy quotations. The first passage that Smith thought worthy of reproduction begins:

> while men contented themselves with their first rustic habitations; while their industry had no object, except to pin together the skins of wild beasts for their original cloathing, to adorn themselves with feathers and shells [etc.] . . . while they applied themselves to such works as a single person could execute, and to such arts as required not the concurrence of several hands; they lived free, healthful, humane and happy, as far as their nature would permit them, and continued to enjoy amongst themselves the sweets of an independent society . . .

and the second passage contains the judgement that

> man, from being free and independent, became by a multitude of new necessities subjected in a manner, to all nature, and above all to his fellow creatures, whose slave he is in one sense even while he becomes their master; rich he has occasion for their services; poor he stands in need of their assistance; and even mediocrity does not enable him to live without them. He is obliged therefore to endeavour to interest them in his situation, and to make them find either in reality or in appearance, their advantage in labouring for his. (*EPS*, 251–2)

Smith is aware that, despite the presence here of what he terms 'rhetoric', Rousseau represents a persistent and important strand in European political thinking. This strand, frequently referred to as civic humanism, linked the ideas of freedom and independence, and identified threats to the latter as inimical to the former. The essence of civic humanism as outlined by John Pocock[1] – the writer who has done most to bring out the presence of this tradition in European thought – lay in the link between virtue and the practice of citizenship as understood by the Greeks and Romans. This link entailed a civic equality and a moral disposition to maintain the public good, so that the (male) human personality was only fulfilled in the practice of active virtue in the *respublica*. Civic equality stemmed from proprietorship of a household, which gave independence; its function was not to promote the accrual of private profit or luxury but to permit the taking on of public tasks such as defence (warfare). This story was re-articulated by Machiavelli and other Florentines and was transported into seventeenth century English republican thought by James Harrington and his associates. By the eighteenth century, the threat to virtue was seen to lie in the growth of credit and commerce, whose fluidity and intangibility were judged to provide an insufficiently stable basis from which the citizen could engage in political action. The riposte to the challenge of commerce was, therefore, to reinvoke the image of the agrarian (thus solidly based) independent republican. It was claimed that without the presence of this foundation for virtuous activity, society, shorn of the bearings needed to direct it to the public good, would be cast adrift on the sea of contingency that an economy based on commerce and credit represents.

Against this backcloth, Smith's coupling of freedom and opulence can be seen as a vindication of modernity, and in that guise his thought is at the forefront of the Enlightenment.[2] The key to the modern world is that it is a world of commerce. It is a world where everyman 'becomes in some measure a merchant' (*WN*, 37). We have in that statement and its implications the key to Smith's vindication. The pursuit of these implications can, therefore, provide a framework for a general overview of Smith's thought. More precisely, our pursuit will proceed by answering the question, 'what are the consequences of living in a society where everyman is a merchant?'

The first and most obvious consequence is that where everyman lives by exchange, there is a network of interdependence. In a 'civilized and thriving country' (a description that is a significant synonym for a commercial society) the 'very meanest person' could not be provided with even his woollen coat without the 'joint labour of a great multitude of workmen' (*WN*, 22–3). To appreciate the full significance of this interdependence it is necessary to appreciate the alternatives. Smith himself does this via an historical analysis, and here Rousseau's work is important.

Smith agrees with Rousseau that the dependence of one individual on another is corrupting (*LJ*, 333). He agrees further that, in the earliest forms of society, there was little if any dependence and that dependency was a subsequent social development. Although there are classical precedents, and Turgot contemporaneously enunciated a similar doctrine in France, Smith's account of this development – the so-called 'four-stages' theory[3] – was seminal and was echoed by many other members of the Scottish Enlightenment, notably John Millar (Professor of Law at Glasgow) in his *Origin of Ranks* (3rd Edition 1779) and the lawyer Lord Kames in his *Historical Law Tracts* (1758). According to this theory, the 'lowest and rudest state of society' is the age of hunters (*WN*, 689), marked by its poverty, which in turn means 'there is scarce any property' and little or no inequality, subordination or dependency (*WN*, 709). In time, pressure of population makes the chase too precarious so that 'naturally' wild animals are tamed, thus initiating the second age (*LJ*, 14). In this age of shepherds there is great inequality, vast disparity in property, and great subordination and dependency:

> Tartar chief, the increase of whose herds and flocks is sufficient to maintain a thousand men, cannot well employ that increase in any other way than in maintaining a thousand men . . . whom he thus maintains, depending entirely upon him for subsistence, must both obey his orders in war, and submit to his jurisdiction in peace. He is necessarily both their general and their judge, and his chieftainship is the necessary effect of the superiority of his fortune. (*WN*, 712)

Once more, population pressure leads 'naturally' to the cultivation of land and the establishment of the third age – the age of husbandmen or farmers. Here there is fixed settlement and a similar pattern of inequality and dependency. Just as the Tartar chief was such by virtue of his being the greatest shepherd, so the leaders in the third age are the greatest landlords (*WN*, 717). The fourth or commercial age sees a decisive change, which stems not from population pressure but directly from the natural human propensity to truck, barter and exchange. Rousseau sees in the commercial age only a deepening corruption but Smith, immediately after having proclaimed the link between dependence and corruption, remarks that 'commerce is one great preventive' of its occurrence (*LJ*, 333). Smith sees in the commercial age not only the re-emergence of independence but also its re-emergence in a form superior to that experienced by a nation of hunters. The explanation of this superiority lies precisely in the social condition that Rousseau abhors, namely, opulence. This is because the conditions that make opulence possible also, in a mutually complementary fashion, make possible a superior form of freedom – that of liberty under law, the hallmark of civilisation.

How, according to Smith, does this conjunction of opulence and civilisation occur? In line with his basic schema, Smith provides an historical account; an account which, Smith explicitly observes, is also to be found in Hume's *Essays* (especially 'Of the rise and progress of the Arts and Sciences', 1742; 'Of Commerce', 1752; 'Of Refinement in Arts', 1752) and is again echoed in other Scots. The focus of this account is the collapse of the age of farmers, in the guise of feudal lords.

A great proprietor perforce uses his surplus in the same way as the Tartar chief, namely, to maintain a multitude of retainers and dependants whose only means of reciprocation is obedience (*WN*, 413). These proprietors

> necessarily became the judges in peace, and the leaders in war, of all who dwelt upon their estates. They could maintain order and execute law within their respective demesnes, because each of them could there turn the whole force of all the inhabitants against the injustice of any one. No other person had sufficient authority to do this. (*WN*, 415)

Since the king was no more than another proprietor, the administration of justice lay in the hands of those with the means to do it. At this point, Smith observes that it is a mistake to see the origin of these 'territorial jurisdictions' in feudal law. The law is a subsequent development and, if anything, is an attempt to moderate rather than to extend the authority of the 'allodial lords'. Instead, Smith declares that this authority 'flowed from the state of property and manners' (*WN*, 417). What makes this statement important is the implicit understanding of social causation that it embodies. The cause of feudal power lies not in the deliberative and purposive decrees of law, but in 'property and manners'. The former are subordinate to the latter. Smith sees in this order of priority the regularity that characterises scientific explanation, since it is duplicated in the histories of the French and English monarchies and is instanced by the case 'not thirty years ago' of Mr Cameron of Lochiel 'a gentleman of Lochaber in Scotland' (*WN*, 416). This priority, therefore, is not a singular event causing wonder and surprise (cf. *EPS*, 37ff.) but is a scientifically expected state of affairs for, as Smith says here, 'such effects must always flow from such causes' (*WN*, 416).

The explanation for the collapse of feudal power – both secular and ecclesiastical (*WN*, 803) – must have an appropriate social cause. Smith identifies it as 'the silent and insensible operation of foreign commerce'. In a celebrated passage, Smith outlines the effect of this commerce

> For a pair of diamond buckles perhaps, or for something as frivolous and useless, they [the great proprietors] exchanged the maintenance, or what is the same thing, the price of the maintenance of a thousand men for a year, and with it the whole weight and authority which it could give them. The buckles, however, were to be all their own and no other human creature was to have any share of them; whereas in the more antient method of expence they must have shared with at least a thousand people . . . and thus for the gratification of the most childish, the meanest and the most sordid of all vanities, they gradually bartered their whole power and authority. (*WN*, 418–9)

As befits an instance in a scientific causal account, Smith elsewhere observes that the sway of the Tartar chief stems from his using his surplus to maintain a thousand men *because* 'the rude state of his society does not afford him any manufactured produce, any trinkets and baubles of any kind for which he can exchange that part of his rude produce which is over and above his own consumption' (*WN*, 712). However, the presence of these 'baubles' in the feudal era results ultimately in the members of a commercial society being free of the thrall of personal dependency:

> In the present state of Europe a man of ten thousand a year can spend his whole revenue, and he generally does so, without directly maintaining twenty people, or being able to command more than ten footmen not worth the commanding. Indirectly, perhaps, he maintains as great or even a greater number of people than he could have done by the antient method of expence . . . He generally contributes, however, but a very small proportion to that of each, to very few perhaps a tenth, to many not a hundredth, and to some not a thousandth, nor even a ten thousandth part of their whole annual maintenance. Though he contributes, therefore, to the maintenance of them all, they are all more or less independent of him, because generally they can all be maintained without him. (*WN*, 419–20)

Once the tenants had attained their independence, the proprietors 'were no longer capable of interrupting the regular execution of justice'. This process of social change, which Smith calls 'a revolution of the greatest importance to the publick happiness', cannot be put down to any deliberative individualistic explanation.

Neither proprietors nor merchants had 'the least intention to serve the publick' and neither had 'knowledge or foresight of that great revolution' (*WN*, 422). The public happiness, the general good, was not brought about by human will. For Smith this is a general truth about social life, and it serves, as we shall note again, to expose the moralism of the civic humanists as unscientific.

As a consequence of this series of events, individuals in a commercial society enjoy a liberty from dependence on particular masters. They enjoy independence but, and this is what distinguishes commercial society, this independence is achieved through an interlocking social system (the market) so that these individuals (merchants) are truly interdependent. We now need to pursue how it is for Smith that opulence and freedom are consequences of this interdependence where everyman is a merchant.

To take opulence first: the natural propensity to 'truck, barter and exchange one thing for another' produces slowly and gradually the division of labour (*WN*, 25). The bigger the market for goods, the greater the specialisation, and the greater the specialisation, the more the productivity. Hence in the famous example of pin manufacture, through the division of labour ten individuals could make 48000 pins a day – equivalent to 4800 each – whereas each working on their own could not have produced twenty a day. What this means in a developed market society is the presence of that 'universal opulence which extends itself to the lowest ranks of the people' (*WN*, 22). By contrast, those who best embody Rousseauan independence are 'miserably poor' and frequently resort to the policy of 'directly destroying, and sometimes of abandoning their infants, their old people, and those afflicted with lingering diseases, to perish with hunger, be devoured by wild beasts'(*WN*, 10). Indeed, Smith pitches the advantages of commercial society even higher. The presence of this universal opulence means that the accommodation of even the lowest 'exceeds that of many an African king, the absolute master of the lives and liberties of 10000 naked savages' (*WN*, 24).[4] It is true that the abodes of the lowest rank in commercial society are far inferior to those of the rich but, though there is this inequality, there is also the second great human blessing of liberty.

This brings us to the next consequence of Smith's position: the character of the liberty enjoyed in commercial society. There are two related dimensions to this liberty. If those in the lowest rank partake in the universal opulence, it means that they are supplied 'abundantly' with what they have 'occasion for' (*WN*, 22). This abundance gives them choice and discretion. Since individuals are not tied into relationships of dependence they enjoy, for example, changing trades as often as they please (*WN*, 23). In this regard, Smith comments on the 'violent' 'police' of Indostan and ancient Egypt in forcing a son to follow his father's occupation (*WN*, 80). The freedom to change occupation, like the freedom to dispose of one's property by testament, is a private liberty not enjoyed in other ages. Indeed the presence of these liberties makes individuals free 'in our present sense of the word Freedom' (*WN*, 400). The maintenance of this freedom itself depends on the liberty that each man has to better his condition, because that liberty is the source of opulence (*WN*, 343). More pointedly, this will be effective only as long as individuals are left free from political directives; it is the 'highest impertinence and presumption' of kings and ministers 'to watch over the economy of private people' (*WN*, 346). Smith remarks that the 'private interests and passions of individuals naturally dispose them to turn their stock toward the employments which in ordinary cases are most advantageous to society'; crucially, this advantage will accrue 'without any intervention of law' (*WN*, 630). What Smith has done, therefore, is to yoke together the two great blessings of opulence and freedom with the private, self-interested life of economics. In so doing, he has also implicitly devalued the public or political life, with its goals of honour and glory, as the unique and privileged arena of human *eudaimonia*.[5] Smith, however, by no means neglects politics, because the second dimension of the liberty enjoyed in commercial society is concerned precisely with that.

While the African chief is the 'absolute' master of his dependents, this superiority is not enjoyed by the rich in an interdependent commercial society. The reason for this is that commerce, as evidenced by Europe, has brought in its wake justice and the rule of law. Their presence is the hallmark of a 'well governed society', and constitutes the political liberty enjoyed by all in commercial society. One of the major distinguishing characteristics of absolute power is the possession in the same hands of judicial and executive power. The feudal lords, it will be recalled, controlled the jurisdiction in their lands. In that circumstance justice cannot be expected, because justice requires impartial administration and it is upon this impartiality that the 'liberty of every individual, the sense which he has of his own security' depends (*WN*, 722–3). The separation of judicial from executive (military) power is, Smith declares in another course of lectures, 'the great advantage which modern times have over ancient' and is a product of 'the increase of refinement and the growth of society' (*LRBL*, 176). Commerce having undermined the power of the feudal landlords, requires, if it is to flourish for any length of time, a 'regular administration of justice'. This is because only where there is such regularity do people 'feel themselves secure in the possession of their property' and have confidence in the 'faith of contracts' and the 'payment of debts' (*WN*, 910).

The crux is the presence of confidence. Commerce depends on confidence not only so that credit can be extended, but more fundamentally because the division of labour itself depends on confidence. To specialise is to commit oneself to the interdependence of market relationships. Put crudely, I will only specialise in making shoes in the expectation that others are specialising in other goods, so that I can take my surplus to market to exchange for theirs. This means acting *now* in expectation of future return, but without the stability that attends 'regular administration' this would be irrational. Where the future is uncertain, where the actions of others are not predictable, then it is better to be independent and self-sufficient and not rely on anyone. But, of course, that option means forgoing the blessing of the opulence that comes from interdependence.

It could be rejoined that Smith has missed the real thrust of Rousseau's indictment to the effect that commercial society has debased human relationships and, in the mainstream of civic humanism, that it has undermined virtue. The case against opulence or luxury was that as private goods they directed the citizen's attention away from the public weal. The roots of this argument lay in Aristotle's strictures against the acquisition of wealth for its own sake (accumulation), which perversely turned what should only be a means to the end of enjoying the good life into an end-in-itself.[6] The good life is the political life of participation in the common affairs of the *polis*, which is genuinely an end-in-itself. To Aristotle, those who lived the political life were free men, since the *polis* itself is definable as an association of freemen.[7]

It should be clear how Smith's position repudiates this. In shorthand terms, he assigns a different meaning to 'liberty' by restricting its requirements while extending its application.[8] Smith's liberty under law is a liberty to be enjoyed by all, but as he points out, the Aristotelean political liberty was only enjoyed by a few and was only sustainable by the enslavement of a sizable proportion of the population (*LJ*, 226). Slavery is not only morally objectionable (as Rousseau – though not all civic humanists[9] – would agree) but also economically unproductive (*WN*, 387;684). Wealth is increased by the 'liberal reward of labour', since where wages are high 'we shall always find the workmen more active, diligent and expeditious' (*WN*, 99). Given further that 'servants, labourers and workmen' (*WN*, 96) constitute the bulk of a society's population, then what improves their lot makes for a happy and flourishing society. It is, indeed, in the context of a discussion of slavery that Smith declares opulence and freedom to be mankind's greatest blessings.

Rousseau, however, might still regard this as begging the question. But the further consequences of Smith's identification of commercial society with everyman being a merchant relate to a new assessment of individual relationships. In a civilised (market) society, the individual 'stands at all times in need of the co-operation and assistance of great multitudes, while his whole life is scarce sufficient' to gain the friendship of a few persons' (*WN*, 26). This means that the individual in a market society deals preponderantly with other individuals who are strangers to him. In that circumstance, individuals must, as Rousseau had lamented, appeal to advantage. Hence it is that

> It is not from the benevolence of the butcher, the brewer, or the baker, that we expect our dinner, but from their regard to their own interest. We address ourselves, not to their humanity but to their self-love, and never talk to them of our own necessities but of their advantages. Nobody but a beggar chuses to depend chiefly upon the benevolence of his fellow-citizens. (*WN*, 26–7)

This now commits Smith to upholding the position that commercial society does not rely on benevolence for its bedrock cohesiveness. Smith, of course, does not deny the virtuousness of benevolence, but society can subsist without it, though it will indeed be as a consequence 'less happy and agreeable' (*TMS*, 86). What is necessary for social existence is not the positive virtue of beneficence, since a company of merchants can subsist without it (*TMS*, 86), but the negative virtue of justice. This is because society cannot subsist at all amongst individuals who are ready to injure each other, that is, where injustice is prevalent. Justice, therefore, is 'the main pillar that upholds the whole edifice. If it is removed, the great, the immense fabric of human society . . . must in a moment crumble into atoms' (*TMS*, 86). Justice is negative because it requires abstention from injuring others, indeed 'we may often fulfil all the rules of justice by sitting still and doing nothing' (*TMS*, 82).[10]

Contrary to both Rousseau and Aristotle, who stressed active participation, we can fulfil our public/political duties by doing nothing. In our conduct with others it is sufficient to follow rules in order to practise the virtue of justice. Furthermore, by making few demands in this way the just life can be in the reach of all, and need not be reserved to those with the resources necessary to underpin an active political life.

Since for Smith civilised societies enjoy liberty under law, he does not share the qualms of the civic humanists that rule-following will be detrimental to the civic spirit. Indeed, Smith is sceptical of this spirit, resting as it does on an unjustified and overblown conception of the human will. As the collapse of feudalism testified, the public good (Rousseau's 'general will') does not depend upon being willed as such. Rather, the public good will be promoted through (in Rousseau's terms) particular wills. This, of course, is the force of Smith's evocation of the 'invisible hand': the individual 'intends only his own gain' but society does not suffer, because through pursuit of his own interest he 'frequently promotes that of the society more effectually than when he really intends to promote it'. Indeed, Smith goes on the offensive: 'I have never known much good done by those who affected to trade for the publick good' (*WN*, 456). Politicians, who exercise their will in directing others, are in fact a threat to the liberty enshrined in the rule of law. They will pursue policies that will affect their citizens differentially – as in the prohibition of wool exportation to promote manufactures – and which will, as such, be 'evidently contrary to the justice and equality of treatment which the sovereign owes to the different orders of his subjects' (*WN*, 654). In Smith's view, political will should confine itself to external defence, the maintenance of justice internally through 'regular administration', and the provision of 'certain publick works' (*WN*, 687–8). Once again, Smith's position here can be fruitfully interpreted as the product of his social science. The complexity and systematic interdependence of commercial society makes redundant the individualist, politically activist, approach of the civic humanists.

What sustains Smith's view that the just life is within reach of all is his sociological account of moral sentiments. Justice, as we have noted, consists in rule-following and Smith, in one place, likens the rules of justice to the rules of grammar in their precision, accuracy and indispensability (*TMS*, 175). This precision makes both grammar and justice susceptible to instruction; we 'may be taught to act justly'. This is important because the 'coarse clay of the bulk of mankind' means that ideal conduct is not to be expected, but

> there is scarce any man, however, who by discipline, educa-
> tion, and example, may not be so impressed with a regard to
> general rules, as to act upon almost every occasion with
> tolerable decency, and through the whole of his life to avoid
> any considerable degree of blame. (*TMS*, 163)

The very efficacy of this process in ensuring adherence to general rules means that it must be found in all ages, just as the very indispensability of justice means that all societies experience it. But, and this is the crucial point, rudeness and barbarism hinder the 'natural sentiments of justice from arriving at that accuracy and precision which in more civilized nations they naturally attain to' (*TMS*, 341).

The repetition of 'natural' here is no accident. 'Nature' for Smith frequently appears in a prescriptive role. It is central to the normative superiority of commercial society that it is also the most natural society. This identification stems from Smith's postulates that, firstly, it is a natural human propensity to truck, barter and exchange and, second, that in a commercial society everyman is in some measure a merchant, so that, when these are combined, it follows that it is only in commercial society that human nature is able to exhibit directly and centrally this propensity. Though exchange has always occurred (cf. *WN*, 27), just as justice is ubiquitous, yet it is only in commercial society, the very rationale of which is to make things for exchange, that the propensity will be fully exercised. This provides crucial ammunition against 'unnatural' government interference, and sustains the basic rectitude of the system as 'the natural system of perfect liberty and justice' (*WN*, 606). It was, of course, this identification of commercial society and its values with the 'natural' society that led Marx, in particular, to accuse Smith of being a bourgeois apologist.

For Smith to be so confident about the rectitude of commercial society means that he must also be confident that general rules will be adhered to in a society where self-love is prevalent. The explanation of Smith's confidence takes us to the heart of his account of moral psychology, which is devoted to showing how social interaction humbles the arrogance of self-love (*TMS*, 83). The lynchpin of this psychology is Smith's analysis of the principle of sympathy. Sympathy, in Smith's technical sense, is the human faculty of compassion or fellow-feeling. By use of imagination, one individual sympathises with another and feels what the other feels (or should feel) (*TMS*, 10). What makes this feasible is the commonplace idea, but one particularly prominent in the Enlightenment, of the uniformity of human nature.[11] Thus upon hearing that someone's father has died, one is able to sympathise, even if the bereaved is a complete stranger (a significant point as we shall see). The greatest consolation for the bereaved is to see others sympathise with him, 'to see the emotions of their hearts, in every respect, beat time to his own' (*TMS*, 22). There is, however, an inevitable shortfall between the two, since no compassion can ever match the original grief. The consequence of this is that (to continue this example) the bereaved learns to lower the pitch of his grief so that spectators can the more easily sympathise.

It is important that this is a learning exercise. Men learn from experience of life (through 'discipline, education and example') what is proper. In line with Smith's account of social causation, the social phenomenon of morality must have an appropriately social cause. In a key passage, with strong overtones of Rousseau, Smith remarks

> were it possible that a human creature could grow up to manhood in some solitary place, without any communication with his own species, he could no more think of his own character, of the propriety or demerit of his own sentiments and conduct, of the beauty and deformity of his own mind, than of the beauty or deformity of his own face. Bring him into society and he is immediately provided with the mirror which he wanted before . . . and it is here that he first views the propriety and impropriety of his own passions (*TMS*, 110–11).

Morality thus becomes a matter of socialisation, of 'insensible habit and experience' (*TMS*, 135). The effects of social intercourse teach the individual what behaviour is acceptable and, in due course, the individual internalises these social judgements as conscience, viewing his actions and motives as an 'impartial well-informed spectator' would (*TMS*, 130). Through the dynamics of this social interaction the emotions of the agent and the spectators can be harmonised. Although it is impossible that their emotions will ever be as one, yet there will be a concord which, significantly, is sufficient for 'the harmony of society' (*TMS*, 22).

The extent to which emotions will harmonise differs with the circumstances, and it is Smith's claim (though this is implicit rather explicit) that the circumstances of commercial society are well suited to maintain harmony. It is this fit, so to speak, that explains Smith's confidence that the general rules of justice will be adhered to in a society where everyman is a merchant. As we have seen, the bulk of relationships in a commercial society take place between strangers. On Smith's account of the dynamics of sympathy, an agent can expect less sympathy from a stranger than from a friend. The effect of this is to make the agent moderate his emotions to a greater extent, so that more tranquillity is called forth in the presence of strangers than of friends (TMS,23).

This ability on the part of the agent to tone down his emotions is the source for Smith of the virtue of self-command, the virtue from which 'all the other virtues seem to derive their principal lustre' (*TMS*, 242). A commerical society, where most men are strangers one to another, will call forth greater self-command than the more tribal or clannish character of earlier forms of society. Commercial society, for example, weakens family ties because the authority of law provides sufficient security, thus making the provision of mutual defence, which was the prime motive for keeping families together in earlier ages, redundant. It is, Smith declares, the case that 'regard for remote relations becomes in every country less and less according as this state of civilization has been longer and more completely established' (*TMS*, 223). Nevertheless, though familial ties weaken and individuals mingle increasingly with those who are strangers to them, they remain, because of this necessary mingling, subject to its moralising constraints. Indeed, the 'pursuit of riches' itself is prompted chiefly by 'regard to the sentiments of mankind', to 'being the object of attention and approbation' (*TMS*, 50).

Self-command, like all the virtues, is also a product of socialisa-tion. The ubiquity of strangers in a commercial society will have the effect of strengthening the character, by making habitual the need to moderate one's emotions (cf. *TMS*, 147). A stranger is more like the impartial spectator (cf. *TMS*, 153–4), who corrects 'the natural misrepresentations of self-love' and who 'shows us the propriety of generosity and the deformity of injustice' (*TMS*, 137). Moreover, commercial society need not go to the extremes of 'savages and barbarians' where self-denial is cultivated at the cost of humanity (*TMS*, 205). Indeed, when self-denial expresses itself in suffering torture without any complaint whatsoever, then the whole merit of self-command is taken away (*TMS*, 245).

There is thus a wide difference between the degrees of self-command required in 'civilized and barbarous nations'. The latter – as the case of the passive victim of torture exemplifies – 'necessarily acquire the habits of falsehood and dissimulation' and when they give way to anger their vengeance is 'always sanguinary and dreadful' (*TMS*, 208). The former, by contrast, become 'frank, open and sincere'. It is in the world of commerce that honesty is the norm. This point is made explicitly in the *Lectures*: 'when the greater part of the people are merchants they always bring probity and punctuality into fashion, and these therefore are the principal virtues of a commercial nation' (*LJ*, 539). The very interdependence of that world contributes to the maintenance of such virtues, because there is a preponderance of men 'in the middling and inferior stations of life' none of whom can ever be great enough to be above the law but are, rather, overawed into respect for 'the more important rules of justice'. Furthermore, in that condition personal success depends on the favour and good opinion of neighbours, and without that opinion 'a tolerably regular conduct' cannot be expected (*TMS*, 63). Regularity, of course, is fundamental to a commercial society, where individuals must act in expectation of future return. The prime source of such regularity is, as we have already noted, adherence to the general rules of justice.

Justice, moreover, is self-supporting in commercial society. This is borne out in practice (Smith affirms) by 'that equal and impartial administration of justice which renders the rights of the meanest British subject respectable to the greatest, and which by securing to every man the fruits of his own industry, gives the greatest and most effectual encouragement to every sort of industry' (*WN*, 610). It is also borne out in theory, because the 'reward' for acting justly, for keeping to the rules, is 'the confidence, the esteem and love of those we live with . . . it is not in being rich that truth and justice would rejoice but in being trusted and believed' (*TMS*, 166). To act justly, therefore, brings forth trust and confidence and they, in their turn, make it rational and feasible to specialise and thus create opulence. The fact, furthermore, that it is 'the gentler exertions' of self-command which find expression in commercial society means that it is there that both the 'amiable virtue of chastity' and the opulence-creating 'respectable virtues of industry and frugality' will be found (*TMS*, 242).

There is one final set of consequences of Smith's interpretation of commercial society as a society of merchants that needs mentioning. Despite Smith's confirmed support for the superiority of commercial society, he is not blind to its drawbacks, and in some much-discussed pages in the *Wealth of Nations* he draws attention to them. A consequence of specialisation is to confine some individuals to 'performing a few simple operations', the very simplicity of which makes them incapable of 'conceiving any generous, noble or tender sentiments and consequently of forming any just judgement concerning many even of the ordinary duties of private life' (*WN*, 782).[12] This is serious, given the importance that Smith attaches to private concerns. It is likely that the obligations of justice will suffer and that the pervasive 'torpor of the mind', and attendant ignorance, will enervate the self-command of these individuals and will fuel 'enthusiasm and superstition', a frequent source of 'dreadful disorders' (*WN*, 788).

Confronted with these consequences, while firmly accepting

the desirability of their causes, Smith seeks to palliate their impact. He sees it, accordingly, as a legitimate task of government (one of its public works) in commercial society to finance the instruction of those 'in the lowest occupations' that they might acquire the 'most essential parts of education' ('read, write and account' together with some 'elementary parts of geometry and mechanicks'; *WN*, 785). The effect of such instruction, he believes, would be to instil self-respect and to promote thereby decency and order. This, in its turn, would further the stability of the entire society because that ultimately rests, as we have seen, on confidence. What lies behind this advocacy of education is Smith's subscription to one of the most characteristic of all Enlightenment tenets, namely, that encapsulated in Voltaire's slogan *écrasez l'infâme*. Science, Smith declares in this definitive Enlightenment idiom is 'the great antidote to the poison of enthusiasm and superstition'. Accordingly, Smith advocates the state making almost universal 'the study of science and philosophy' among the middling (and superior) ranks. Since this would make these ranks immune then, thanks to their example, 'the inferior ranks' too would be little exposed to the poison (*WN*, 796).

We can best draw to a close the threads of this deliberately synoptical and inevitably coarse-grained treatment by highlighting one of its themes. It is Smith's attempt (never realised in its entirety) to establish 'the general principles of law and government' (*TMS*, 342) by means of a social scientific approach that marks off his thought from that of Rousseau and the civic humanists.[13] The hallmark of scientific explanation is the discovery of regular connecting principles (cf. *EPS*, 45). For the Enlightenment, the paradigm of such explanation was provided by Newton, and the desire to emulate his achievement in the natural world by arriving at a few simple but general explanatory principles for the social world was common. For example, it was the animating force behind the great Encyclopedia project of Diderot, as is unambiguously apparent from d'Alembert's *Preliminary Discourse*. In Scotland, this desire is seen clearly in Hume's *Treatise of Human Nature*, which he subtitled 'An attempt to introduce the experimental method of reasoning into moral subjects'. This ambition – as with much else – Smith shared with Hume.[14]

As the full title of his major work: – *An Inquiry into the Nature and Causes of the Wealth of Nations* – testifies, Smith's search for regular and general principles put a premium upon causal analysis.[15] The evident constancy and cohesiveness of the social world must, being an effect, have an appropriately constant cause. Such constancy could not be found in isolated, individual human will or reason which, in itself, is both too weak and too fickle to provide the causal premiss for scientific generalisation. Instead, Smith locates the requisite solidity and generality in 'natural' facts and processes. Such natural facts (like population pressure on resources) 'necessarily' produce their outcomes (like changes in the mode of subsistence).

Thus the division of labour was not the effect of 'any human wisdom' but the necessary consequence of the uniform and universal human 'propensity' (a Newtonian term) or 'natural disposition' to truck, barter and exchange (*WN*, 25 cf. *LJ*, 493). Thus, also, government was not the product of any deliberate human will or agreement but was made 'absolutely necessary' by the effect of the 'natural progress' of private property (cf. *LJ*, 207). Similarly, being a political subject is not a product of choice – for no one chooses their place of birth – but is the effect of being 'born and bred up under the authority of the magistrates', together with the 'natural modesty' of mankind which disinclines them to dispute the title of their superiors (*LJ*, 317–8). Finally, morality itself cannot be explained as the product of reason but rather 'it is by finding in a vast variety of instances that one tenor of conduct *constantly pleases* in a certain manner and that another *constantly displeases* the mind that we form the general rules of morality' (*TMS*, 320 my emphases). This experiential constancy coalesces insensibly into habits, so that the social phenomenon of morality is best understood as the habituated response to social circumstances.

In the trading circumstances of a commercial society, the operant morality was one of prudence and probity although these same circumstances could also lead to 'mental mutilation'. But none of this was a matter of human will. No one decided to put great weight on honesty or to establish 'alienating' work conditions. These are both the natural effects of life in society, in the same way that the different characters of the philosopher and the porter arise gradually 'from habit, custom and education' (*WN*, 29). The circumstances where human will might seem to have some moment – when there was room for heroes or Machiavellian princes suffused with *virtù* – no longer obtains.[16] Yet it is just such times that the civic humanists presuppose in their critique of credit or commerce. To this critique, Smith is able to rejoin that it is not only anachronistic but also unsoundly (unscientifically) based. It is true, in one sense, that Rousseau fares better because he realises that it is the very circumstances of the world of commerce that makes political will redundant. He aims to establish his virtuous republic among a people not yet moulded by customs, so that the values of economically independent small-holders can entrench themselves as the customary norm. But, and this brings us full circle, such an enterprise, aside from being mere wishful thinking (you cannot stop the world and get off at a destination of your own choosing), prevents mankind enjoying both of their greatest blessings – opulence and freedom. The modern world of commerce, even with its drawbacks, still offers the prospects of those twin delights.[17]

NOTES

* The following abbreviations of Smith's works are cited in parentheses in the text:

WN: An Inquiry into the Nature and Causes of the Wealth of Nations, eds R.H. Campbell and A.S. Skinner (Glasgow Edition of the works and correspondence of Adam Smith). Indianapolis: Liberty Classics edition, 1981.

EPS: Essays on Philosophical Subjects, ed. W.P.D. Wightman and J. Bryce (Glasgow Edition). Indianapolis: Liberty Classics, 1982.

LJ: Lectures on Jurisprudence, eds R.L. Meek, D.D. Raphael and P.G. Stein (Glasgow Edition). Indianapolis: Liberty Classics, 1982.

TMS: The Theory of Moral Sentiments, eds A.L. Macfie and D.D. Raphael (Glasgow Edition). Indianapolis: Liberty Classics, 1982.

LRBL: Lectures on Rhetoric and Belles Lettres, ed. J.C. Bryce (Glasgow Edition). Indianapolis: Liberty Classics, 1985.

1 Cf. *The Machiavellian Moment* (Princeton University Press, 1975). More recent essays that continue to elaborate his argument and which concentrate on the eighteenth century are collected in J.G.A. Pocock *Virtue, Commerce and History*, (Cambridge University Press, 1985). One essay not included in the collection, and the one which bears most directly on the Scottish Enlightenment, is 'Cambridge paradigms and Scotch philosophers: a study of the relations between the civic humanist and the civil jurisprudential interpretation of eighteenth-century social thought' in *Wealth and Virtue: The shaping of Political Economy in the Scottish Enlightenment*, eds I. Hont and M. Ignatieff (Cambridge University Press, 1983) 235–52. For comment on Pocock's account of the Scottish Enlightenment, and the debate in which his essay engages, see C.J. Berry 'The Nature of Wealth and the Origins of Virtue', *History of European Ideas*, vol. 7 (1986) 85–99.

2 Cf. P. Gay *The Enlightenment*, two volumes (London: Weidenfeld and Nicholson, 1966, 1969), who characterises the

'family' of the philosophes as engaged in 'The Pursuit of Modernity'.

3 Cf. R.L. Meek *Social Science and the Ignoble Savage*, (Cambridge University Press, 1976); R.L. Meek *Smith, Marx and After*, (London: Chapman and Hall, 1977); A.S. Skinner *inter alia* 'Adam Smith: an Economic Interpretation of History' in *Essays on Adam Smith*, eds T. Wilson and A.S. Skinner (Oxford: Clarendon Press, 1975), 154–78; 'A Scottish Contribution to Marxist Sociology?' in *Classical and Marxian Political Economy*, eds I. Bradley and M. Howard (London: Macmillan, 1982), 79–114.

4 Cf. *LJ*, 489, 'when the nation is cultivated and labour divided a more liberal provision is allotted them; and it is on this account that a common day labourer in Brittain has more luxury in his way of living than an Indian sovereign'. That the poor in commercial societies enjoyed a better standard of living than in earlier ages was crucial to Smith's defence of the modern commercial world is well maintained by I. Hont and M. Ignatieff 'Needs and justice in the *Wealth of Nations*' in *Wealth and Virtue*, 1–44.

5 According to Smith what constitutes the 'real happiness of human life', namely, 'ease of body and peace of mind' is enjoyable by all, regardless of rank. This statement occurs at the end of a long paragraph which opens with a vivid description of how industry has 'entirely changed the whole face of the globe' (*TMS*, 183–5). The editors point out how Smith's wording recalls that of Rousseau in a passage from the *Discours* that Smith translated in the *Edinburgh Review*. Cf. M. Ignatieff *The Needs of Strangers* (London: Chatto & Windus, 1984) for a perceptive discussion of Smith's relationship to Rousseau.

6 Aristotle *The Politics*, 1258a.

7 Ibid. 1279a.

8 Cf *inter alia* K. Haakonssen, *The Science of a Legislator: The Natural Jurisprudence of David Hume and Adam Smith* (Cambridge University Press, 1981), 140; J. Robertson *The Scottish Enlightenment and the Militia Issue* (Edinburgh: John Donald, 1985), 12. The differing interpretations of liberty (as of property) is one of the benchmarks Pocock uses to distinguish the civic humanist and jurisprudential paradigms, see his essay in *Wealth and Virtue* cited above n.1. J.H. Hexter had picked up this point in his review essay of Pocock's *Machiavellian Moment* in *History and Theory*, vol. 16 (1977), 306–37 at p.331.

9 For example, Andrew Fletcher of Saltoun in his *Second Discourse on the affairs of Scotland* (1968) in *Fletcher of Saltoun: Selected Writings* ed. D. Daiches (Edinburgh: Scottish Academic Press, 1979) advocated as part of his package of economic reforms that estates should directly employ vagabonds, who, if in local excess, should be sold to other estates where there was a

lack. While Fletcher denies that he was thereby advocating slavery he makes clear that this was the policy of the 'ancients'. Pocock included Fletcher in his civic humanist camp in *Machiavellian Moment* (427–32) and Fletcher's importance to the Scottish Enlightenment has been maintained by G.E. Davie *The Scottish Enlightenment* (Historical Association pamphlet No. 99; London, 1981) and N. Phillipson 'The Scottish Enlightenment' in *The Enlightenment in National Context* ed. R. Porter and M. Teich (Cambridge University Press, 1981), 19–40.

10 The inclusion of 'often' here indicates that Smith is not committed to any unqualified assertion of this principle and it is clear, in the *Moral Sentiments*, that he thinks 'bare observance' of rules without more positive acts of virtue is to lack certain feelings of humanity (*TMS*, 82). But justice and benevolence are not inversely related; one who acts justly will also exhibit great humanity and benevolence (*TMS*, 218), as well as being the recipient of esteem (see text below).

11 Cf. C.J. Berry *Hume, Hegel and Human Nature* (The Hague: Nijhoff, 1982), Chap. 1.

12 Though Smith does in this context use the term 'corruption' this does not mean he is thereby adopting the conceptual framework of civic humanism (not even as 'transforming' it, *pace* J. Robertson 'Scottish Political Economy Beyond the Civic Tradition: Government and Economic Development in the *Wealth of Nations*' in *History of Political Thought* vol. 4 (1983), 451–82). Those who are vulnerable are not those (i.e. independent labourers) who would have qualified for citizenship and their 'corruption' affects not their economic independence but their ability to adhere to the requirements of propriety. Cf. E. Harpham 'Liberalism, Civic Humanism and the case of Adam Smith' in *American Political Science Review* vol. 80 (1984), 764–74.

13 The weakness of Donald Winch's admirably conceived attempt to view Smith resolutely in eighteenth-century terms is that he says little about Smith's – impeccably 'enlightened' – scientific pretensions. *Adam Smith's Politics*(Cambridge University Press, 1978).

14 That the *Wealth of Nations* had succeeded in emulating Newton was a judgement passed by contemporaries. For example, John Miller, who was Smith's former pupil, observed 'The great Montesquieu pointed out the road. He was the Lord Bacon in this branch of Philosophy. Dr. Smith is the Newton' quoted in W.C. Lehmann *John Millar of Glasgow* (Cambridge University Press, (1960), 363; Governor Thomas Pownall opened his pamphlet on the *Wealth of Nations* by remarking how Smith had achieved the task of fixing 'first principles in the most important of sciences' so that his work 'might become *principia*

to the knowledge of politick operations,' – 'A Letter from Governor Pownall to Adam Smith' affixed as Appendix A to *Correspondence of Adam Smith* eds. E.C. Mossner and I.S. Ross (Oxford: Clarendon Press, 1977), 337, cf. 354.

15 Cf. T.D. Campbell *Adam Smith's Science of Morals* (London: G. Allen & Unwin, 1971), Chap. 1.

16 Cf. *TMS* 241–2 where Smith observes that 'the most intrepid valour may be employed in the cause of the greatest injustice'. Courage, while sometimes useful, is 'equally liable to be excessively pernicious' and will be called upon when law and justice are 'in a great measure impotent', that is, 'in times of great public disorder'.

17 This paper has benefited from comments from my Glasgow colleague, Professor Andrew Skinner.

8

PETER JIMACK

Voltaire

If ever the hackneyed phrase 'a legend in his own lifetime' could be applied to anyone, it is surely to Voltaire. When he died in 1778 at the age of eighty-three, he had dominated the literary and intellectual scene, not just of France but of Europe, for well over a quarter of a century. He had long been considered pre-eminent as a poet, a dramatist and a historian. But he was also regarded as virtually the father of the anti-establishment movement which came to be known loosely as 'the Enlightenment', and whereas his reputation in the purely literary sphere did not much survive the eighteenth century, it is above all as the supreme representative of the Enlightenment that he has been seen ever since.

Voltaire's anti-establishment credentials were certainly impressive: he was imprisoned twice in the Bastille, and then spent most of his life in exile, at least from Paris; and many of his published works were condemned by the authorities. Yet in many ways, he could be seen as an establishment figure. The violent overthrow of the *Ancien Régime* has undoubtedly influenced subsequent perception of the movement which preceded it and which (to a disputed extent) prepared the intellectual ground for it, and it is often assumed that the French Enlightenment was more overtly political and implicitly revolutionary than it generally was. Voltaire himself became a very rich man, and led a decidedly aristocratic life. He was a friend of monarchs, and in effect knew everybody who was anybody in Europe; indeed the most eminent of his contemporaries were flattered to be received by him. He was not, like Montesquieu, Rousseau and Diderot, a political theorist, but he did from time to time touch directly or indirectly on the subject of politics, and in so far as one can draw conclusions about his opinions, they seem to have been far from radical – not surprisingly perhaps: although he spoke out warmly in favour of the freedom of the individual, he appears in general to have been in favour, not just of a monarchy, but of some form of benevolent despotism.

In what sense then was Voltaire enlightened? The Enlighten-

ment was characterised above all by a sense of intellectual
excitement and enthusiasm, by a pride in human achievement
and potential; scientific progress and discoveries confirmed and
reinforced a growing confidence in man's capacity to understand
the mysteries of the universe and to dominate his environment.
Inevitably, though, such an attitude involved a challenge to
certain traditional ways of thinking, and particularly those of the
Church, which not only insisted on the literal truth of the Bible
and the inadequacy of human reason, but was prepared to put to
death those who disagreed with it. So conflict with the Church
became one of the most marked features of the Enlightenment.

Certainly both of these characteristics are to be found in
Voltaire. Particularly in his early works, he expressed great
confidence in man and his achievements. He brought back from
his exile in England (1726 to 1728 or 1729) great enthusiasm for
the scientific thought of Newton, and in the years that followed he
engaged in much scientific work, especially experimental physics,
together with his mistress, Madame du Châtelet, herself a mathematician and physicist of some repute. His poem *Le Mondain*,
written at this time (around 1735), admittedly a rather light-
hearted work, was a hymn in praise of luxury and modern
civilisation. But at a more serious level, many of his works of this
period reveal a basically similar attitude, and his great history of
the world, the *Essai sur les Mœurs*, on which he had already
worked for over twenty years when he published it in its first
complete version in 1756, while it is in no way complacent, is
infused with a belief in the possibility and the reality of human
progress. It is interesting to note, incidentally, that Voltaire's
approval of the development of modern civilisation made him a
fundamental adversary of Rousseau, who was probably the most
intellectually influential of his Enlightenment contemporaries. In
his first *Discourse*, published in 1750, Rousseau maintained that
the development of science and the arts had contributed to the
moral corruption of mankind, and in the second, five years later,
he evoked the vision of an ideal primitive man, arguing that the
formation of civilised society had led inevitably to his corruption
and unhappiness. When he sent Voltaire a copy of this work, the
latter replied with heavy irony that reading it had made him want
to go about on all fours!

But even more than his enthusiasm for the achievements of
modern man, it is Voltaire's hostility to the Church, and indeed,
in many respects, to Christianity itself, that forms the principal
basis of his reputation as one of the major representatives of the
Enlightenment, and no account of Voltaire can ignore this second

aspect of his thought and activity. It is important, though, to bear in mind that both aspects stem from a deep concern for man and from a firmly anthropocentric view of the universe. It is this concern, in my view, that provides the key to understanding not just his thought, but virtually all his philosophical and polemical work.

Discussion of Voltaire's thought is difficult not because it is particularly complex or obscure, but for two very practical reasons: firstly, he wrote a vast amount – his complete works fill many library shelves, even without his enormous correspondence; and secondly, his thought is rarely formulated in a systematic way in works of theory, but must rather be deduced and synthesised from ideas diffused throughout his voluminous writings, and often expressed in ambiguous terms, for example through satire and irony. This in itself is revealing: Voltaire was not primarily interested in abstract philosophical truths, but more concerned with what people today call 'the real world' – a phrase usually implying contempt for the false 'ivory-tower' world of academics and philosophers. To some extent Voltaire's own impatience with metaphysics reflected a similar attitude: rather than a philosopher, he was in many ways a kind of polemical journalist, who devoted himself to a campaign of propaganda for the causes he embraced and fierce attacks on what he saw as the forces of evil.

One of Voltaire's rare systematic theoretical works was his *Traité de Métaphysique*, written around 1734 but not published in his lifetime. It is difficult to know what importance to attach to the work: critics have argued that the fact that Voltaire did not publish it points to its being a work of deep personal commitment rather than mere propaganda for public consumption; but one might equally well argue that, while it may have represented a serious attempt to sort out his thinking at the time, he did not attach enough importance to its subject matter, or was simply not confident enough about it, to think it worth publishing. In fact, rather than a genuine speculative enquiry, it seems to me an attempt by Voltaire to provide a coherent philosophical justification of a number of beliefs which appeared to him either as axiomatic, or as so desirable that to abandon them was unthinkable.

The theoretical starting point of the *Traité* is the demonstration of the existence of God. Voltaire gives two proofs. The first, which had been used by Newton and which Voltaire saw as the more accessible, was the watchmaker argument, based on the obvious order of the universe and the plausibility of final causes: if looking at a watch leads one to the conclusion that it was created by an intelligent being and that its hands are intended to show the time, it is reasonable to conclude from contemplation of the human body that it too was created by an intelligent being, that the eyes were meant for seeing, and so on. It is worth noting that Voltaire saw this argument not as conclusive, but as indicating only the probability of the existence of an intelligent creator. His second proof of the existence of God, which was derived in part from Locke and which Voltaire described as 'more metaphysical', was the first cause argument: I exist, therefore something exists, therefore something has existed since all eternity; for either what exists is necessary and eternal, in which case it is God, or its being has been communicated to it by something else, to which the same argument applies. Since the material world is manifestly neither eternal nor unchanging, it is not necessary by itself but contingent, and must owe its existence to a being which *is* necessary, i.e. God. By a similar argument, movement, thought and feeling must all have been communicated to matter by God.

Despite the attractiveness of its apparent rigour, however, Voltaire never subsequently made much use of this second proof, and indeed, in a letter written in 1737, he showed himself to be unconvinced of its soundness;[1] it is clear on the other hand that he was greatly attracted by the first, the proof from final causes, which was to become one of his favourite arguments, no doubt because it depended on a common-sense interpretation of everyday experience rather than on abstract reasoning. In the *Traité*, he returns to the final cause argument to defend it against some apparent objections. If, for example, one protests that meadows are not made for horses, this merely proves that we do not always know what the final causes are; and if one argues that there is no *proof* that stomachs are made for digestion, Voltaire retorts that there is certainly no proof that they are not, and that common sense would surely indicate that they are. Such arguments of course, seem to imply a prior conviction both that God exists and that he is beneficent – Voltaire states explicitly that it would be absurd to accuse God of injustice – and there appears to be a certain circularity in using final causes to prove the existence of such a God.

Moving on to a discussion of man, Voltaire emphatically rejected the 'absurd belief in innate ideas', usually associated with Descartes, and accepted the sensationalist theories of Locke, according to which all our knowledge comes from the experience of the senses. But he firmly rejected two theories which other thinkers derived from Locke's sensationalism. To begin with, he maintained that the external world exists: although he appears here to be refuting the ancient Pyrrhonians, he was probably thinking mainly of Berkeley, who had recently argued that we can have no sure knowledge of the material world. Voltaire's common-sense approach made short work of such subtleties, and he ended this chapter, with characteristic wit, by saying that if the Pyrrho-nians would not allow him a belief in the existence of the corporeal, he would have to deny that they themselves existed. Secondly, whereas some of Voltaire's contemporaries, like Diderot, argued that if man acquires everything through his sense experi-ence, then he must be totally determined by his environment, concluding that human freedom is an illusion, Voltaire, at least for the time being, clung resolutely to a belief that man is indeed free. As with final causes and the existence of the external world, he appealed to common sense: since man feels that he is free, then he is; it would be absurd to believe that God has deliberately deceived us. As for the problem of reconciling this freedom with the prescience of God, Voltaire took convenient refuge in man's limited understanding – a humility he was quite willing to adopt when it suited him.

Now both these arguments are based on moral considerations as well as on common sense. Firstly, social morality is inconceiv-able if the existence of the outside world is in doubt; and secondly, if man's behaviour is determined, how can he be held morally responsible for his actions? That morality was indeed Voltaire's ultimate concern is confirmed by what he wrote to Frederick the Great when he sent him a summary of the *Traité*: 'As far as I can, I always bring back my metaphysics to morality'.[2] The work concludes with a discussion of virtue and vice, which begins by arguing that they are not absolute but relative notions, to be understood in a social context: 'Virtue and vice, moral good and evil, are in every country what is useful or harmful to society'.[3] So that not only are the crimes of one country some-times the virtues of another, but acts which are normally thought of as intrinsically wicked, such as murder, may occasionally be seen as good if they serve the public interest: thus, 'a brother who kills his brother is a monster; but a brother who sacrificed his brother as the only means of saving his country would be divine.'[4] But the drift of the argument is obviously that such cases are the exception rather than the rule, and implicit in it is the assumption that prior to being assessed by the criterion of public utility, actions do have an intrinsic moral worth. Voltaire comes close to recognising this explicitly when he proceeds to affirm the existence of universal 'natural laws': a benevolent God, having destined man for a social existence, had given him the instincts which were necessary for the creation and perpetuation of societies. Thus, for example, men are naturally well-disposed towards their fellow men and will behave accordingly – so long as it is not contrary to their own interests.

Most of the beliefs enunciated in the *Traité de Métaphysique* were to remain more or less constants in Voltaire's thought. But some were to change, and others he would have difficulty in maintaining in the face of what looked like contrary evidence. Much as he may have wanted to believe in human freedom, for example, he fairly soon moved towards an acceptance of determinism. It was some years later, in *Le Philosophe Ignorant* (1766), that he gave perhaps the most succinct statement of his position on the subject. He reduced discussion of freedom to what he saw as its essentials, a question of practice and behaviour, dismissing the metaphysical aspects as incomprehensible. Freedom consists in action, in acting in accordance with one's will: 'When I can do what I will, that is freedom for me'.[5] The will is determined in the sense that there can be no effect without a cause: Voltaire dismisses as absurd the notion that the will can be described as free; you might just as well, he says, describe it as blue or square. No doubt this means that human freedom is limited, but it was a limitation he professed himself well content with, and it did not seem to diminish his confidence in man's natural inclination to virtue. The example he used to illustrate his conception of practical freedom is significant: 'My freedom lies in not performing a wicked action when my mind perceives it as necessarily wicked'.[6] Despite Voltaire's hostility to Christianity, this notion of freedom consisting in the ability to resist temptation to evil is of course very close to the Christian concept of free-will.

The faith in man's natural inclination to virtue was indeed one that Voltaire was particularly attached to, despite his consciousness of apparent evidence to the contrary. Faced with the difficulty of reconciling this belief, which appeared to imply that virtue and vice were absolutes, and therefore universal, with the principle of the social relativity of morality, it was the latter that he jettisoned, though his thinking remained somewhat ambiguous on this point. In the *Eléments de la philosophie de Newton*, for instance, published in 1738, he affirmed his conviction that all men have an innate moral sense, and dismissed as unreliable travellers' tales of barbaric practices in far-off lands. But even if such tales were accurate, they did not disprove the universality of a moral sense: Voltaire was even prepared to defend the reported practice of cannibals eating their parents as their (no doubt) misguided way of showing their affection for them – saving them from the worse fate of being eaten by enemies or just dying of old age! Which could, of course, be seen as a defence of the relativity of morality.

There is a similar defence of universal morality in the *Poème sur la Loi naturelle*. Written probably in 1751, but not originally intended for publication, this long poem was a response to a work entitled *L'Anti-Sénèque ou le Souverain bien*, by the materialist La Mettrie, who had tried to demonstrate that virtue, vice, and especially remorse were merely prejudices produced by social conditioning. Voltaire maintained that God had endowed all men, throughout the world and since the beginning of time, with an innate moral sense, a 'uniform morality' as he called it. He recognises in the poem the difficulty posed by the evidence of human wickedness, of which he gives various examples, including the execution of King Charles I. No matter, all these individual crimes are just temporary deviations from the norm of virtue, and all men have received from God a conscience and a sense of justice. As for the objection that everything in man is acquired from his experience, Voltaire simply affirms that the basic sense of virtue 'comes from another hand', and falls back on the analogy with the instinct of animals.

Now it is apparent throughout this discussion that, for Voltaire, belief in a universal moral sense and belief in a benevolent God were interdependent. In fact, we are back to final causes: Voltaire argued in the poem that the moral sense had been given to man, along with other faculties, as part of God's provision for all his needs. Even the elements bear witness to the general disposition of the world for the benefit of man: 'Heaven to his needs submits the elements'.[7] However, although Voltaire was to go on, virtually for the rest of his life, expressing roughly similar views, it would be quite misleading to say that that is what he believed and leave it at that. It is apparent, even in the *Poème sur la Loi naturelle*, dedicated though it was to defending the principle of a universal moral sense, that Voltaire was troubled by the abundant examples he saw of human wickedness, and it is very clear from a number of other works written at about the same time that he was finding it increasingly difficult to reconcile belief in natural virtue and a benevolent God with the irresistible evidence of human suffering and of man's cruelty to man.

In the story *Zadig*, which appeared in 1746, he recounts the tale of a virtuous and gifted young man for whom everything seems to go wrong: again and again he is a victim of the cruelty and injustice of his fellow-men. Just when he is at his lowest ebb and beginning to protest against Providence, he meets a hermit with whom he keeps company for several days. The hermit perpetrates what appear to be a number of wickedly ungrateful acts: he burns down the house of the man who has shown them generous hospitality, and drowns the nephew of the virtuous woman who received them charitably the following night. Eventually, in response to Zadig's reproaches, the hermit turns into an angel, representing Providence, and explains that beneath the burned-down house, its owner will find an immense treasure, and that the drowned boy, had he lived, would have gone on to murder first his aunt and then Zadig. In other words, the angel goes on, men judge from faulty and incomplete knowledge: 'there is no evil from which good does not result',[8] all that happens is necessary in a world in which 'there is no such thing as chance',[9] and everything is in its rightful place in the divine scheme of things. Zadig (to his credit, we may well think) is not very convinced, but the angel flies off, telling him to continue on his way to Babylon. Which he does, marries the woman he loves, becomes king, and lives happy ever after.

Now the message delivered to Zadig by the angel is clearly a potted version of the so-called Optimism of Leibniz, or rather of the simplified and distorted account of it which appeared in Pope's widely read *Essay on Man*. At least in this form, the doctrine had become very popular, and given the importance it seems to have had in the evolution of Voltaire's thought, it is worth quoting the key section of Pope's poem:

All Nature is but Art, unknown to thee;
All chance, direction, which thou canst not see;
All discord, harmony not understood;
All partial evil, universal Good;
And, spite of Pride, in erring Reason's spite,
One truth is clear: whatever is, is right.

As far as Voltaire's attitude to Optimism is concerned, it is difficult to know how to interpret *Zadig*, but it is hard to believe that the reader is expected to be any more convinced than the hero by the angel, and the latter's explanations, particularly of his own apparently unjust acts, approach the caricatural. And despite the story's happy ending, the dominant impression is one of an immense amount of injustice and suffering that it is difficult to square with the existence of a benevolent God and a natural inclination to virtue. One is left with the feeling that Voltaire is here already dissatisfied with the explanation offered by Pope, however reluctant he is to abandon it.

Some two years after *Zadig*, the dissatisfaction seemed even greater in the short tale entitled *Memnon*, the story of the man who foolishly tried to be perfectly wise. As with Zadig, everything goes disastrously wrong, culminating in Memnon losing an eye, and this time there is no happy ending. However, a celestial being appears to Memnon in a dream and explains all. In a grotesque distortion of Leibniz's idea of an infinity of possible worlds, he tells him that there are a hundred thousand million carefully graduated worlds, ranging from the one in which perfect wisdom is indeed to be found, to the one in which everyone is mad – and our one, he admits, is nearly the worst. 'So the poets and philosophers who maintain that all is good are quite wrong?' asks Memnon;[10] not so, retorts the spirit, they are quite right with regard to the order of the universe as a whole. 'I shall believe that,' Memnon replies, 'when I get my eye back!'[11]

Now Memnon's last word is of course quite 'illogical', in that no amount of empirical evidence can have any logical impact on the kind of argument used by the celestial spirit, which is, in a sense, designed precisely to discount empirical evidence. The answer given to Zadig by the angel, that man does not have enough knowledge to judge the ways of God, remains unanswerable on the level of human experience. Yet the message of *Memnon* is a powerful one: Voltaire is clearly saying that the metaphysical explanation of evil provided by theories such as Optimism is unacceptable (which is not to say it is untrue) because it is irrelevant to human experience, and it is human experience he is interested in, and human suffering in particular that disturbs him.

The ultimate argument against Optimism as far as Voltaire was concerned came on November 1st 1755 with the Lisbon earthquake disaster, which could scarcely even be blamed on human folly – or, more theologically, on the abuse of free-will. His immediate reaction was one of outraged indignation at the inhumanity of a philosophy which seemed to make light of human suffering, even when it was on so vast a scale. As he wrote in a letter a few weeks after the earthquake, 'If Pope had been in Lisbon, would he have dared to say that all is right?'[12] It was this attitude which underlay his *Poème sur le désastre de Lisbonne*, which appeared shortly afterwards. Never was the emotional and subjective nature of Voltaire's thinking more apparent than in this deeply-felt poem, which was written in a sombre, impassioned tone, very different from the ironic detachment of *Memnon*. Yet the message of the work was virtually the same: it was an insult to the plight of the thousands of wretched victims to try to console them with reassurances about the good order of the universe as a whole. This factor of consolation highlights the pragmatism of Voltaire's position. Optimism was unacceptable not on any metaphysical grounds, but simply on the basis of human experience and human need; it was, as he realised, 'a cruel philosophy under a consoling name',[13] since if things were for the best, there could be no hope of any improvement.

It is ironic that it was precisely on the score of consolation that Rousseau took issue with Voltaire's response to the Lisbon disaster. Voltaire, he protested in his letter to him, had attacked the idea of Providence, which was all very well for the rich and comfortable Voltaire, but he, Rousseau, poor and unhappy, needed a belief in Providence as a consolation for his woes. The arguments he used to defend Providence were banal enough, and not unlike those Voltaire himself had used in his defence of a universal morality: for example that the magnitude of the disaster was not the fault of God, but entirely due to the folly of man in constructing cities – nobody paid any attention to earthquakes which happened in the middle of the desert. Rousseau subsequently complained that Voltaire did not do him the courtesy of replying to the substance of his letter; except, he claimed, in *Candide* (which Rousseau boasted he had never read).

Although it is unlikely that Voltaire was thinking of Rousseau when he wrote *Candide*, certainly his most famous work, the latter was in a sense justified in seeing it as a reply to his letter, since its central theme was a restatement and development of the attitude and argument of the Lisbon poem. It is of course quite different in tone, reverting, though much more effectively, to the cool irony of *Memnon*. Candide is a naïve and innocent lad, a pupil of the philosopher Pangloss, who teaches that all is for the best in the best possible of worlds, a doctrine he supports with the evidence of final causes: noses, he points out, were obviously made to bear spectacles. Candide's long string of misfortunes begin when he falls in love with Cunégonde, the Baron's daughter, and is literally kicked out of her father's castle. Candide, and indeed all the other characters in the story, undergo or witness the most terrible suffering, mostly, it is true, as a result of man's inhumanity to man (slaughter in battle, rape, torture and burning at the stake by the Inquisition, etc.), but also because of natural calamities (the Lisbon earthquake). In the course of his incredible adventures, Candide arrives by accident in the wonderful land of Eldorado, where all is beauty, harmony and happiness. When he questions the statutory wise old man about the local religion, he is told that the Eldoradans do not pray to God, 'we have nothing to ask from him, he has given us all we need'.[14] But, ironically, Candide is not content to stay in this best of all possible worlds, mainly because he wants to search for Cunégonde, who of course is not the virtuous maiden he imagines, and who will have grown ugly by the time he finds her again. And once he has left Eldorado, it is quite impossible to return there.

Finally, Candide and a little group of companions, each of whom has suffered the most appalling hardships, settle on a small farm near Constantinople, where they argue continually about metaphysical matters. One day, led by Pangloss, they go to consult a famous dervish, and their conversation is instructive. When Candide asks the dervish about the terrible amount of evil there is in the world, the dervish replies: 'What does it matter whether there is good or evil? When His Highness sends a ship to Egypt, does he worry whether the mice in the ship are comfortable or not?'[15] And when Pangloss tries to get this second wise man to discuss matters such as causes and effects, the nature of the soul and pre-established harmony, he shuts the door in their faces. The message is clear, and not much different from that of the end of *Memnon*: God is concerned with the good order of the universe as a whole, and not with man. As for metaphysical questions, these are just a waste of time. So Candide and his companions at last realise that the only thing to do is to cultivate their garden: by doing this they finally make life tolerable, and even discover talents they never knew they had: Cunégonde, for example, by now very ugly, becomes a first-rate pastry-cook!

There is a certain ambiguity about this famous ending of *Candide*. What does Voltaire mean by 'cultivate their garden', or rather, how big is the 'garden'? Is the maxim to be taken in the very limited sense of looking after one's own immediate concerns and ignoring the rest of the world? Or is Voltaire telling us to occupy ourselves with the world we live in and thus with our fellow-men, rather than waste our time seeking to know the unknowable? Given Voltaire's involvement, in the years that followed *Candide*, in matters that went far beyond his own immediate self-interest, the second seems the more likely interpretation to me, but the text is inconclusive and critics are divided. What is clear, however, is the emphatic rejection of philosophical speculation and the picture of a man virtually abandoned by God, dependent only on his own activity.

The obvious contrast between this position and what Voltaire seemed to have believed some years earlier is made even more striking by the fact that the religion of the unattainable, unreal Eldorado closely resembles views that he himself had expressed in, for example, the *Poème sur la Loi naturelle*. Similarly, all the emphasis in *Candide* was on the widespread cruelty and wickedness of men, which Voltaire had previously been at pains to discount. Had he then changed his mind? Well perhaps, but only temporarily. There is ample evidence in his writings after *Candide* of the kind of deism (or theism – Voltaire seems to have used the terms practically interchangeably) he had expounded in his earlier works, namely belief in a God closely concerned with the well-being of man, and in a universal God-given moral sense. It was the latter point that he was probably most attached to, his standard position being expressed for example in the short work entitled *Profession de foi des Théistes* (1768): 'Our religion was engraved in our hearts by God himself, who said to the Chinese, to the Indians, to the Tartars, and to us: Worship me and be just'.[16]

Voltaire continued too to defend the doctrine of final causes, which amounted to seeing the world as designed specifically for the convenience of man. In *Des Singularités de la Nature* (1768), echoing what he had written more than thirty years earlier in the *Traité de Métaphysique*, he poured scorn on those who denied that the stomach was made for digesting, the ears for hearing and so on, with a homespun, common-sense (and totally specious) argument that is characteristic of his philosophical approach: 'These people nevertheless admitted that their tailors made them suits to clothe them, and their masons houses for them to live in; and they dared to deny to nature, to the supreme Being, to the universal intelligence, what they granted to the least of their labourers'.[17] No doubt it was ridiculous to maintain with Pangloss that noses were made for spectacles, but they *were* obviously made for smelling. And the grand design extended to the world man lived in: mountains and rivers are as much evidence of divine providence as the ear-drum and the retina of the eye. Totally resisting the evolutionist theories which were beginning to be propounded by Buffon and others, Voltaire defined the 'true system' as the existence of a supreme being 'who made everything, and who gave to each element, to each species, to each kind, its form, its place and its eternal functions'.[18]

In short, *Candide* seems to mark the extreme point in a temporary pessimistic deviation from a fairly consistent philosophical position, a pessimism, or more accurately, perhaps, a bewilderment, brought on by Voltaire's increasing consciousness of the prevalence of evil in the world. This sense of bewilderment, which was accentuated not just by the Lisbon earthquake but also by the Seven Years War (1756–63), is nowhere more succinctly expressed than in a letter he wrote to the Duchess of Saxe-Gotha in February 1756: 'The more I think about the evil that covers the face of the earth, the more I retreat into my sad ignorance.'[19]

But if the earthquake had shaken Voltaire's belief in a deity concerned with the doings of men, the war no doubt reinforced his conviction that such a belief was essential for the moral order of society. Most of the misfortunes of Candide and his companions are indeed due to human wickedness, and if this scarcely reflected a belief in a universal morality, it made the need for some kind of universal sanction against universal immorality all the more obvious. The God Voltaire described in the *Profession de foi des Théistes* was one who rewarded virtue and 'avenged crime' – and the use of the term 'crime' instead of 'vice' is perhaps a clear indication of the social direction of Voltaire's thinking. His attitude to the social desirability of a belief in God was given perhaps its most pithy formulation in a dialogue published in 1762, entitled *l'A.B.C.*: 'I want my lawyer, my tailor, my servants, even my wife, to believe in God, and I suspect that I shall thus be less robbed and less cuckolded.'[20]

Given such views, it is scarcely surprising that Voltaire reacted with considerable anxiety to the overt preaching of atheism in the writings of some of his contemporaries, particularly those of d'Holbach, and a good many of his later works were aimed at refuting them. But Voltaire's conviction of the social necessity for people to believe in a policeman-type God inevitably poses the question of the nature of his own deism. When he declared that 'If God did not exist, we should have to invent him',[21] was he not perhaps revealing his own doubts about the very existence of God? The question is a difficult one to answer, and the fact that this celebrated formula occurs in a poem which was actually an attack on atheism scarcely helps, any more than does the fact that Voltaire had a church built on his estate at Ferney, since the firmness of his belief that atheism was morally and socially dangerous is not in doubt. Despite the abundant evidence of his declarations of a belief not only in a deity, but in a deity closely concerned with man, it is still possible to argue that whatever views he expressed publicly, he was probably in reality an atheist, or at best believed only in the remote God of *Candide*. One of Voltaire's most important biographers, Theodore Besterman, has concluded that 'Voltaire was at most an agnostic', and clearly suggests he was an atheist:[22] I do not find Besterman's case convincing, but once we start trying to establish a thinker's secret thoughts as distinct from his declared ones, proof becomes unascertainable, and the question must remain unresolved.

In any case Voltaire was not much bothered about the establishing of metaphysical truths; like the God he declared he believed in, he was concerned above all with the well-being of man, and he found atheism unacceptable on the same kind of pragmatic grounds as Optimism: Optimism seemed to discount human suffering, and atheism potentially created it by undermining social morality. But the dangers of atheism remained somewhat hypothetical for Voltaire, whereas he saw a far more direct source of human suffering in the Catholic Church. Particularly after *Candide*, one might say that he heeded his own message: rather than indulge in philosophical speculation, he set about cultivating his garden – and the principal weed as far as he was concerned was what he called 'fanaticism', in other words religious intolerance.

Many years earlier, on his return from England, Voltaire had used the religious toleration he had found there to make an implicit attack in his *Lettres philosophiques* (1734) on the very different situation in France (e.g. 'An Englishman, as a free man, goes to heaven by whichever route he chooses'[23]), and the denunciation of religious intolerance had figured prominently in many subsequent works, often side by side with the defence of deism, as in the *Poème sur la Loi naturelle*. It was too an important theme in *Candide*, particularly in the mocking chapter devoted to the 'bel auto-da-fé' organised by the Inquisition (and which really took place) as 'a sure remedy for preventing earthquakes'.[24] But Voltaire was not just concerned with intolerance in general, and he devoted much of his considerable energy to involvement in a number of campaigns against specific cases of injustice. His most important work on the subject, the *Traité sur la Tolérance* (written 1762, published 1764) was triggered by the most famous of these cases, the Calas affair. Jean Calas, a Toulouse Protestant, had been condemned, tortured and executed in 1762, for allegedly having murdered his son to prevent his conversion to Catholicism. The evidence was non-existent and the trial a travesty of justice (it is virtually certain that the young man had committed suicide), and thanks almost entirely to Voltaire's persistent campaigning, the verdict of the court was eventually annulled and compensation paid to Calas's widow.

In fact, however, Voltaire's attacks were by no means confined to the intolerance of the Catholic Church, and extended to other and quite fundamental aspects of Christianity. To some extent, no doubt, this was because the Church's intolerance was based, coherently enough, on Christianity's claims to uniqueness, to a monopoly of truth via divine revelation. Perhaps too, Christianity in general simply suffered in Voltaire's eyes from the phenomenon of contamination by association. But he was particularly contemptuous of miracles and indeed of virtually any alleged manifestation of the supernatural – especially the virgin birth and the divinity of Christ – and I would suggest that the very nature of the miraculous was offensive to his commitment to a common-sense approach to philosophy. Whatever the explanation, Voltaire embarked on a very deliberate campaign against Christianity, under the slogan, which he regularly used in letters to his friends, of 'écrasez l'infâme' (literally, 'crush the infamous one').

From among the many works he devoted to this campaign, the *Sermon des Cinquante*, dating from around 1762 and described by Besterman as 'his first frontal assault on Christianity',[25] provides a good illustration of the approach. The work is a systematic attack on the Bible. Voltaire makes the point that 'any religion whose tenets offend morality is certainly false',[26] and then shows that the Old Testament is full of obscenity, immorality, murder and other crimes. Lot's daughters, for example, got their father drunk two nights running so that they could sleep with him (Genesis, 19). Jacob, presented as the model of men, forced his brother, who was dying of hunger, to give up his birthright for a dish of lentils; deceived his father on his death-bed; deceived and robbed his father-in-law; and slept with all the servant girls (Genesis, 25, 27, 31, 30). And we are expected to believe that God blessed all this infamy. Besides, the Old Testament is equally full of total implausibilities: a snake speaks, a woman is changed into a pillar of salt . . . and enough food is stored in the Ark to feed more than two thousand times fourteen birds and beasts for ten months! And so on. Furthermore, the books allegedly written by Moses speak of things which happened long after his death. As far as the New Testament was concerned, Voltaire's principal charge was its implausibility. Not only is it full of miraculous occurrences, but there are contradictions between the different Gospels over virtually every aspect of the life of Christ, which was in any case a tissue of 'puerile and odious things';[27] anyway, not a single contemporary historian even mentions Christ or his apostles. Needless to say, this common-sense approach might be seen as scarcely appropriate in a discussion of a book which purports to be of divine origin. And to say that a miracle is an event contrary to the ordinary observable laws of the universe sounds more like a definition than a refutation.

But of course, works like the *Sermon des Cinquante* were not part of a serious philosophical enquiry: Voltaire's object was to attack the Christian religion, and to do so he chose whatever method seemed the most effective. Most of his writing on what might be termed philosophical topics was indeed polemical, and wit and ridicule were undoubtedly his preferred weapons. A fair idea of his technique will, I hope, already have been gained from some of the examples I have given in the course of this essay. Above all, he was a master of the lapidary, witty formula which, because it made people laugh and because it was memorable, was often far more effective than a lengthy philosophical treatise. What could be better as an attack on mindless tradition than Sétoc's defence of suttee with the question he puts to Zadig: 'Is there anything more worthy of respect than an ancient abuse?'?[28] And what more telling as a comment on judicial injustice than the reply Candide received to his enquiry about the execution of Admiral Byng: 'in this country it is a good thing to kill an admiral from time to time to encourage the others?'[29] Perhaps the best example of Voltaire's brilliantly unfair destruction of ideas he disapproved of was his attack on Optimism in *Candide*. Rather than attempt to refute the doctrine, he simply made fun of it. Pangloss teaches 'métaphysico-théologo-cosmolo-nigologie', with 'nigologie' being a play on the word 'nigaud', and equivalent to, say, 'doltology'. He argues that since individual evils contribute to the general good, 'the more individual evils there are, the more everything is good';[30] and that in this best of possible worlds, the baroness is 'the best of possible baronesses'.[31] The result is that the very phrase 'the best of possible worlds' becomes irremediably tarnished and can never again be taken seriously.

How one assesses Voltaire's significance as a thinker depends on what one is looking for. No doubt his thought was neither particularly original nor particularly profound, and it could certainly be argued that he was not an important philosopher. And this conclusion might appear to be reinforced by the argument that is sometimes used, that his thought was above all negative and destructive. Yet it is clear that behind the attacks – on Optimism, on atheism, on Christianity, on intolerance – there lay very positive values. Voltaire believed in conventional enough virtues – justice, tolerance, kindness, and above all a respect for human suffering; but he believed in them with an uncommon intensity, and he had the capacity to attack what he saw as the forces of evil hostile to his beliefs with a quite remarkable power. It seems to me a near certainty that he had more influence on the minds of his contemporaries and of ordinary men and women in the centuries that followed than any true 'philosopher' of his period.

NOTES

Unless otherwise indicated, quotations are from: Voltaire, *Œuvres Complètes*, ed. Moland (Paris 1877–85).

1 Quoted by R. Pomeau, in *La Religion de Voltaire* (Paris, 1956), 200. This excellent book is the best work available on Voltaire's thought in general, as well as on his religious views.

2 'Je ramène toujours, autant que je peux, ma métaphysique à la morale.' Quoted by H.T. Mason in *Voltaire* (London, 1975), 137. Professor Mason's short but masterly book provides the best general survey of Voltaire's work in English; it would be ideal for further reading.

3 'La vertu et le vice, le bien et le mal moral, est . . . en tout pays ce qui est utile ou nuisible à la société': *Traité de Métaphysique*, ed. H. Temple Patterson (Manchester U.P., 1937), 57.

4 'Un frère qui tue son frère est un monstre; mais un frère qui n'aurait eu d'autres moyens de sauver sa patrie que de sacrifier son frère, serait un homme divin' (ibid., 59).

5 'Quand je peux faire ce que je veux, voilà ma liberté' (Vol. 26, 56).

6 'Ma liberté consiste à ne point faire une mauvaise action quand mon esprit se la représente nécessairement mauvaise' (ibid.).

7 'Le ciel à ses besoins soumet les éléments' (vol. 9, 444).

8 'il n'y a point de mal dont il ne naisse un bien': Voltaire, *Romans et Contes*, ed. H. Bénac (Paris, 1960), 56.

9 'il n'y a point de hasard' (ibid.).

10 'Eh mais! dit Memnon, certains poètes, certains philosophes, ont donc grand tort de dire que *tout est bien?*' (ibid., 86).

11 'Ah! je ne croirai cela, répliqua le pauvre Memnon, que quand je ne serai plus borgne' (ibid.).

12 'Si Pope avait été à Lisbonne, aurait-il osé dire, tout est bien?': Voltaire, *Correspondence*, ed. Besterman, *The Complete Works of Voltaire* (Genève, Banbury, Oxford 1968–77) vol. 28, 166.

13 'une philosophie cruelle sous un nom consolant' (ibid., vol. 29, 72).

14 'nous n'avons rien à lui demander, il nous a donné tout ce qu'il nous faut' (*Romans et Contes*, 178).

15 'Qu'importe . . . qu'il y ait du mal ou du bien? Quand Sa Hautesse envoie un vaisseau en Egypte, s'embarrasse-t-elle si les souris qui sont dans le vaisseau sont à leur aise ou non?' (ibid., 220).

16 'Notre religion . . . a été gravée dans nos coeurs par Dieu même, . . . qui a dit au Chinois, à l'Indien, au Tartare, et à nous: Adore-moi et sois juste' (vol. 27, 55–6).

17 'Ces gens-là, pourtant, avouaient que les tailleurs leur

faisaient des habits pour les vêtir, et les maçons des maisons pour les loger; et ils osaient nier à la nature, au grand Etre, à l'intelligence universelle, ce qu'ils accordaient tous à leurs moindres ouvriers' (ibid., 138).

18 'qui a tout fait, et qui a donné à chaque élément, à chaque espèce, à chaque genre, sa forme, sa place, et ses fonctions éternelles' (ibid., 141).

19 'Plus je réfléchis sur le mal qui inonde la terre, et plus je retombe dans ma triste ignorance' (*Correspondence*, vol. 29, 67).

20 'Je veux que mon procureur, mon tailleur, mes valets, ma femme même, croient en Dieu; et je m'imagine que j'en serai moins volé et moins cocu' (vol. 27, 399–400).

21 'Si Dieu n'existait pas, il faudrait l'inventer' (*Epitre à l'auteur des trois imposteurs*, vol. 10, 403).

22 *Voltaire* (London, 1969), 223. Besterman's book contains a vast amount of valuable information, but the author's judgements sometimes need to be viewed with caution.

23 'Un Anglais, comme homme libre, va au ciel par le chemin qui lui plaît': *Lettres Philosophiques*, ed. F.A. Taylor (Oxford, 1956), 14.

24 'un secret infaillible pour empêcher la terre de trembler' (*Romans et Contes*, 149).

25 *Voltaire*, 398.

26 'toute religion dont les dogmes offensent la morale est certainement fausse' (vol. 24, 439).

27 'choses puériles et odieuses' (ibid., 450).

28 'Y a-t-il rien de si respectable qu'un ancien abus?' (*Romans et Contes*, 30).

29 'dans ce pays-ci il est bon de tuer de temps en temps un amiral pour encourager les autres' (ibid., 199).

30 'plus il y a de malheurs particuliers, et plus tout est bien' (ibid., 146).

31 'la meilleure des baronnes possibles' (ibid., 138).

9

I.D. LLOYD-JONES

Charles Fourier: Faithful Pupil of the Enlightenment

The usual categorisation of Fourier is that which Marx and Engels formulated to distance themselves from the preceding generation of social theorists in France: an Utopian socialist. Together with what is known about his maverick career and obsessive personal characteristics, this has confirmed his position amongst the more extravagant figures of Romanticism. So he certainly appears to be the joker in a pack of Enlightenment thinkers. But it is an enlightening corrective for us to consider the debts he owed (and acknowledged) to central aspects of the Enlightenment.

An exposition of his theory is a way of illustrating and assessing the effects of that élitist movement on popular culture. We shall see an ordinary educated bourgeois trying to assimilate the mass of empirical scientific discoveries of his time into a framework which, while originally orthodox in its logical premises, becomes more and more extravagantly imaginative until it provides a paradigm of romantic speculation. The principles of his analysis are typical of Enlightenment methodology, but his discursive style overlays these with details of contemporary scientific controversy and speculation which he held could be shown to prove his premises by their overall coherence, once interpreted according to the correct criteria.

The first educational influence on Fourier – his mother – was, typically, not an example of enlightenment; being devout and puritanical. But we can see Fourier as personally influenced by Enlightenment attitudes in his commitment to self-culture, in preference to the concentration on worldly wealth (gained by commercial specialisation and speculation) that was in fact his patrimony. Both parents came from prominent commercial families in Besançon. In this thriving market for the prosperous independent peasantry of the Franche Comté, the local college was run by secular priests who emphasised the traditional culture of rhetoric, Latin and theology. The evidence of these three disciplines remained strong in all his writings. Theology provided the Deistic basis as well as the telos of his argument. Latin culture furnished many traditional examples and tropes for his rhetoric. This self-conscious attempt to be attractive and persuasive to different types of readership still gives his writing a compelling charm, despite the problems his eclecticism today presents to someone not a specialist in the thought and arguments of his times. More centrally though, the traditional discipline of rhetoric has always been aware of the mechanism of metaphor whereby Man's creative understanding advances analogically. This logical insight underpins the whole of Fourier's construction of a synthesis of the particular sciences engendered by the Enlightenment: and our invocation of the hypotheses of his predecessors and contemporaries shows the place that metaphor has in reaching towards explanations of novel phenomena.

But it was his mathematical aptitudes that led him to aim for the military college of engineering at Mezières. Not being an aristocrat, however, thwarted his chances of military promotion, so he used his mathematical concepts in the development of his social analysis. He was a cousin of the distinguished mathematician J.B.J. Fourier, whose serial principle Charles Fourier tried to use to articulate the basic concept of movement that informs his entire theory. But his idiosyncratic use of scientific and technical terms reminds us that, like many creative thinkers, he needed always to adapt these as his theory developed encyclopedically. He was as sophisticated as Rousseau or Bentham in recognising that his new view of science required its own set of terms. 'Does not a new science have the right to make use of a few new words . . .? Many subalternate occupations have their own unmethodical collections of technical terms . . . My terminology will be adapted to that which is already accepted in the precise sciences.'[1]

Like Rousseau, he had the single-mindedness and imagination to use the skills of an ordinary education for an extraordinary creativity of vision and design. Or one might compare him with his own contemporary, Restif de la Bretonne, the erotic novelist. They share obsessions, and some similarities of style. But whereas the self-styled 'perverted peasant' indulged in an imaginative orgy of softly pornographic adventures in the new world of urban artisans, Fourier made his critique of the hypocrisy of bourgeois sexual mores and corrupt commercial practices (which he sees as causally connected) the springboard for a whole theory of historical change and ecological relationships. The outcome of that meditation of a free mind upon the knowledge made available not in institutions such as Academies but in bookshops and libraries, was his very characteristically Enlightenment faith in his own encyclopedic theory of social relationships. This theory was also a science for him, because – besides being comprehensively systematic – it arose from the demands of real, felt, needs. It was illustrated by everyday experiences and would be proved by its practical results: in the community life of his proposed 'phalansteries'.[2]

The two cardinal principles of his scientific system were faith in the Deist maxim that the world of nature must be coherent, and the praxis of the Cartesian notion of absolute doubt.[3] These two principles may seem hard to reconcile logically. But the optimism of the first is probably a necessary condition for the practice of the critical scepticism of the second. Fourier was clear that it was through the suspension of belief, while an hypothesis is tested, that enlightenment had been spread. The expansion of this scientific method had only been limited by the fearful pessimism of the authorities – religious and philosophical – who had not the faith to allow this inquisitive activity into every aspect of customs, habits and beliefs. Fourier's main criticism of philosophy – and he was consistently scornful of most of its practitioners, whom he characterised as sophists – was that this refusal to practice what it preached showed its continued subservience to the double standards, or hypocrisy, of institutionalised religion.[4] Consequently 'civilised' societies were still ruled by superstitions and prejudices that acted as a binding force, obscuring the pure demands of nature, which reflected God's creative harmony. Fourier's writings were both a detailed exposé of the shortcomings of the practices of philosophers in relation to social theory, and a demonstration of how this perverted world could be subverted and inverted to release the psychological and cosmological energies which create an harmonious, universal system.

In attempting to understand his synthesis of contemporary ideas, cleansed from these philosophical and religious misperceptions, we will see which scientific ideas were popular at the time; the fruits of enlightened speculation. Thus William Herschel's great advances in astronomy, and Charles Cuvier's disputes with Hutton in palaeontology and his demonstration of comparative anatomy had caught the imagination of the public in the first decade of the nineteenth Century. Cuvier's laws on the subordination of organs and the correlation of forms, and his dispute with Geoffrey Saint-Hilaire as to whether there is a general law to describe a unity of organic compositions, were topical questions in the learned journals. It seemed to Fourier as though the mystery of the physical origin and development of the universe would be solved by the developments of scientists in his century. Consequently, he argued, it had become as fashionable to enunciate one's own cosmological theory as formerly, during the Revolution, it had been obligatory to construct one's own constitution![5]

Fourier was a great admirer of F.W. Herschel, whose theories contained many ideas very amenable to his own system. Thus Herschel's discovery that the orbits of planets were circular while those of comets were parabolic, seemed to re-inforce the Keplerian theory to which Fourier was so indebted for the general analogy between the forms of movement in the heavens and those within the social sphere. Herschel's discovery of the binary systems was taken by Fourier to support his argument that the composite order was inherent in the universal system. The revelation in 1785 that the nebulae were 'island universes', each one a group or cluster like our galaxy, seemed to illustrate Fourier's belief that the group was the fundamental social unit. The discovery in 1811 that there were thirty-one groups in a transitionary series of nebulae seemed to confirm Fourier's confidence in the numerical significance of thirty-two. So on the principle of analogy, Fourier predicted that two satellites of Uranus remained to be discovered. The success of this prediction was hailed by Fourierists as a verification of his general theory of numerical analogies.

For Fourier, the universe is to be perceived as a 'societas' because man is in fellowship with the creative forces of the universe.[6] The 'socialism' – as it came to be called – of theorists who emphasised the productive consequences of social co-operation, is a practical consequence of this approach. Thus the concept of Association is to be found at the heart of Fourier's theory, in the necessity of God and Man's co-operation in history. Man as a composite being has the power to choose; he has Free Will. In order that man's will may not clash with the Divine purposes, Fourier desires to show how we can co-operate with these forces, which are manifest in the natural world that the sciences of the Enlightenment were revealing, rather than in the 'word' of the Gospels – whose meaning has been obscured by theology. These manifestations of divine energy are observable in the field of social activity as well as the realms of physics. Morality is thus but the application of the laws of movement; and is subject to the same general necessity as natural science.

Since God is just, His activity is not arbitrary and obeys the principles of economy. Mathematics thus describes, even if it does not explain, the universal tendencies of will or force observable throughout the creation. Man is the lowest in the scale of harmonic creatures, those who are marked by the possession of freedom to choose between possible ends. He is thus also an example of the cosmic mathematical laws of the Contact of Extremes, and of the significance of the Infinitesimal, in that the Divine inheres in the individual and man associates with God as well as other men.[7]

In Fourier, the Enlightenment goal of a society that is balanced and static (once it is peopled by rational human beings) is transformed into one of imaginative, progressive creatures, thanks to the workings of a mathematical system, Pythagorean in its assurance of justice. The 'serial law' was supposed to express how the passional calculus of individual needs and desires can be seen to be related to an increasingly complex and sophisticated set of social situations, tabulated by Fourier both historically and futurologically. But the sophisticated criteria he developed to distinguish societies from one another remind one that the Enlightenment had already investigated the significance of demography, productivity and cultural factors in this respect.

Fourier makes distinctions between societies, derived from the way the twin needs to produce and re-produce are institutionally related to one another. Thus in the patriarchal stage of societies, the family unit is the nexus of both economic and sexual relations.[8] The coherence of needs makes for a stability which ensures a degree of happiness. This synthesis breaks down when the dialectic between society and nature leads to a new form of economy: commercial civilisation. Here economic developments reflect the involvement of the passions, but these become perverted because their free interaction with the environment is prevented by the tyrannical hold of the previous ideology, whereby the monogamous sexual mores of the previous period are retained. The unhappiness and friction generated by his disharmony makes sexual habits and desires a pivotal feature of the present social system. So Fourier's emphasis on the permissive, innovative and serial character of sex in the phalanstery is seen to be a perfectly 'scientific' appreciation of one of the ways to move towards a new set of social structures.

These possible combinations of productive and re-productive activities are generally arranged by Fourier in a serial form, according to the amount of happiness possible in each – sometimes measured by the degree of independence of women.[9] Here again one sees not only the Utilitarian concept of quantifying (or at least correlating) a quality such as happiness, but also the emergence of the grand design of providence in the guise of progress. But, while very aware of progress as a manifestation of the change and

movement inherent in human nature and the universe, Fourier is
critical of the theory of the inevitability, irreversibility and
unlimited attributes of progress, such as is associated with
Condorcet. Also, unlike Enlightenment figures in France particularly, he does not see historical periods and progress as
primarily distinguished in terms of political ideologies. Here
Saint-Simon is more characteristic of the French tradition. But
Fourier does recognise that the modes in which we enjoy happiness are conditioned by the ideology through which our education
and religion confine our passions. Hence the freedom to imagine
and experiment with new relationships is the real road to the
extension of happiness. Like Rousseau, he recognises that language is the first of the social relations, the first link in the 'vast
chain of unities'. If we cannot perceive and express ourselves
correctly, if we cannot settle even the alphabet of a natural logic,
we cannot hope for a true science. Like most Enlightenment
theorists Fourier uses the association of ideas as the basic
explanation of how we extend the frontier of experience. But, we
shall see, he extends this cognitive technique into the metaphysical realms by means of analogical connections.

In the '*Social Contract*', Rousseau had emphasised that association is more than aggregation because it is an agreement of wills.
Saint-Simon expresses the development of this concept of a
'general' will:

> Society, is not at all a simple conglomeration of living beings
> whose activities have no other cause but the arbitrariness of
> individual wills . . . It is above all a veritable organized
> machine, all of whose parts contribute in a different way to
> the movement of the whole; . . . a veritable being . . .
> according to whether its organs acquit themselves more or
> less regularly of the functions entrusted to them.

The idea that society is in this way an organism created by the
willing subordination and co-operation of parts for a defined end,
was a characteristic borrowing from such late eighteenth-century
naturalists as Cuvier and Saint-Hilaire.

This notion of a functional system is expressed by Fourier in
his basic, pseudo-Newtonian, formula: 'Attractions proportionate
to Destinies'. The Destinies are the present, past and future
outcomes of God's mathematical laws operating on the principle
of universal movement. This law is equated with the sidereal
harmony. But Fourier claimed an advance on the Newtonians.

> They explained nothing about the causes of the distribution,
> distance and conjugations of the stars. They have only
> described a harmony of effects. They have ignored those

causes of distribution regulated by aromal affinity, from which is born a counter-equilibrium in direct and inverse proportions.[10]

Fourier's 'aromal' theory will be discussed later. Here we note that the serial law (by which all things are distributed functionally) is conceived as a form of movement. This law explains the behaviour of the macrocosmos and is evident in each of us in the operation of our *distributive passions*. These are the psychological mechanisms which, according to Fourier's analysis of human nature, regulate our instincts. They are the three propensities for intrigue, alternation and composition through which a will to enjoy the other nine basic passions is expressed in a succession of acts that can be analysed as a serial pattern.

All science is thus derived from a sort of comparative psychology. The science of Passional Attraction is the 'romantic' science because it recognises that God is love and that this is the key to an understanding of Cause and Destiny. Fourier calls the principle of Attraction – 'God in Action'; the guide and motor of the universe. In a myriad of examples in his works he was always trying to show the mechanics of this universal phenomenon. 'I every day discover new beauties, and everything in it leads wonderfully to unity of system', he wrote in 1817. 'I can now say that the science was but an embryo when I published the Prospectus.' He was thus unwilling to let contemporaries judge his scientific and cosmological ideas on their first expression in the 'Four Movements' of 1808. His continual attempts to concretise this universal theory makes a study of his general science difficult; but at the same time it is essential to attempt to grasp his primitive attempt at a logic that is proved by such a synthesis.

The encyclopedic details of Fourier's theory are supposed to relate in an 'holistic' way, so that ultimately man's relationship to the natural world has to be seen as dialectical. Various ecological transformations are envisaged in his earliest work, as expressions of his 'Theory of Four Movements and General Destiny'. These effects are also sketched in the more specific 'political economy' of his 'Treatise on Homesteading Agricultural Associations' of 1822. Throughout the 'New Industrious and Associative World' of 1829 runs the theme of universal unity, or indivisibility of practical schemes from the ultimate concepts of science which give meaning to them, by establishing the correct relationships or proportions between all things. This unity expresses God's plenitude of creation. Understanding of the means by which it is achieved results in the development of an harmonious – in the original musical sense – era which will develop all potential relationships.

But then the analogy of the life cycle indicates that exhaustion will set in, so that the serial movement of the cosmos leads to a disintegrative phase again.[11]

The implicit but pervasive pantheism of Fourier's cosmological dimension may seem to distance him from more sober Enlightenment analysts. But they almost all accepted, *a priori*, the goodness and coherence of God's activity. Fourier's recognition that the doors of perception can only be opened by freeing educational and religious teaching of all prejudice aligns him with such an Enlightenment radical as L.S. Mercier, who advocated a bonfire of books and hence the reprobation of all authorities. Instead of received wisdom, Fourier – again like Mercier in his 'Picture of Paris' – builds up his new view of the world by enumerating and relating a thousand details of everyday experience. He actually credits Bacon with this alternatively analytic and synthetic methodology that he came to call the serial law. Empirical data are seen – by commonsense – to arrange themselves thus.

Such respect for the practical experience that constitutes commonsense marks the immediate aim and endeavour of the '*Encyclopedia*' and is, of course, also characteristic of that branch of Enlightenment theory that Bentham concerned himself with, particularly in his penological works. Utilitarianism generally is the philosophically abstract formulation of the view that values cannot be ranked according to same A PRIORI criterion, other than the equal validity of everyone's search for pleasure or happiness. Given this undogmatic tolerance, practical proofs become centrally important to an argument's persuasiveness. So Bentham's *Panopticon* and Fourier's *Phalanstery* are to be the working proofs of how efficient and rational are the arguments of their authors. The reason why Newton – in Fourier's argument, as in that of other Enlightenment social theorists – symbolises the highest achievement, is because he not only related the manifold data of science in simple and coherent laws, but also thereby enabled the great practical transformation of the material world that seemed to justify the optimism of Enlightenment theorists. What have been described as the agricultural, industrial and political revolutions were made possible by science. They were the necessary conditions for the free, creative artistry that nineteenth-century poets, philosophers and statesmen saw as the genius of the modern era. Fourier's life and career intersected with all these 'revolutionary' experiences. They provided the materials for him to express the new form of creative artistry – a scientific imagination – in articulating a 'newfoundland' in his extrapolation of the 'Harmonious' era of history. He did not characterise this as Utopian, but as a scientific hypothesis.

Utopianism, in the sense of the depiction of a possible set of human relationships derived from an actual theory of human nature, was central to the methodology of Enlightenment social theorists. Morelly derived 'garden cities' from his 'Code of Nature', and Mably, Volnay and Restif de la Bretonne all composed what L.G. Crocker has termed 'non-primitivist Utopias'.[12] But whereas Rousseau's critique of the origin of inequality led him merely to posit the imperative of a revolutionary expression of the new social contract, derived from the basic instincts of uncorrupted nature (as recovered by the critical analysis of reason), these more optimistic – and perhaps more simplistic theorists – were prepared to deduce their social plans from psychological absolutes. It was not the notion of psychological absolutes, but the simplistic concept of them that made Fourier apply the term Utopian to these theorists, in almost as derogatory a way as Marx and Engels subsequently did to him. Utopia he defined as 'the dream of social harmony in a fabulous land'. When he attacks tentative contemporary agricultural reform experiments, or the belief in violent revolution as a panacea, he stigmatises them as Utopian. It is not because they are visionary that they are criticised; but because they are only partially developed fragments of what should be a complete attitude to life and a coherent plan of campaign. Their unsophisticated and unscientific nature means that Utopias in general are characterised by the vice of rationalistic simplification.[13]

This simplistic method is the original sin of philosophy, the cause of intellectual blindness. It leads to logical absurdities, 'Simplistic action, without counterweights operates against itself.'[14] It arises from a misunderstanding of the complex nature of the mechanism of things. Its application by philosophers and theologians to the study of man and society is exemplified in Utopian literature. But society's endemic need to fabricate such visions is itself a result of treating simplistically what is complex. Because the present social system is unable to embody the virtues which man's nature demands, such imaginative creations are needed to help clarify the conditions of social good. They are abstracted models depicting what is lacking – but as simplistic as the realities they criticise or satirise. Of course, Fourier's Phalanstery, depicted in such vivid detail, seems just such a model, though this community's exemplification of the calculus of the passions is by no means abstract or simple. He, therefore, claims it is scientific, being the result of a methodologically coherent and comprehensive analysis of the springs of all action and all potential outcomes.

Fourier's criticism of previous Utopias is directed mainly against Fénélon, for his arbitrary regulations, deduced from an unscientific psychology and ethics. Fourier argued that this Utopia had been tried in 1789 and found wanting. Delille's contemporary rural idylls are also scornfully castigated – chiefly for their author's false view of the principles upon which the universe is grounded; but also for the disordered picture that results; and it is characterised as poetic licence.[15] These criticisms illumine the main issues of Fourier's science: a sociology deduced from a scientific psychology, and tied by broad ethical and methodological principles to the nature of the universe.

Like most Enlightenment theorists, Fourier's psychological theory is supposed to provide the key that unlocks the mechanism whereby the desired reconstruction of society can be achieved. His conception of 'passions' seems to derive directly from de Jaucourt's definition in the *Encyclopedia*. The twelve basic desires are the elements that combine or compete to form the various depictions of that 'vortex of the passions' that motivates all societies, whether historical or futuristic. This psychological categorisation derives from Descartes' reformation of the medieval humours. He had spoken of 'passion' as the union of body and soul which gives rise to action. Similarly, Fourier regards the passions as composite, and as the prime sources of activity. Rousseau had distinguished between the sensual and the spiritual or intellectual; Fourier between the sensual, the social, and what were originally described as the 'mechanisers' and were later called the 'Distributors'. This threefold distinction between groups of passions comprises the prime series that everyone experiences. Condillac's view that, through the manipulation of these drives, a range of human types may be created is echoed in Fourier's insistence that in operating this series in a 'controlled' situation – the Phalanstery – new social relationships and consequently new types of personality will develop. His emphasis is on the creative freedom which understanding of these drives, and of the serial mechanism for developing them, gives to every individual in the phalanstery. In this fundamental emphasis he is nearer to the Rousseauist quest for individual self-fulfilment than to the detailed determinism of such as D'Holbach – or the modern Utopia of B.F. Skinner's '*Walden Two*'.

The material world, for Fourier, is experienced through the four sensitive passions. These sensations are co-ordinated by affective passions, which lead us to enjoy them in various forms of social relationship, so that an individual's composite nature can only be expressed through belonging to a series of groups. These are the sexual, familial, friendly, and emulative situations (where ambition and competition are expressed). Friendship and ambition were the dominants among men. But among women it is love and family feeling that predominates. Each of these affective passions, being composite, consists of a material and spiritual component. Ambition, for example, finds fullest expression and satisfaction among the groups in which people are joined together by material considerations of interest and spiritual considerations of glory.

Ambition has been regarded as one of the prime expressions of personality at least since Hobbes. Helvetius – whose views where now acceptable to society, Fourier noted – had particularly emphasised the power of this passion; Glory, as he called it. In spite of this, Fourier argued, the philosophers with their republican ideal of equality, had tried to suppress 'this most redoubtable of all the passions'. So its expression in our society is characterised by hate, and its repression produces, in the political field, Jacobinism. It is impossible to ignore such cardinal passions. Thwarted, they find a dangerous and vicious outlet. Thus in contemporary society Ambition disrupts the family, which is the fundamental sexual group of contemporary social organisation. This demonstrates the duplicity of our conventions. They are only the perverted expression of the ontological principle of duality or compositeness.

The dialectic between the group tendencies on the one hand and the *distributives* faculties on the other, leads to an almost infinitely variable number of possible expressions of individual personality. Only almost, however; since as these twelve motivations are found in everyone (each with their own genetic dispositions towards a particular grading of them), it is mathematically possible to organise a calculus. This will both reflect the Divine principle that God and Nature create nothing in vain, and express the potentialities for humanly constructing humane spaces in which freedom will be enjoyed; the phalansteries. In these communities individuals, spontaneously forming groups, interact with the material and social worlds, thereby creating new types of personality and new configurations between man and the universe. Thus Fourier opens up almost unlimited vistas of potential pleasure. Groups are created, grow, diminish and disappear in a kaleidoscopic expression of social needs and desires and opportunities.

Instead of the traditional concept of reason as the regulator of our desires, Fourier (reflecting Rousseau again in his suspicion of a reasoning faculty corrupted by its thrall to convention and power), discerns a natural balancer at work in the psyche, in what he calls the 'distributive' impulsions. A set of natural instincts in everyone ensures the changeability and re-grouping of relationships once an individual is temporarily satiated or satisfied by a particular combination of his needs. The popular novelist Bernadin de Saint-Pierre is criticised for not seeing that these distributors lead to inspiration and joy; joys transcendent and joys most earthy. They are the 'organic springs'; 'in truth the lawgivers of harmony'. Through them the principles of justice are made manifest.

The purpose of the serial technique is to ensure a just distribution of whatever matter it organises. As instruments of this operation the distributive or 'mechanizer or neuter passions are the *CAUSES* that form the passional series,[16] (Here Fourier echoes Rousseau's characterisation of 'the power to judge' as an ultimate cause.) These three distributive operations may be compared with the basic principles of resemblance, contiguity and causation of which Hume said, 'they are to us the cement of the universe'.

'Attraction between passions is the impulsion nature gives anterior to reflexion and it persists despite the opposition of reason, duty, prejudice etc.'[17] The essential pattern of the passions – as distinct from accidental variations in terms of the degrees of strength of each – is to be found in all people at all times. A conceptual grasp of this calculus will banish from our studies 'vagueness, or sophistry, and enable all knowledge to be related on an unified basis'. Thus if Fourier does not say that reason is the slave of the passions, he tacitly agrees with Hume that this most complex faculty of man has developed in order to register and collate the degrees of passion, and hence express the decrees of 'the serial law'. Like Pascal, he shows that 'the heart has its reasons, which reason knows not of': because philosophical rationalism is too simplistic in the sources that it takes into consideration. It follows that our perceptions ought to create our conceptions, rather than the latter constraining the former – as in the world ruled by philosophical and religious institutions.

'Matter may not improperly be said to be the image of our minds', said Malebranche, developing the logic of Cartesian dualism. For Fourier, matter is passive, until informed by the 'motor principle' of God or spirit: and 'justice or mathematics' provides the 'regulative principle for movement'. Like Descartes, he believed that a coherent system of knowledge was beyond the reach of the atheist. But Fourier also argued that understanding of God's purposes was impossible without the technique of analogy. The analogical relation arises from the Distributive faculty's processes of comparison, differentiation and composition.

Thus analogy is the 'link that unifies the universe', the pivot of the 'four coherent sciences'. It is through comparison of our basic experiences that we test the truths of hypotheses and eventually recognise the wider correspondences that lead to a conviction of truth: a conviction subsequently tested by practical experimentation.

'The study of analogy must proceed, like algebra, by a chain of reason and by comparisons.'[18] The calculus of analogy, suggested Fourier, reveals new fields for the physiologists and could give direction to the studies of the naturalists. This sense of direction and of interconnection is what distinguishes a positive science from 'scientific illusions'. Here Fourier (like the St Simonists and Comte), is implying that synthetic, conceptual methods of science mark the 'Organic' phases of history, in contrast to the emphasis on analytical, empirical and inductive methods of the 'Critical' period in which the Enlightenment had flourished.

Thanks to the Composite passion, extremes meet; so that there exists – as Wordsworth put it – 'another and finer connection than that of contrast. It is a connection formed through the subtle process by which, both in the natural and the moral world, qualities pass insensibly into their contraries, and things revolve upon each other'. This is the connection by correspondence or analogy. The imaginative characteristic of this process is illustrated, according to Fourier, by the recognition that dreams can 'in certain cases initiate man into the sensual faculties of other worldly beings, according to the laws of extremes and of diffraction . . .'.[19] Normally, however, our attractions are given coherence by the serial patterns activated by the Distributors, 'the distinct powers whose function it is to control, determine and modify the phantasmal chaos of association'. Thus Fourier 'shows the *nature* of the universal link' between the intuitive passions, or unconscious will, and the rational process of willing through conceptualisation and policy. The ability to strike analogies, and so link the world into new and creative patterns, is peculiarly the mark of genius. One is reminded of Coleridge's description of the poet. 'The primary imagination', he writes, 'I hold to be the living power and prime agent of all human perception, and as the representation in the finite mind of the eternal act of creation in the infinitive I AM. The secondary I consider as an echo of the former, coexisting with the conscious will . . . It dissolves, defuses, dissipates, in order to re-create . . . it struggles to idealise and to unify. It is essentially vital . . .'.[20]

Our attempt hereafter to describe Fourier's cosmic analogies (and his arguments that these are attributable to a scientifically

evident 'aromal' chemistry), respect his conviction that these are
the marks of his genius, even though others have regarded them
as fantastic speculations akin to science fiction! The Enlightenment developed the model whereby Kepler and Newton had
explained the static equilibrium of the planets. In Fourier's day,
interest was shifting to questions concerning the genesis and
development of the cosmos. The concept of the vortex had
become current again thanks to Laplace's 'nebular hypothesis'.
Laplace emphasised rotation as the cause of development of the
planetary system from an original chaotic substance. Fourier's
basic principle of movement echoes this conception. Laplace's
theory of the continuous creation of planets, Fourier saw as
progressive, 'raising the system from the 3rd to the 4th power',
just as in his own theory the passional vortices are perfected by
the generation of more and more complex combinations of
passions and characters. Apart from this analogy, however, the
cosmological theory is used at first (in the 'Four Movements' of
1808) to give support to the belief in other worlds where souls
may exist.

Justice, in the shape of Leibniz's principle of plenitude,
demands that every individual develop his potentialities to the
full. Since this is clearly not achieved in this world, the Pythagorean and Buddhist notion of the transmigration of the soul, or
metempsychosis, may be the answer. The universal belief in some
sort of immortality is a presumption in its favour, or so Fourier's
notion of common sense indicated. There does seem to be a
tension here with Fourier's general attack on the current concept
of 'compensations'. But there he is attacking what he calls the
doctrine of the sophists; that is, an ideological use of the concept
of immortality to counterbalance actual injustice, and hence the
justification of the constraints of 'civilisation'.

It would seem at first sight that Fourier's 'Phalanstery', were it
ever to be realised perfectly, would dispose of the necessity for
metempsychosis. But apparently the possibilities of development
are endless. The most complete characters in this world are only
at the bottom of the scale of 'harmonic creations'. Their composite expression of 'unificatory' motivations qualify them to graduate to a qualitatively higher series. Thus the idea of metempsychosis – or 'composite immortality' – is called the 'pivot' of the
Harmonious Society. The knowledge of progress, or regress, in
another existence according to one's achievements in this life will
be a powerful incentive to good and industrious behaviour.
Fourier has often been criticised for apparently neglecting incentives in his optimistic theory of attractive labour. In fact, he make

use of one of the oldest and most general of incentives: that occasioned by the hope or fear of what may be 'when we have shuffled off this mortal coil'. But in so doing he does seem to come dangerously close to the sophists of civilisation whose negative simplism he wished to expose.

Other arguments in favour of metempsychosis are provided by the needs of the alternating passions, and by the myths of the more instinctive periods of history. Finally, the Leibnizian arguments for a scale of beings, witnessing to God's plenitude of power and the ultimate unity of creation, clinch these considerations. In an humorous article on the 'Métempsychoses of hares' Fourier's fantasy recalls the idea of 'palingenesis'.[21] This notion of self-sustaining creativity had been given currency by the biologist Charles Bonnet, whose 'Palingénésie philosophique' had been published in 1770. Fourier reviewed approvingly an article by his contemporary, the leading romantic novelist Charles Nodier on resurrection and palingenesis. This theory of the process whereby the variables in a situation continually re-dispose themselves to compose new configurations for development, accords with Fourier's view of social history as an infinite cycle, analogous to the metempsychosis of the individual soul.

There was much dispute at this time about the nature of the basic constituents of physics. In 1789 Rumford had cast doubt on the 'calorific' theory of heat. In 1801 Thomas Young showed the validity of the wave theory of light. It is therefore not surprising that Fourier's ideas in this area are unclear and perhaps contradictory. From the many current scientific theories he was trying to find an explanation of the composition and behaviour of the basic substance of existence. Thus in his first work, primary matter is spoken of in terms of 'atoms'. But even in the 'Four Movements', Fourier had noted that light is decomposed into twelve rays, seven visible (like the seven pronounced notes of the musical octave) and five invisible. In this way he tried to account for the 'X-rays' discovered by Herschel in 1800. By 1822 Fourier designates the field of the physicists the 'aromal kingdom'.

Newton had written of 'the highly subtle spirit which pervades crass bodies . . . by whose force the particles of bodies attract each other . . . and cohere, electrical bodies act, . . . light is emitted, reflected, refracted, inflected, and sensation is excited as the limbs of animals are moved at will by vibrations in this spirit . . .'. Fourier calls this medium through which the great chain of being is effected, and connection established between the earth and the rest of the universe, the 'aromal' fluid.

The 'aromal movement's' significance in his system is apparent from this definition: it is the 'system by which known and unknown aromas are distributed, directing man and the animal kingdom and forming the germs of outbreaks and epidemics, registering the sexual relationships between the stars and furnishing the germs of all the species in creation'.[22] It was in 1814 that he added this 'movement' to the original four: the social or passional, animal or instinctual, organic and material. In that year he copied a description of atoms from '*Le Moniteur*'. The hypothesis that matter is formed as a result of pressures, may thus have provided the clue that enabled him to claim that in this year he discovered the 'general scale of creation', a compass for his cosmogonical calculations, and the 'verifying formula'.

In 1807 Young had first applied the term 'energy' to the velocity of a mass, an idea hitherto 'conveyed by the term living or ascending force. The same idea is somewhat more concisely expressed by the term *energy*, which indicates the tendency of a body to ascend or to penetrate to a certain distance in opposition to a retarding force'.[23] Similarly the patterns of Fourier's series are always of ascending and descending vibrations. The mid-term or apogee thus represents the effective force of the series, the result of the expenditure of the energy within it, against that of its immediate environment.

In 'The Grammar of Science', Karl Pearson in 1892 criticised 'that unfortunate metaphysical conception *force* . . . not infrequently a fetish which symbolizes more or less mental obscurity'. So if we find it hard to see the connection Fourier makes between his 'aromal' theory and physical notions of force, we should recall that Engels points out that Hegel preferred the term 'soul' to 'force'. At this time the concept of force or energy was still shrouded in anthropomorphic assumptions. Thus Sir John Herschel identified gravitation with will. Throughout the eighteenth century various metaphorical concepts were advanced:– the 'appetitive conatus' of Leibniz's *monads*; *Toland's* pantheism of active energy overcoming all barriers between matter and spirit; Swedenborg's basic substance consisting of points of force or activity in incessant movement, transmuted into substances by the varying pressures that result from this; this 'vortex of vitality' as Cuvier called it;[24] the 'luminiferous ether, rare and elastic' of Young; the 'ether vortex-ring' of Thompson's prime atom'. These are the ancestors of our picture of the molecular basis of physics.

Swedenborg's explanation of chemical affinity as due to pressure resulting from an increase in the amount of movement, which at a certain point produces a qualitative change, was an hypothesis commonly accepted by both astronomers and chemists. Fourier – who admired his contemporary Philippe Lebon's work on the isolation of gases – adopts it. For him it accounts for the apparently discontinuous transmutations in the scale of created beings, and the apparently strange correspondences or influences between different forms of matter. It thus seems to us that his 'Aromal theory' deals with two apparently different things.

On the one hand it is the most extensive of the basic elementary substances. Along with earth, water and air it forms fire. Corresponding to love, and an 'occult' – in the sense of hidden – element, distinct from the material and passional elements, it has properties similar to Hegel's 'chemism'. It is connected with sexual and spiritual relations as well as with meteorological affairs. Investigations in this field, says Fourier, should be entrusted to physicists and chemists rather than naturalists or geometers. It seemed to him that the synthetic substances created by Chemistry illustrated the potentiality of this substance.

On the other hand it connects with the popular definition of an 'Aroma' – 'a subtle, pervasive quality or charm'. Here it is another sort of essence, as appears in Marx's description of religion as 'the spiritual aroma of the other world'; perhaps this is also the 'aroma' by which a dog knows his master. It thus seems to be the medium through which attraction operates, whether physically as in Newton's gravitational observations or psychologically, as in Fourier's discovery of the 'composite' social dimension of those laws.

When Fourier's analysis of the structure and mode of operation of the 'aromes' is forgotten, a scientific concept – quite plausible when considered in relation to contemporary knowledge – quickly becomes a mysterious 'force'. It must be remembered that Fourier conceives of all being in terms of movement. Thus different substances and forces are basically different patterns of movement.

Fourier's contemporary, the distinguished naturalist Geoffrey Saint-Hilaire thought that the 'unity of composition' upon which he based his classificatory system, was finally to be explained by a similar power emanating from the movements of atoms and elements of unalterable character. These various states of existence may be fundamentally described in terms of movement, since they represent the effects of degrees of force. Although Fourier does not make exactly the same distinction as the Saint-Simonian Buchez between circular, serial and spiritual forces, his description of the spectrum of force also proceeds from an analysis in terms of geometric forms towards a purely functional and moral criterion. As with Turgot, Helvetius and Comte, the 'vicious circle' symbolises a regression from the progressive movement man is destined to create, a falling back to the type of movement characteristic of natural phenomena. Engels' variant is to compare the vicious circle of society to the spiral movements of the planets. We have already noticed the importance for Fourier of the passional vortex as a creative movement, and of the spiral as the shape of the dialectical progression to Indivisibility or Wholeness – that fusion of attractive forces.

Fourier, like Comte, tried to measure the intensity of an activity – mental or physical – by discerning the amount and type of exertion involved. Thus what he calls the 'Powerful Module' is the standard from which the variations in psychological pressure may be calculated. Descending in the series from this, energy in its mixture with other elements takes manifold forms. The statistician Jacques Quetelet (1796–1874) noted how Rousseau had tried to show mathematically the place of political force, in its numerous forms. Fourier's variant of this is to point out that the force of sexual attraction and feminine blandishments operates in inverse proportion to physical force. In religion, faith gives force to intelligence. The passions are forces, to be treated as a problem of dynamics. His concern was to show how the forces within society could be so balanced that their 'influences' would result in justice. The result of the development of individual centres of vitality is the functional unity of society, conceived as a 'brilliant engine'.

In 1826, Fourier noted that 'if everything is connected in the system of the universe, there must exist a means of communicating between creatures of the other world and thus . . . a communication of faculties'.[25] This he regarded as the fundamental argument for the 'animal magnetism' that Gall, the physiologist, was so persuasively demonstrating. At the same time Mesmer described 'animal magnetism' as a continuous fluid, with mutual influence upon the earth, animate and heavenly bodies. Its properties were similar to those of the magnet; it had an alternating rhythm, and the capacity to be intensified and reflected like the waves of light and sound. Quetelet calls animal magnetism an 'imponderable fluid'; Fourier calls the aroma a 'magnetic fluid'. The similarity of his concept to Mesmer's is clinched when he adds that people in a hypnotic state can actually see the 'aromal ribbons'.

Fourier asserted that through this force God is able to direct the spiritual sphere – that of the passions and society – as well as the material components of the universe. Without it God could not be 'one and indivisible'. A force similar to this forms the continuum whereby in the psychological field the dichotomy between mind and body, is overcome. The individual becomes absorbed in the primary activity of this electro-magnetic force in proportion to his capacity for personal activity; activity that makes fullest use of the physiological and environmental circumstances. Thus an intense involvement both in specialised activities and over a series of activities, marks the most progressive human beings.

Fourier criticised Chateaubriand for having in his '*Martyrs*' (1809) restricted the power of vision into ultimate Causes to the dead. Apart from his own claims, Rousseau, Napoleon and Caesar possessed such capacities in differing measures. So of course, did prophetic figures such as Christ, St Augustine, and Muhammad – who had succeeded because of his energy or fanaticism. It is this strenuous involvement in particularities that enables heroic types to achieve the synthesis – whether in thought or action – that leads to qualitatively new possibilities. Fourier also emphasises the role of chance – the opposite extreme to speciality, and thus joined according to the Law of the 'contact of extremes' – in revealing occult qualities. Thus coffee, quinine and mercury have been found, by chance, to possess undreamed of qualities!

The series by which the Aromal connection with other worlds is made, begins at the level of touch. The water-diviner is affected by the Aroma from the spring. The series ascends via extremely sensitive social personalities, to the 'transmondains'. They are compounded of aromal substances and the ether – 'the subtle and superior aspect of our atmosphere'. Finally, the Ultra-mondaine, demonstrates that – as religion teaches – the quality of the 'resurrected body will be steadiness, clarity, agility and subtlety'.

The vagueness of scientific hypotheses concerning creation and evolution in his own day gave Fourier great scope to lose himself in 'the brilliancy of his imagination', as the American Fourierist Brisbane realised.[26] Fourier was quite aware that what he called the 'colossal and romantic' sections of his work laid him open to satire, giving grounds for complaints that his science was only a fairy-tale, or an abstruse vision in which the main points were submerged in the fantastic accessories. In his attempt to develop the 'scientific' concept of an 'aromal fluid' Fourier tried to provide a material explanation of the imaginative or psychological faculty for making analogies. It was not that this supreme logical – or metaphorical – faculty should be reduced to such an explanation. But his theory of the composite or binary nature of everything implied such an alternative explanation. It is poetic justice that in trying to elaborate a theory of aromes he should have particularly relied on the wildest analogies!

But in his own view these sections established his claim to have 'invented' a new and ultimate science, 'romantic' in that it linked the personal and particular to the universal by means of the composite experiences of eros and agape. Cosmology was the 'most romantic and most interesting' part of his theory because Causes are regulated by aromal affinities. But if this cosmogonical theory becomes a stumbling block, rather than a help, to the understanding of the societal condition, (in affinity with which Nature had distributed all attractions), Fourier was prepared to say that it might be tacitly ignored. This, however, was rhetorical tactics, not a scientific reformulation. He did not thereby renounce his 'cosmogony'.

All science demands initiation before it can be fully understood. Fourier wanted to encourage people to graduate to the necessarily esoteric core by means of the immediately beguiling examples and stories he provided. These are 'emblems of our passions' and preferable to the sophists' 'analogical frivolities entitled the Language of Flowers'.[27] Thus Fourier envisages a telegraphy as the unitary, harmonic language enabling communication between the stars, thanks to the pivotal position of Mercury as a reflector of radio waves, and the existence of the 'aromal shell', as a sort of 'Heavyside Layer' between air and ether. Today this seems comparatively mild science fiction and, like so much science fiction, a vivid pre-figuring of subsequent developments. But the new creations he imagined, such as the 'anti-lion', and the seas 'of a substance like lemonade', are still dismissed as ludicrous by analysts of Fourier's social theory. They were never intended to be other than fabulous. 'We can leave it to the literary small fry to solemnly quibble over these phantasies', as Engels suggested, and concentrate on the 'grand thoughts and germs'.

Creation is defined as a 'work of general intervention for all planets, each according to its entitlement'. The American Fourierist Silberling quotes Lamarck as asserting that 'nature carries out certain direct and significant creations at the beginning of each of the kingdoms of living beings'.[28] Cabanis, the popular contemporary medical theorist, described how nature 'every day starts to form again the first sketches of an organization, which we call "spontaneous generations" '. Lamarck thought that these 'infusions' or 'Monads' might reveal the nature of force. The mathematical analogy of the music of the spheres describes Fourier's idea of the cause of creations. The 'redoubled octave' – i.e. thirty-two units of the planetary system – shows that every star exudes one of the thirty-two types of aroma responsible for all creations. The different varieties of fruit, for example, result from the differing proportions of combinations of these thirty-two basic substances in its composition. The cherry is a product of the masculine aroma from the North Pole and the feminine from the South. But there are many gaps in the scale of creation because of the inability of the earth in its present state to nourish the germs received from other planets.

The idea of the 'germ' – both intellectual and physical – is important in Fourier's theory. The analogy is with the 'seeds' of Hippocrates, (whom Fourier thought had foreshadowed Linneus's sexual system of classification). Fourier speaks of the germs of stars as scattered in the Milky Way and developing under certain conditions – certain pressures, according to Swedenborg – into comets which may eventually be attracted into a planetary system or vortex. In the same way, in history and sociology germs await favourable conditions to develop and find their appointed places. Fourier's contemporary Charles Babbage, inventor of the calculating machine, insisted creation is not an arbitrary act of God, but the operation of a mathematical law whose principles we have not yet grasped. Similarly, in Fourier's theory, God limits himself to the just principles of mathematics. Apparent miracles are thus examples of the working of what Fourier calls the Law of Exceptions.

If creation results from a synthesis – or 'fusion' as both Fourier and Faraday described it – at a certain degree of association, it requires a convenient environment to develop these germs by 'rumination and investigation'. Jenner, as Fourier saw, had demonstrated the possibilities of immunisation. Similarly the task of sociology is to transform germs of malady into germs of vigour. A mild dose of some undesirable social state might be a useful prophylactic; though in general Fourier thought it safer to stifle all such germs. Subversive creations or destructive 'investigations' are the result of man's misuse of good materials. This may be due either to simplistic ignorance of what the time and conditions demand, or to man's wilfulness, his refusal to co-operate in the harmonic process with God.

In biblical language the Flood is a consequence of man's disobedience. It is also, according to Fourier, an inevitable phase in the natural development of every astral body. As usual he tries to reconcile free will and an overall determinism. The flood, in our case, was caused by the aromal confusion resulting from the death of the moon. But the moon's 'death' followed man's departure from the 'harmonic' state of Eden, and thus may be attributable to man's will. The lacunae in the aromal scale caused by the absence of the moon's aromes led to very imperfect creations on earth in the period following the flood. Amongst such were the wolf and the lion. The recent appearance of Vesta, as a replacement of the dead moon, is one of the indications that a new creative period is imminent. In this Harmony the earth will 'conjugate' with additional moons – Mercury, Ceres, Juno and Pellas. One of the products of the new phase of 'replenishing creations' thus indicated may be the 'anti-lion'.[29]

Fourier was very interested in the controversy between Cuvier and Hutton as to whether geological history was a series of catastrophes or a more uniform development. The theory of 'replenishing creations' – basic structural and elemental changes at certain points in the life cycle of a planet – seems to favour the catastrophic theory. There have been two such creative periods since the Flood. These periods must not be confused with the normal reproductive cycle. The Flood is an example of catastrophic change; and Fourier held that the entrance of a new planet into our cosmological vortex could upset the 'natural' succession of social periods. Thus catastrophes may be of great importance in altering the direction of movement or progress. But their infrequency indicates that, like other manifestations of Chance, they are subject to the Law of Exceptions.[30]

At the level of historical and sociological phenomena Fourier's views are analogous to the evolutionary theory. He says that useful creations may be conserved from one epoch to the next. Apart from this, within the historical time-scale the creative possibilities are limited by the 'furniture' of each epoch of creation. Fourier thus agrees that adaptation, or evolution, occurs through the preservation of chance beneficial variations. The serial organisation of all types of movement allow for all variations to prove their functional value.

Since the thirty-two aromes 'correspond' to the social functions described by the passional calculus at its third power, we may assume that every period within the historical epoch has its dominant function or character determined by the particular aromal proportions of its time.[31] Thus there is indeed a 'materialist' basis to history and it can be read as part of a general science. The distribution of the basic 'materials' of an epoch or era has been determined; but within these aromal limits there is considerable freedom to manoeuvre. 'If one admits that creatures can create like God, employing the germs distributed by Him, they may make mistakes'.[32] But apart from man's participation in the aromal essence of his own planet, and his subsequent power to control to some extent the general movement of the universe through this, the framework of his own existence is definitely set by the conditions created by the aromal or cosmogonical situation.

Meteorology was a branch of science that Fourier felt had been neglected. He was convinced of the influence of human cultivation upon the climate. 'The air is a field open to industrial exploitation quite as much as the earth.'[33] Just as leaves are essential to trees, so healthy individuals are necessary if the globe is to function properly. It should take about 120–130 years to change the climate after the achievement of Harmony; to make good the depredations of civilised society by re–afforestation, and to recapture the warmth, which Arctic fossil remains showed to have been the climate in former times. He suggested that the prize money offered by Britain for the discovery of a North–West passage should be devoted to the foundation of Associations (i.e. phalansteries) – the same result would be achieved. The seas of lemonade – a drink Fourier happened to be partial to – might be the attractive outcome of these climatic changes.

Man's influence on the climate through the aromal fluid is expressed by magnetic variation, according to Fourier's understanding of Malte-Brun, the geographer. Our 'aromal corruption' affects the other heavenly bodies in contact with us – hence the sun-spots of 1785.[34] Because of man's repressed condition there has been a suspension of 'aromal exercises' between earth and the other heavenly bodies. The world is in a state of quarantine. But all planets in their life-phases of puberty and senility – when there are no 'creative replenishments' – pass through this condition of isolation. The danger is that this period will be unduly prolonged by man's blindness or ignorance. The aim of Fourier's Cosmogony is to be the 'medical science' of the planets. A knowledge of geological and cosmological time, or proportion, thus sets the true scale for history and sociology.

The 'grand speculations', as he calls them, of his science have made commentators liken him to the theosophists; and he does appear to have had connections with the important sub-culture of 'illuminés' at Lyons in the post revolutionary period.[35] This raises the question of whether such groups – including the Free Masons who made a cult of the path to enlightenment – can justly be ruled out of a consideration of the fertilising effects of 'the Enlightenment'. The orthodox 'philosophers' attack on the established Church has perhaps led to the unjustified marginalisation of those contemporaries who were more permeated by pietistic and mystical religious attitudes than the rationalistic Deism of the former could tolerate. But should such criteria continue to exclude ideas demonstrably widespread and influential, when we construct the canon of intellectual development?

The survey undertaken here of Fourier's science reveals that his grandiose works are also full of enchanting details, designed specifically to entertain readers. They were aimed especially at women and adolescents, who cannot cope with much abstract theory, but whose sympathetic and imaginative qualities are as essential to social life as the analytical talents of enlightened man. But these episodes serve as illustrations of possibilities (when they are not satirical descriptions of contemporary society's hypocrisy and pretensions), rather than as blue-prints to be authoritatively imposed by the wise or the powerful. They are often cameo novels ('romans' – a reminder of how he envisaged his romantic affinities); and they are in the pastoral style of much eighteenth-century fiction. In his sensitive and humorous depiction of real emotions and social desires in intimate situations (as well as in his consciously fantastic and fabulous examples of futurology), his scientific imagination carries him beyond prosaic social and political scientists into a poetry that we may characterise as romantic. But rather than counter-pose science and poetry, we need to counterpoint the complementary aspects of Enlightenment and Romanticism if we are to fairly reflect Fourier's intentions. One result of what he called this 'composite' approach is to liberate him from the charge upon so many Enlightenment thinkers of developing a determinist sociology, despotically imposed – however benevolently – by philosophers and kings.

Many Enlightenment thinkers appealed to benevolent despots to implement their blueprints, or at least assist in rolling back the clouds of superstition and ignorance blinding society. This political tactic was often in fact the most rational one, and we should not be too quick to criticise it as political naivety. Given the authoritarian institutions of pre-revolutionary Europe, such patronage was essential, as even Voltaire recognised. Fourier's science is marked by a significant lack of detail concerning the politics of implementation. His experiences of the Revolution, Directorate, Empire and subsequent Bourbon monarchy made him wary of committing his schemes to any particular political power group. This pragmatic scepticism echoes the fact that his methodology commits him to a public appeal; the universal individual recognition that his theory is deduced from common sense. The perverted passions of fear, hypocrisy and deceit that characterise the play of politics will be converted to the positive aspects of the 'distributive' apparatus for intrigue, competition, emulation and inspiring leadership for co-operation, in future societies. Then the free expression of the Mathematics of the Divine Law will realise all the potentialities of justice.[36]

Given, however, that the dynamic elements in French society when he published were undoubtedly the commercial capitalists who were starting to emulate the British lead into large-scale manufacturing, his Invitation is not so ridiculous as is sometimes claimed. According to this strategy, a persuasive example of the phalanstery can be brought into immediate existence, characteristically, by that product of commercial civilisation – the millionaire. So long as all Fourier's methodological conditions – or should they be called structural requirements? – are met, his science ensures success. Thus his psychological analysis, his philosophical insistence on absolute freedom of individual choices, and his mathematical syntheses of these *a priori* data into the 'law of the series' must be rigorously observed in the structure of the phalanstery – both architecturally and existentially. When, late in his life, attempts were made to put his theories into practice, he always repudiated them on the grounds that these conditions were not being observed. A partial realisation of an essentially comprehensive theory was not possible.

Subsequently, his followers found in his arguments elements of an alternative strategy, whereby existing institutional 'germs' of co-operation might be developed. These would educate attitudes so that people would accept his radical views on freedom of thought and behaviour – especially sexual – as a pre-condition of success for a community. These two strategies may be seen as exemplifying the tension between the mechanistic and the developmentally organic views of social change that marks the thought of much of the Enlightenment.

Fourier was, indeed, interested in contemporary economic developments – particularly in the extension of the division of labour to agricultural life in order to increase productive efficiency, thereby liberating the peasant from enslavement to his family unit and his plot of property. He saw the attempts of his French contemporaries to establish rural banks, with co-operatives to store and market produce, as the 'germs' of the next phase of historical development.[37]

'Garantisme' (or Social Welfare) – which is the prelude to the apogee of full social harmony – is characterised by the social insurance of individual security. All are able thus to be free from basic wants, and secure to start enjoying life by voluntary rather than inevitable participation in the various social groupings that constitute the social series. The development of such a welfare society did not seem to him – any more than many other

enlightened thinkers – a problem, given the revolutionary in-
creases in health and wealth that the previous century had
witnessed.

Man's productive activities – like his reproductive ones – were
essential to ensure the satisfaction of his primary sensual needs.
But Fourier's highly detailed division of labour in the phalanstery
was not aimed primarily at the more efficient manufacture of a
quantity of pins. Its purpose was rather to generate richer social
and cultural relationships through a variety of types of activity.
Fortuitously (or in Fourier's terms, as an example of the composite
nature of existence) the enthusiastic energy of such free associations would lead to a great increase in productivity, thereby
ensuring that the problem of the scarcity of basic goods would be
completely overcome. But the purpose of the agricultural economic activity that Fourier depicts is to satisfy needs of consumption, rather than produce capital or stimulate demand. The
purpose of life is defined in terms of the maximisation of
happiness, rather than the accumulation of things. In this emphasis, Fourier follows directly the main stream of Enlightenment
ethics, with its open admiration for the Spartan model in which
happiness is gained by virtuous participation in the civic culture.

The criticism of Fourier for not anticipating the world of
industrial capitalism is answered if we think of him not as an
utopian prophet but as a 'philosophe', still concerned to develop
themes of Enlightenment thought. His debt to Enlightenment
attitudes is nowhere more evident than in the view that our
material pleasures are easily shown to be merely necessary
conditions for the expansion of the mind and spirit attendant on
social intercourse. The problem, as Fourier saw it, was to ensure
the distribution of a basic minimum, whose availability to all was
only obscured by the fear, greed and power-seeking of the
unenlightened citizens of 'civilisation'. The empire of the distributive passions would ensure this justice within the phalanstery. As
a basically self-sufficient economy, a phalanstery could survive as
an island in contemporary society. Its success in generating
personal and social fulfilment would quickly convert the sceptical.
Then, ultimately, exchange between phalansteries would enable
any scarcities resulting from environmental conditions to be met.

The more fundamental problem was to overcome the exploitation and perversion of the spirit by the unbalanced ecology of our
educational and ideological institutions. Some instincts and emotions are suppressed, others exploited, in the name of a mental
strait-jacket described as reason, but in reality the effect of
religious superstitions and philosophical prejudices bolstered by a

system of power. The institutions of Church and Academy are the truly political power because they control men's conceptions.[38] Their authority can only be undermined by showing people that it is based on a false consciousness, rather than a true science. In this sense, Fourier rejoins the mainstream of Enlightenment concern with the redefinition of understanding. His characteristic optimism about the effects of Enlightenment allow him to assume that the exposition of the real, coherent and cohesive science of human nature, social history and cosmological relationships – together with it proof in the demonstration of a thriving phalanstery – will suffice to subvert the prejudices that are the bastions of power in Church and State.

NOTES

1 *Oeuvres Complètes*, (Paris, 1841–4), Vol. II,84.
2 *Oe. C.* V,873.
3 Ibid. III,131.
4 Ibid. 128–9.
5 Ibid. IV,222.
6 Ibid. III,270.
7 Ibid. II, 'Du Libre Arbitre', xxxix.
8 Ibid. III,33.
9 'Théorie des Quatre Mouvements et des Destinées Générales' (Lyon, 1808), 188.
10 *Oe. C.* V,526.
11 Ibid. II,13.
12 L.G. Crocker, *The Age of Enlightenment*, 1969, 23.
13 OE. C IV,2.
14 Ibid. VI,128.
15 Ibid. V,294 and 499.
16 *Le Nouveau Monde Industriel et Sociètaire*, (Paris, 1829), 14.
17 Ibid. 47.
18 Ibid. 535.
19 Ibid. 436.
20 'Biographia Literaria' ed. G. Watson, 1956, 167.
21 *Oe. C.* II,22
22 C. Pellarin, *Life of Fourier*, 2nd ed., translated by F.G. Shaw (New York, 1848), 228.
23 *Lectures on Natural Philosophy* Vol. I,44.
24 *Anatomie Comparée* I,6, trans. W. Ross, 1802
25 *Oe. C* II,179.
26 A. Brisbane, *Social Destiny of Man* (Philadelphia, 1840), 188.

27 *Oe. C.* IV,223.

28 E. Silberling, *Complément au Dictionnaire de Sociologie Phalanstèrienne*, Mss. 103.

29 *Oe. C* IV,253–4.

30 Ibid. VI,61.

31 Ibid. IV,243.

32 *Publication des Manuscrits*, (Paris, 1851), Vol. I,355.

33 *Oe. C.* III,97.

34 *Les Cahiers Manuscrits de Fourier*, ed. E. Poulat (Paris, 1957), I/9, 13.

35 J. Buche, *L'Ecole Mystique de Lyon 1776–1847*, (1935, 13.

36 *Quatre Mouvements*, 417.

37 *Oe. C.* IV,564.

38 Ibid. 189.

Index